TAKE NXT OVER

DENNIS HOPELESS

JAKE ELPHICK

KENDALL GOODE

HYEONJIN KIM

RODRIGO LORENZO

BOOM!
STUDIOS

WWE: NXT TAKEOVER, April 2019. Published by BOOM! Studios, a division of Boom Entertainment, Inc. WWE is ™ & © 2019 WWE. All WWE programming, talent names, images, likenesses, slogans, wrestling moves, trademarks, logos and copyrights are the exclusive property of WWE and its subsidiaries. All other trademarks, logos and copyrights are the property of their respective owners. © 2019 WWE. All rights reserved. Originally published in single magazine form as WWE: NXT Takeover ~ The Blueprint No. 1, WWE: NXT Takeover ~ Proving Ground No. 1, WWE: NXT Takeover ~ Into The Fire No. 1, WWE: NXT Takeover ~ Redemption No. 1. ™ & © 2018 WWE. All rights reserved. BOOM! Studios™ and the BOOM! Studios logo are trademarks of Boom Entertainment, Inc., registered in various countries and categories. All characters, events, and institutions depicted herein are fictional. Any similarity between any of the names, characters, persons, events, and/or institutions in this publication to actual names, characters, and persons, whether living or dead, events, and/or institutions is unintended and purely coincidental. BOOM! Studios does not read or accept unsolicited submissions of ideas, stories, or artwork.

BOOM! Studios, 5670 Wilshire Boulevard, Suite 400, Los Angeles, CA 90036-5679. Printed in China. First Printing.

ISBN: 978-1-68415-341-1, eISBN: 978-1-64144-194-0

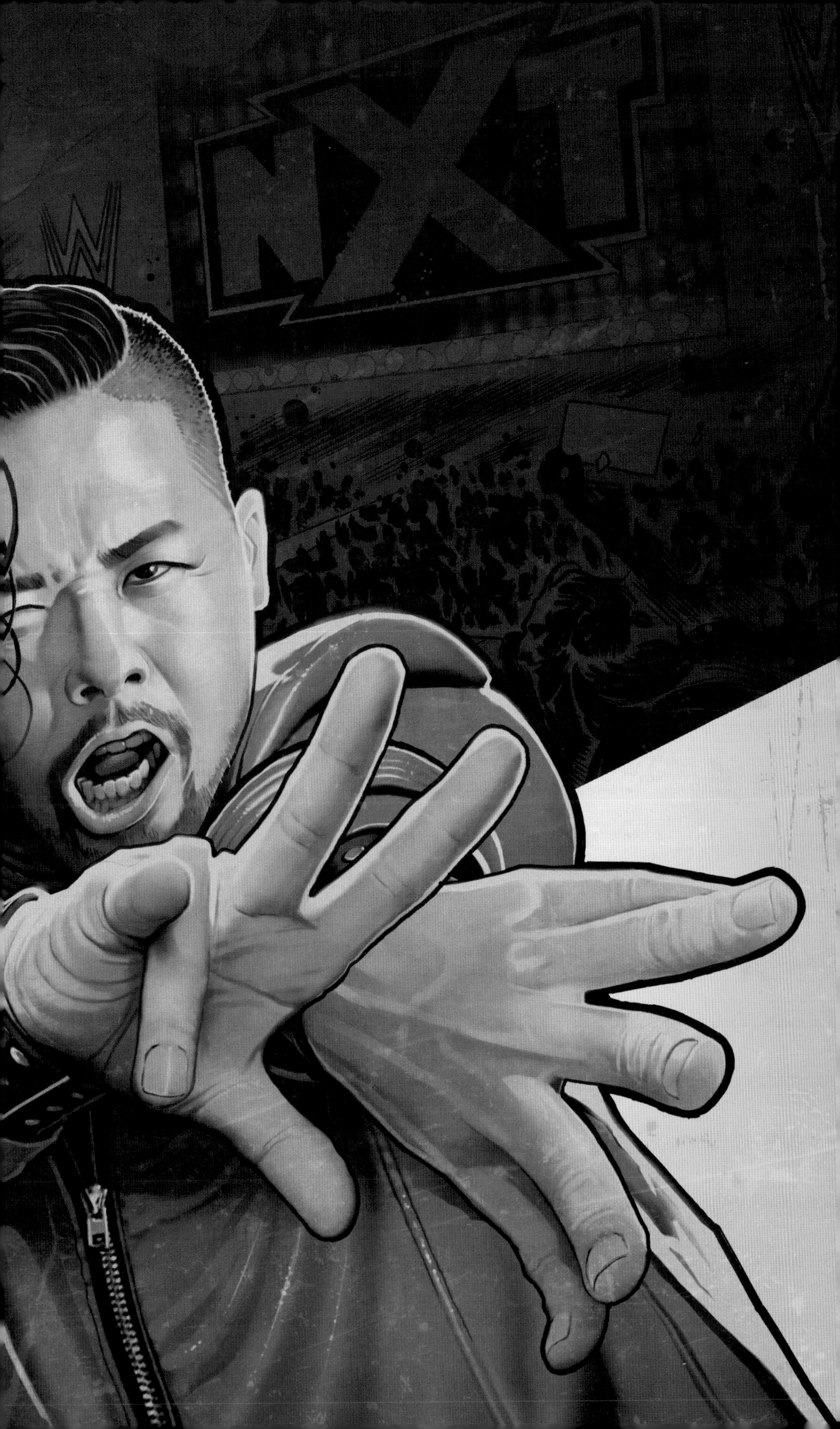
NXT

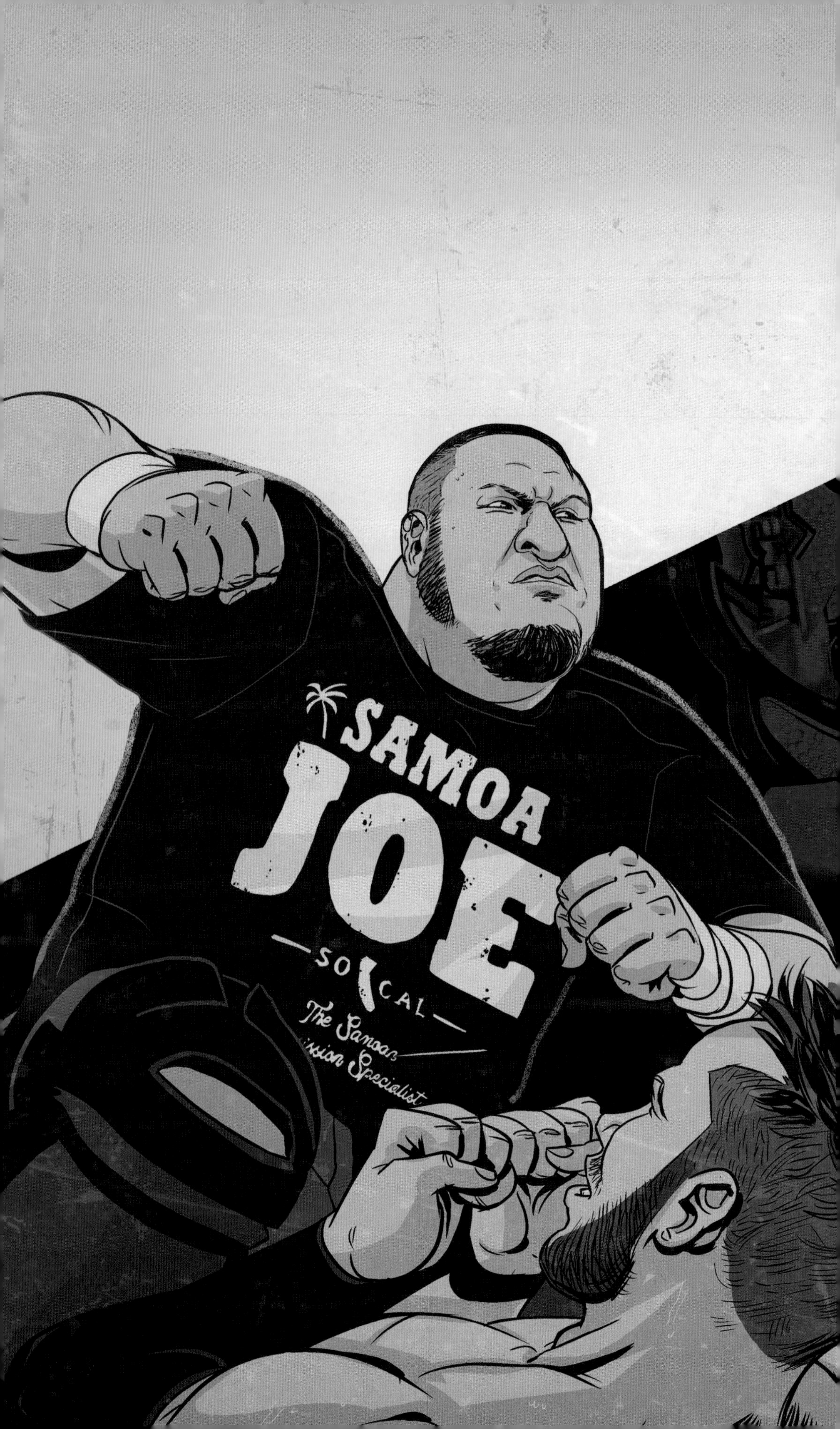
SAMOA
JOE
SO CAL
The Samoan
Specialist

WRITTEN BY
DENNIS HOPELESS

THE BLUEPRINT
ILLUSTRATED BY
JAKE ELPHICK
COLORED BY
DOUG GARBARK

INTO THE FIRE
ILLUSTRATED BY
HYEONJIN KIM
COLORED BY
WESLLEI MANOEL

PROVING GROUND
ILLUSTRATED BY
KENDALL GOODE

REDEMPTION
ILLUSTRATED BY
RODRIGO LORENZO
COLORED BY
WESLLEI MANOEL

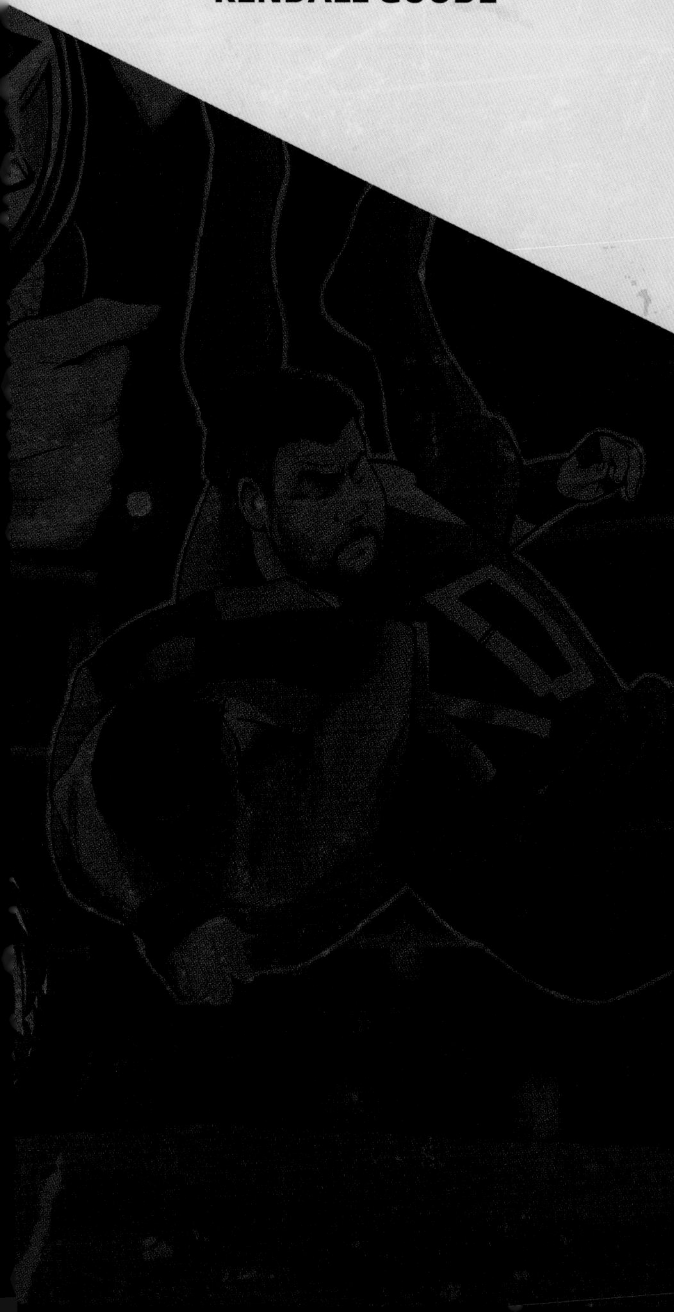

LETTERED BY
JIM CAMPBELL

COVER BY
LUKAS WERNECK

SERIES DESIGNER
GRACE PARK

COLLECTION DESIGNER
JILLIAN CRAB

EDITOR
CHRIS ROSA

SPECIAL THANKS TO
STEVE PANTALEO
CHAD BARBASH
BEN MAYER
JOHN JONES
STAN STANSKI
LAUREN DIENES-MIDDLEN
AND EVERYONE AT **WWE**

THE
BLUEPRINT

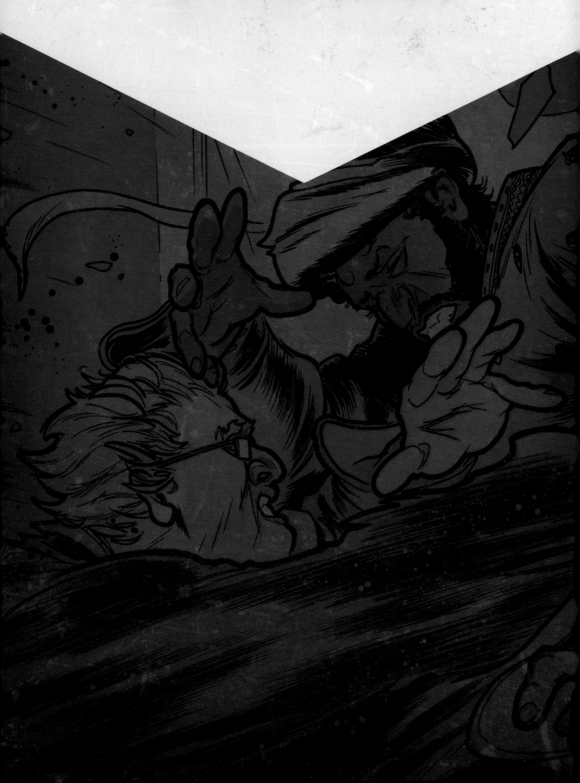

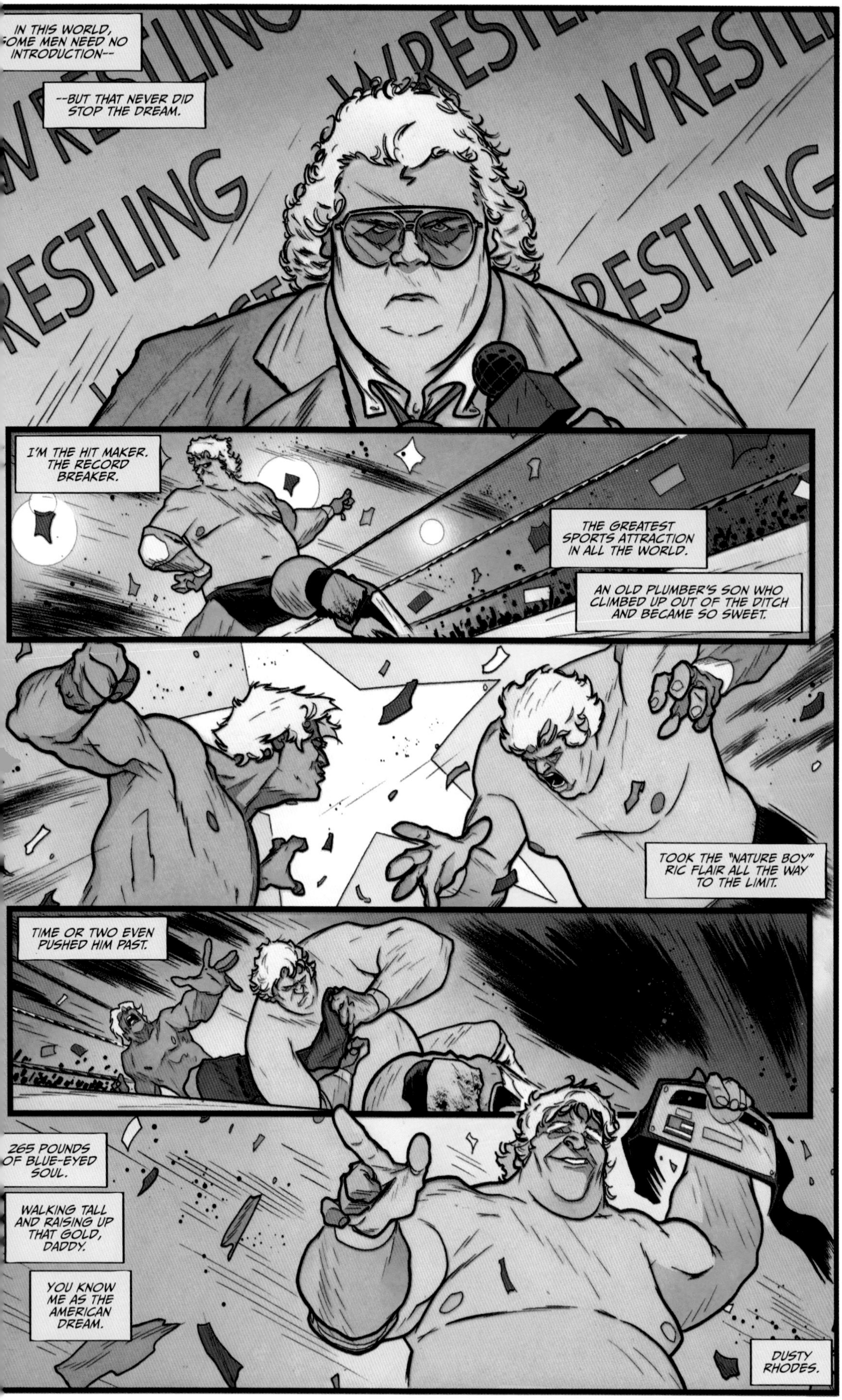
IN THIS WORLD, SOME MEN NEED NO INTRODUCTION--
--BUT THAT NEVER DID STOP THE DREAM.
WRESTLING
I'M THE HIT MAKER. THE RECORD BREAKER.
THE GREATEST SPORTS ATTRACTION IN ALL THE WORLD.
AN OLD PLUMBER'S SON WHO CLIMBED UP OUT OF THE DITCH AND BECAME SO SWEET.
TOOK THE "NATURE BOY" RIC FLAIR ALL THE WAY TO THE LIMIT.
TIME OR TWO EVEN PUSHED HIM PAST.
265 POUNDS OF BLUE-EYED SOUL.
WALKING TALL AND RAISING UP THAT GOLD, DADDY.
YOU KNOW ME AS THE AMERICAN DREAM.
DUSTY RHODES.

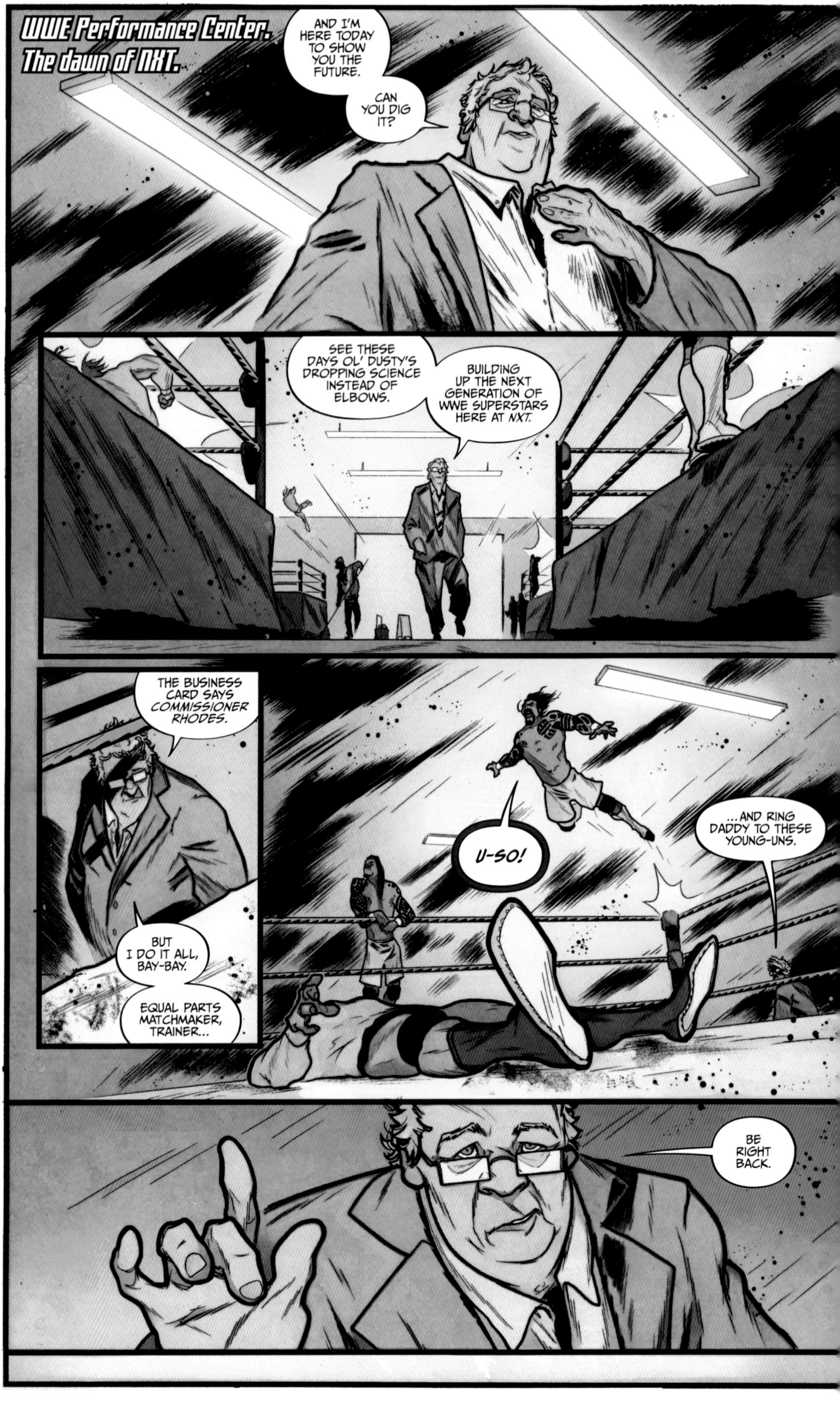
WWE Performance Center.
The dawn of NXT.
AND I'M HERE TODAY TO SHOW YOU THE FUTURE.
CAN YOU DIG IT?
SEE THESE DAYS OL' DUSTY'S DROPPING SCIENCE INSTEAD OF ELBOWS.
BUILDING UP THE NEXT GENERATION OF WWE SUPERSTARS HERE AT NXT.
THE BUSINESS CARD SAYS COMMISSIONER RHODES.
BUT I DO IT ALL, BAY-BAY.
EQUAL PARTS MATCHMAKER, TRAINER...
U-SO!
...AND RING DADDY TO THESE YOUNG-UNS.
BE RIGHT BACK.

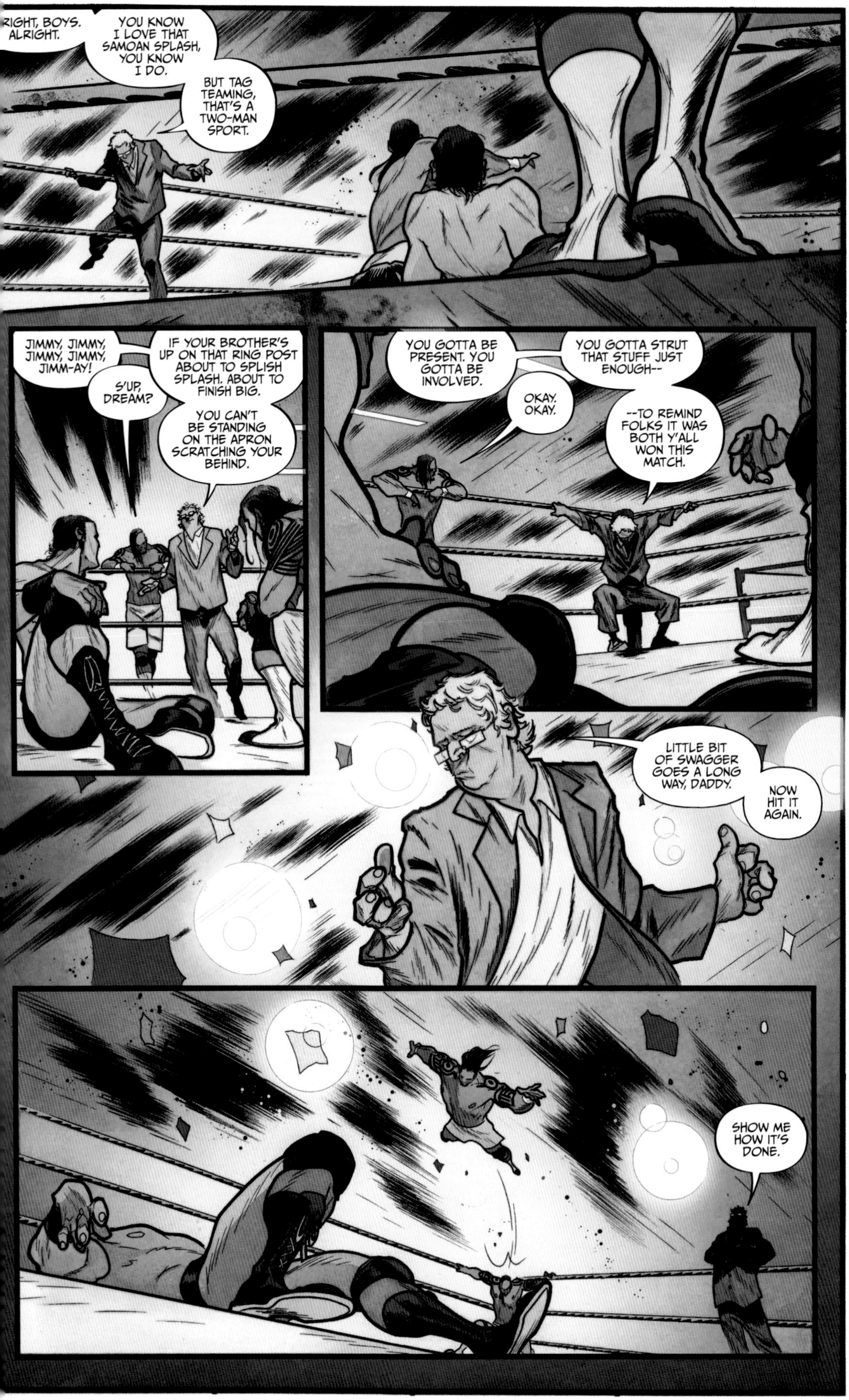
RIGHT, BOYS. ALRIGHT.
YOU KNOW I LOVE THAT SAMOAN SPLASH, YOU KNOW I DO.
BUT TAG TEAMING, THAT'S A TWO-MAN SPORT.
JIMMY, JIMMY, JIMMY, JIMMY, JIMM-AY!
S'UP, DREAM?
IF YOUR BROTHER'S UP ON THAT RING POST ABOUT TO SPLISH SPLASH. ABOUT TO FINISH BIG.
YOU CAN'T BE STANDING ON THE APRON SCRATCHING YOUR BEHIND.
YOU GOTTA BE PRESENT. YOU GOTTA BE INVOLVED.
OKAY. OKAY.
YOU GOTTA STRUT THAT STUFF JUST ENOUGH--
--TO REMIND FOLKS IT WAS BOTH Y'ALL WON THIS MATCH.
LITTLE BIT OF SWAGGER GOES A LONG WAY, DADDY.
NOW HIT IT AGAIN.
SHOW ME HOW IT'S DONE.

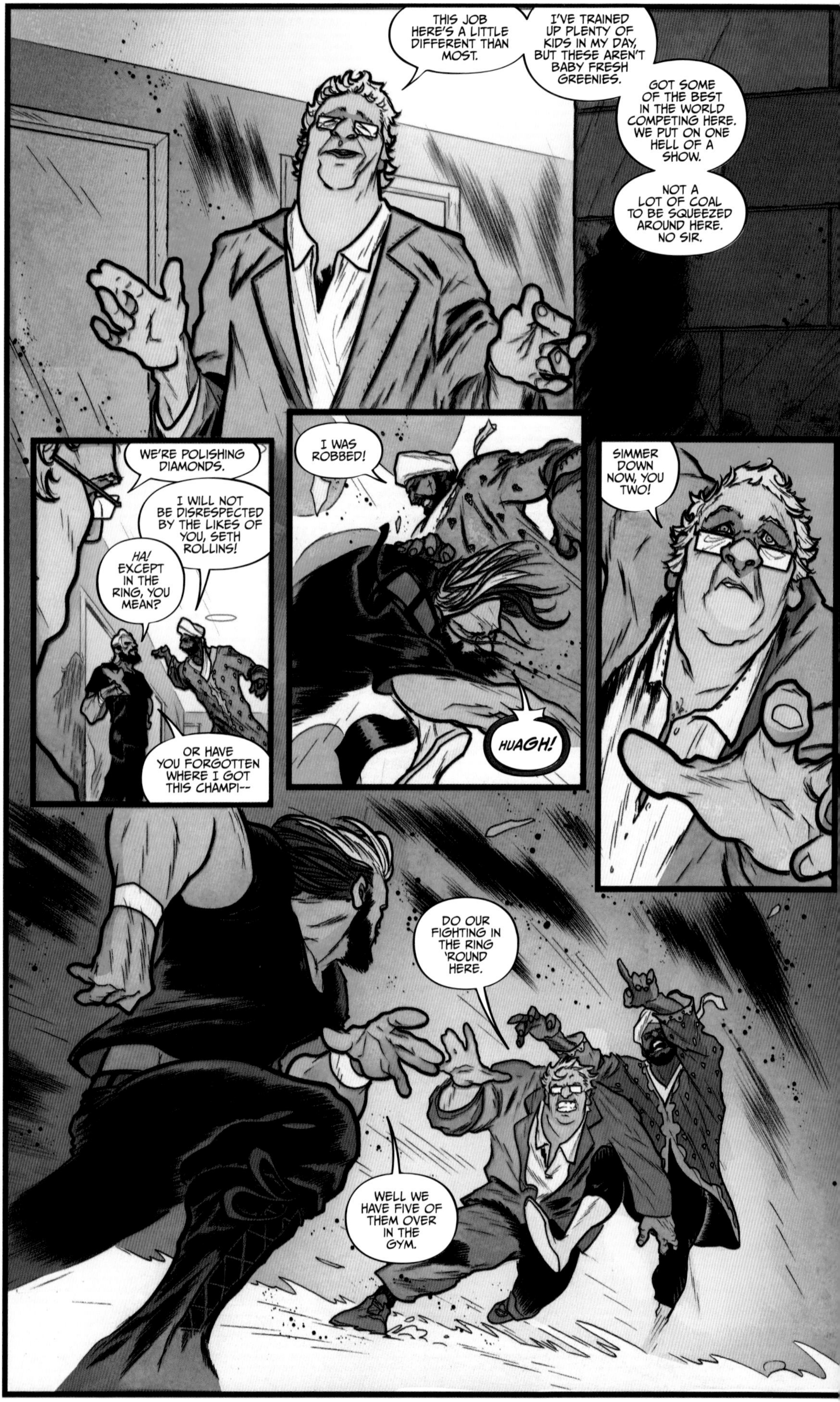
THIS JOB HERE'S A LITTLE DIFFERENT THAN MOST.
I'VE TRAINED UP PLENTY OF KIDS IN MY DAY, BUT THESE AREN'T BABY FRESH GREENIES.
GOT SOME OF THE BEST IN THE WORLD COMPETING HERE. WE PUT ON ONE HELL OF A SHOW.
NOT A LOT OF COAL TO BE SQUEEZED AROUND HERE. NO SIR.
WE'RE POLISHING DIAMONDS.
I WILL NOT BE DISRESPECTED BY THE LIKES OF YOU, SETH ROLLINS!
HA! EXCEPT IN THE RING, YOU MEAN?
OR HAVE YOU FORGOTTEN WHERE I GOT THIS CHAMPI--
I WAS ROBBED!
HUAGH!
SIMMER DOWN NOW, YOU TWO!
DO OUR FIGHTING IN THE RING 'ROUND HERE.
WELL WE HAVE FIVE OF THEM OVER IN THE GYM.

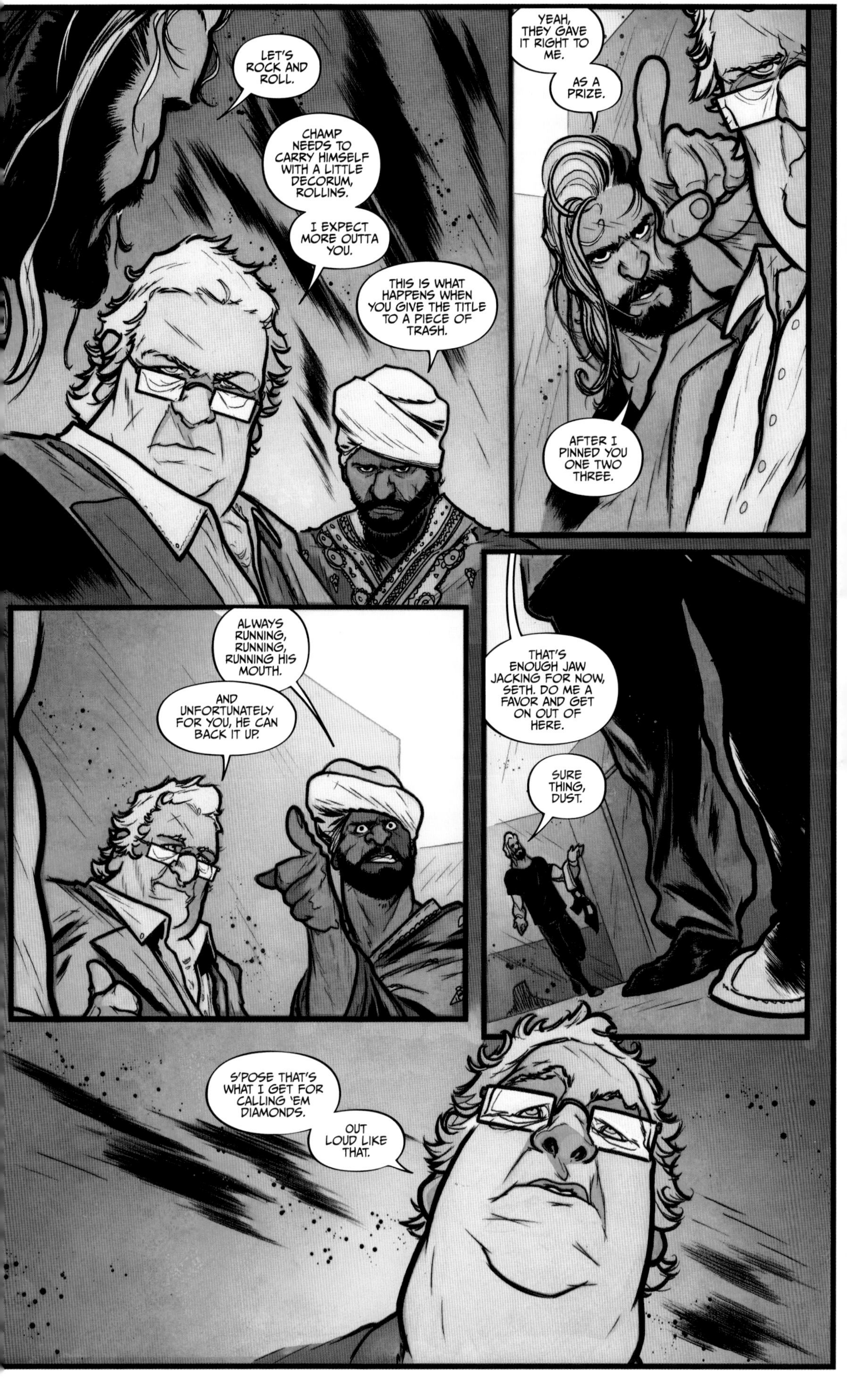
LET'S ROCK AND ROLL.
CHAMP NEEDS TO CARRY HIMSELF WITH A LITTLE DECORUM, ROLLINS.
I EXPECT MORE OUTTA YOU.
THIS IS WHAT HAPPENS WHEN YOU GIVE THE TITLE TO A PIECE OF TRASH.
YEAH, THEY GAVE IT RIGHT TO ME.
AS A PRIZE.
AFTER I PINNED YOU ONE TWO THREE.
ALWAYS RUNNING, RUNNING, RUNNING HIS MOUTH.
AND UNFORTUNATELY FOR YOU, HE CAN BACK IT UP.
THAT'S ENOUGH JAW JACKING FOR NOW, SETH. DO ME A FAVOR AND GET ON OUT OF HERE.
SURE THING, DUST.
S'POSE THAT'S WHAT I GET FOR CALLING 'EM DIAMONDS.
OUT LOUD LIKE THAT.

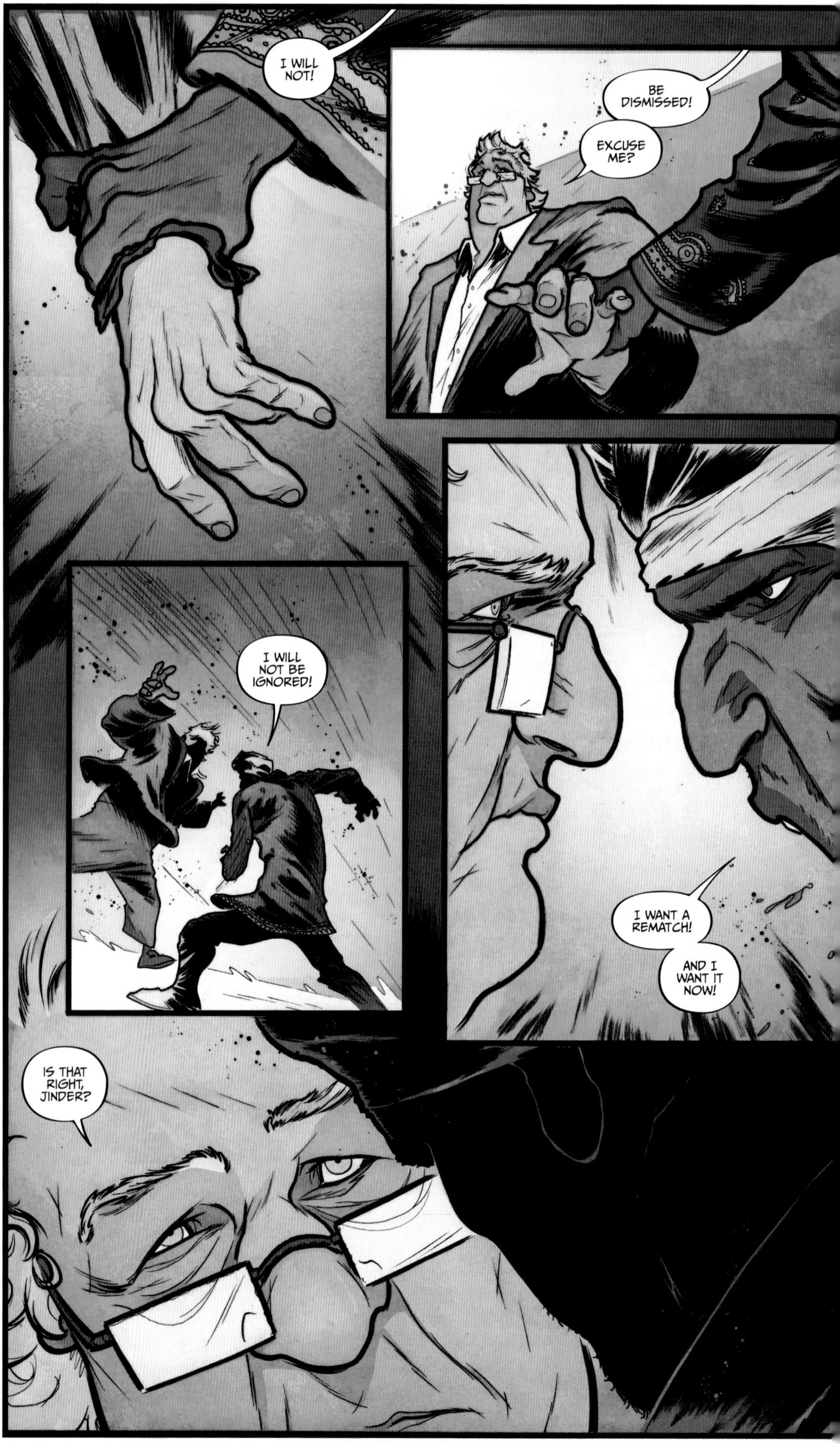
I WILL NOT!
BE DISMISSED!
EXCUSE ME?
I WILL NOT BE IGNORED!
I WANT A REMATCH!
AND I WANT IT NOW!
IS THAT RIGHT, JINDER?

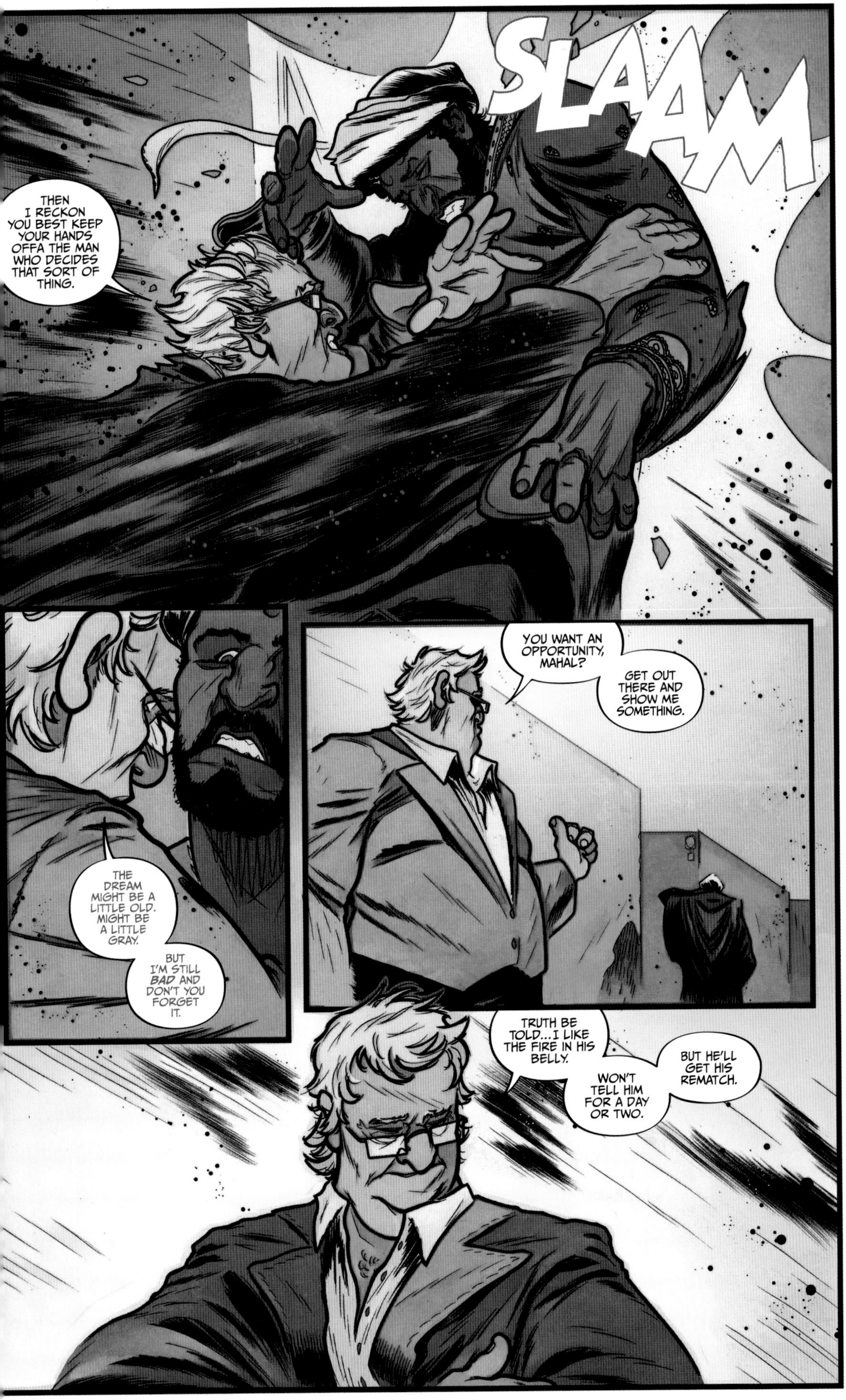
SLAAM
THEN I RECKON YOU BEST KEEP YOUR HANDS OFFA THE MAN WHO DECIDES THAT SORT OF THING.
THE DREAM MIGHT BE A LITTLE OLD. MIGHT BE A LITTLE GRAY.
BUT I'M STILL *BAD* AND DON'T YOU FORGET IT.
YOU WANT AN OPPORTUNITY, MAHAL?
GET OUT THERE AND SHOW ME SOMETHING.
TRUTH BE TOLD...I LIKE THE FIRE IN HIS BELLY.
WON'T TELL HIM FOR A DAY OR TWO.
BUT HE'LL GET HIS REMATCH.

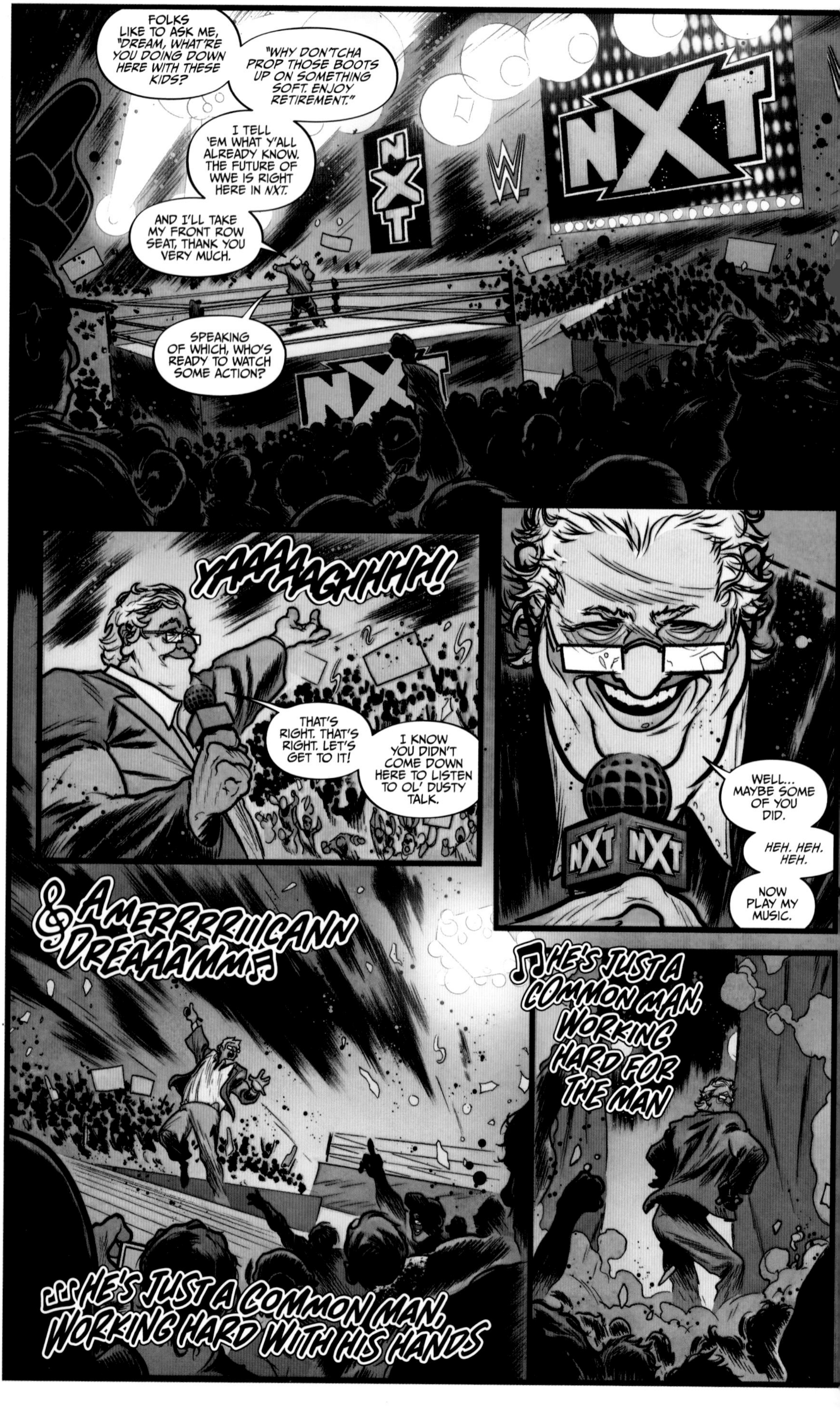
FOLKS LIKE TO ASK ME, "DREAM, WHAT'RE YOU DOING DOWN HERE WITH THESE KIDS?
"WHY DON'TCHA PROP THOSE BOOTS UP ON SOMETHING SOFT. ENJOY RETIREMENT."
I TELL 'EM WHAT Y'ALL ALREADY KNOW. THE FUTURE OF WWE IS RIGHT HERE IN NXT.
AND I'LL TAKE MY FRONT ROW SEAT, THANK YOU VERY MUCH.
SPEAKING OF WHICH, WHO'S READY TO WATCH SOME ACTION?
NXT
YAAAAAGHHHH!
THAT'S RIGHT. THAT'S RIGHT. LET'S GET TO IT!
I KNOW YOU DIDN'T COME DOWN HERE TO LISTEN TO OL' DUSTY TALK.
WELL... MAYBE SOME OF YOU DID.
HEH. HEH. HEH.
NOW PLAY MY MUSIC.
AMERRRRIIICANN DREAAAAMM
HE'S JUST A COMMON MAN, WORKING HARD FOR THE MAN
HE'S JUST A COMMON MAN, WORKING HARD WITH HIS HANDS

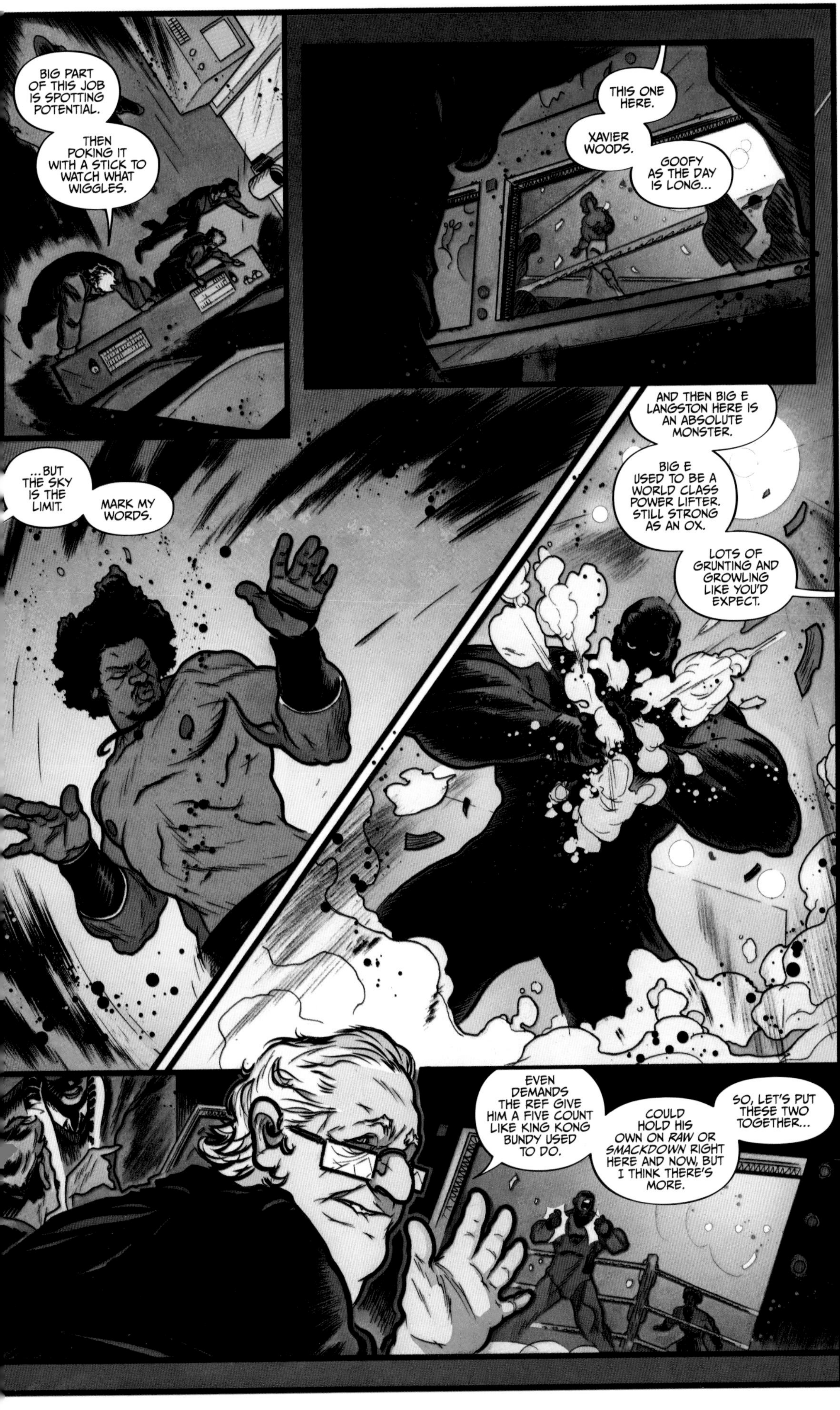
BIG PART OF THIS JOB IS SPOTTING POTENTIAL.
THEN POKING IT WITH A STICK TO WATCH WHAT WIGGLES.
THIS ONE HERE.
XAVIER WOODS.
GOOFY AS THE DAY IS LONG...
...BUT THE SKY IS THE LIMIT.
MARK MY WORDS.
AND THEN BIG E LANGSTON HERE IS AN ABSOLUTE MONSTER.
BIG E USED TO BE A WORLD CLASS POWER LIFTER. STILL STRONG AS AN OX.
LOTS OF GRUNTING AND GROWLING LIKE YOU'D EXPECT.
EVEN DEMANDS THE REF GIVE HIM A FIVE COUNT LIKE KING KONG BUNDY USED TO DO.
COULD HOLD HIS OWN ON *RAW* OR *SMACKDOWN* RIGHT HERE AND NOW, BUT I THINK THERE'S MORE.
SO, LET'S PUT THESE TWO TOGETHER...

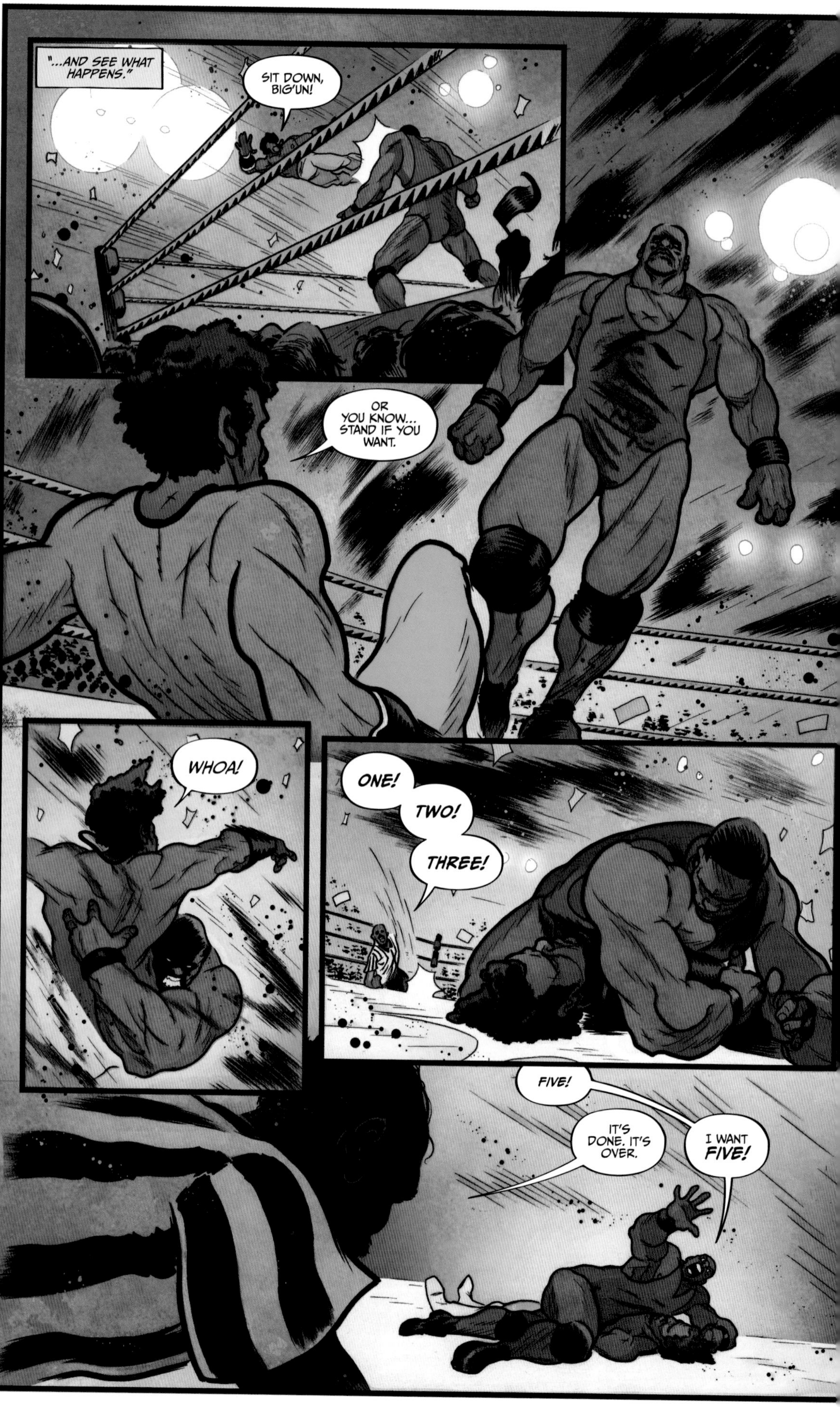
"...AND SEE WHAT HAPPENS."
SIT DOWN, BIG'UN!
OR YOU KNOW... STAND IF YOU WANT.
WHOA!
ONE!
TWO!
THREE!
FIVE!
IT'S DONE. IT'S OVER.
I WANT **FIVE!**

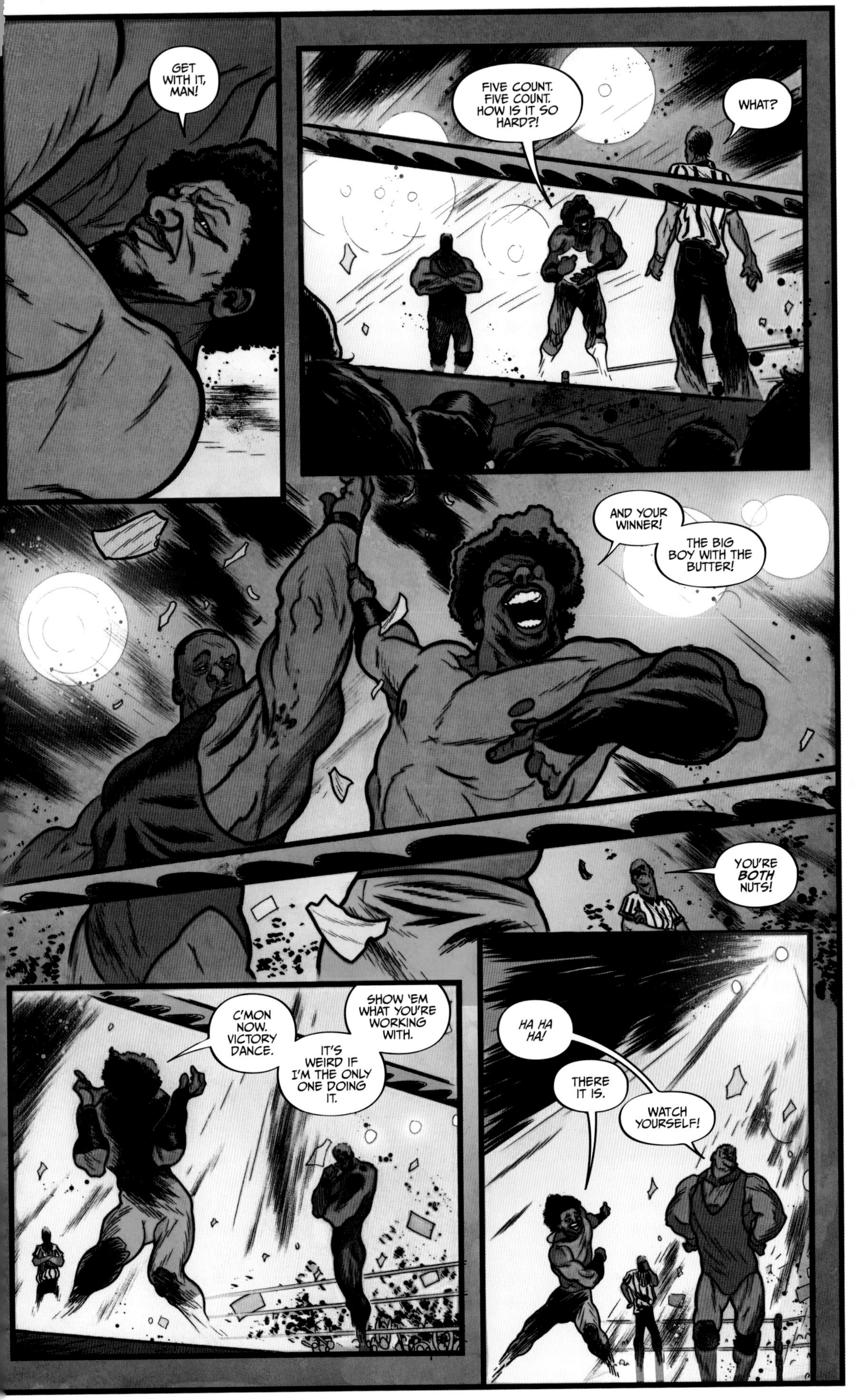
GET WITH IT, MAN!
FIVE COUNT. FIVE COUNT. HOW IS IT SO HARD?!
WHAT?
AND YOUR WINNER!
THE BIG BOY WITH THE BUTTER!
YOU'RE BOTH NUTS!
C'MON NOW. VICTORY DANCE.
SHOW 'EM WHAT YOU'RE WORKING WITH.
IT'S WEIRD IF I'M THE ONLY ONE DOING IT.
HA HA HA!
THERE IT IS.
WATCH YOURSELF!

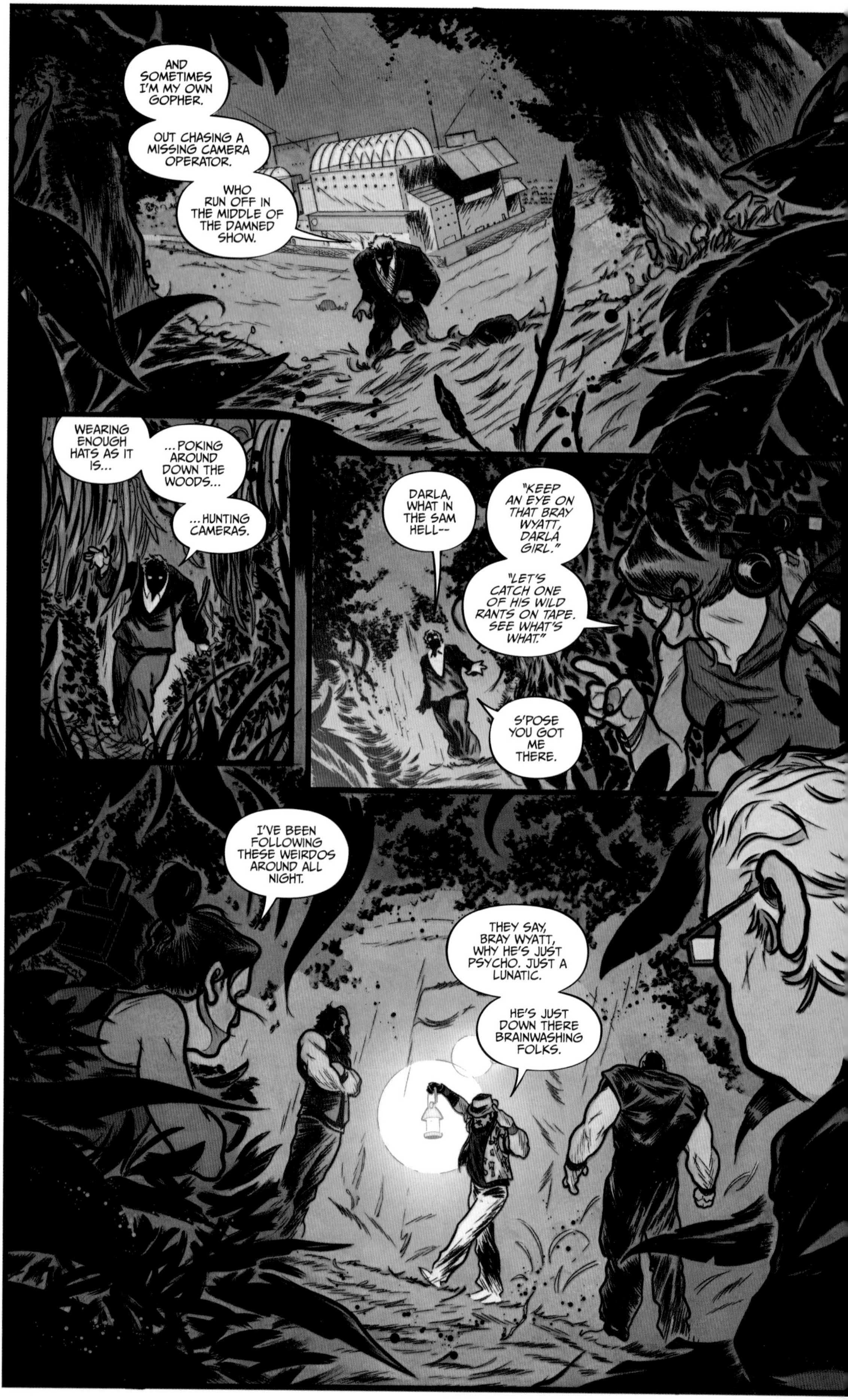
AND SOMETIMES I'M MY OWN GOPHER.
OUT CHASING A MISSING CAMERA OPERATOR.
WHO RUN OFF IN THE MIDDLE OF THE DAMNED SHOW.
WEARING ENOUGH HATS AS IT IS...
...POKING AROUND DOWN THE WOODS...
...HUNTING CAMERAS.
DARLA, WHAT IN THE SAM HELL--
"KEEP AN EYE ON THAT BRAY WYATT, DARLA GIRL."
"LET'S CATCH ONE OF HIS WILD RANTS ON TAPE. SEE WHAT'S WHAT."
S'POSE YOU GOT ME THERE.
I'VE BEEN FOLLOWING THESE WEIRDOS AROUND ALL NIGHT.
THEY SAY, BRAY WYATT, WHY HE'S JUST PSYCHO. JUST A LUNATIC.
HE'S JUST DOWN THERE BRAINWASHING FOLKS.

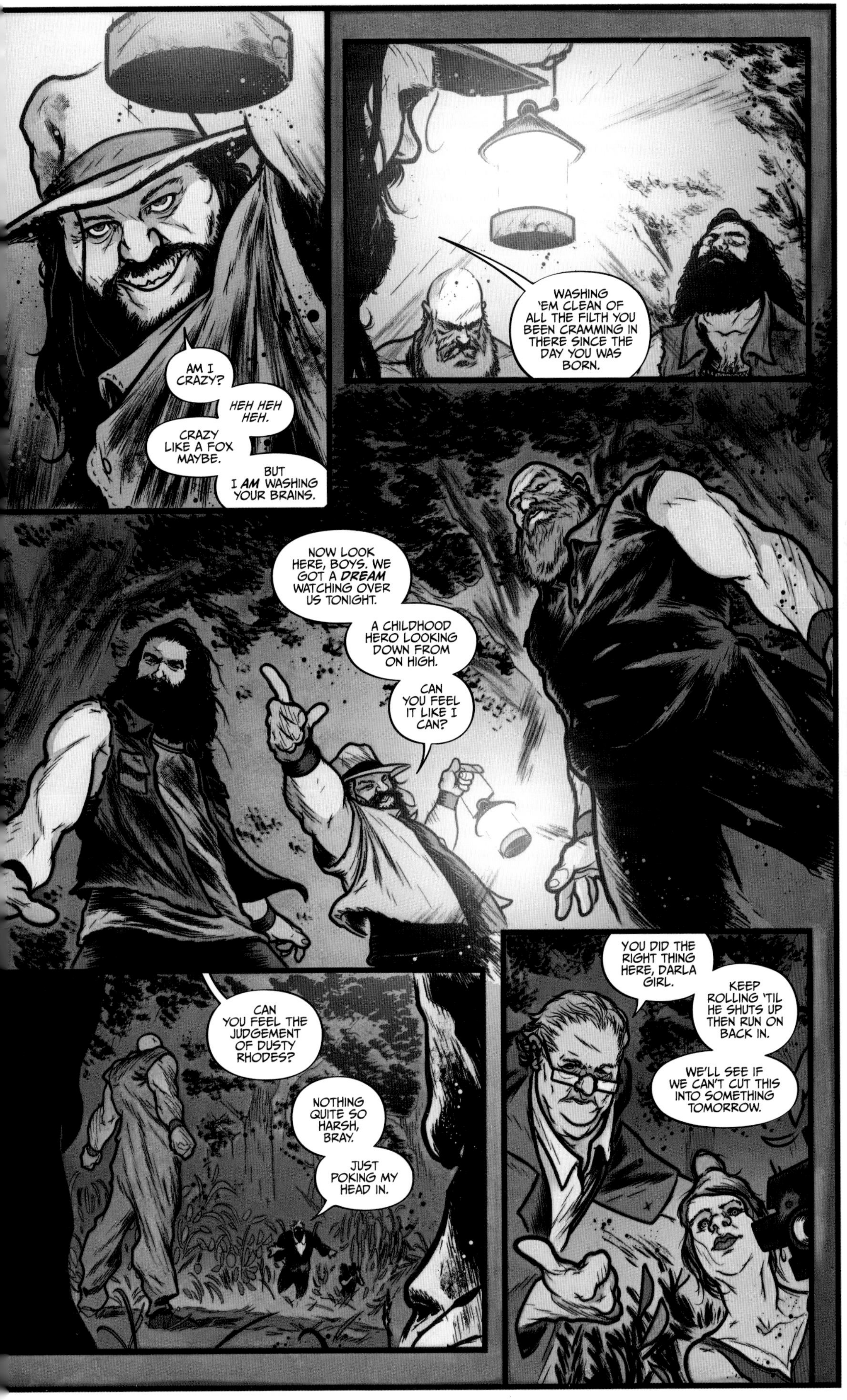
AM I CRAZY?
HEH HEH HEH.
CRAZY LIKE A FOX MAYBE.
BUT I AM WASHING YOUR BRAINS.
WASHING 'EM CLEAN OF ALL THE FILTH YOU BEEN CRAMMING IN THERE SINCE THE DAY YOU WAS BORN.
NOW LOOK HERE, BOYS. WE GOT A DREAM WATCHING OVER US TONIGHT.
A CHILDHOOD HERO LOOKING DOWN FROM ON HIGH.
CAN YOU FEEL IT LIKE I CAN?
CAN YOU FEEL THE JUDGEMENT OF DUSTY RHODES?
NOTHING QUITE SO HARSH, BRAY.
JUST POKING MY HEAD IN.
YOU DID THE RIGHT THING HERE, DARLA GIRL.
KEEP ROLLING 'TIL HE SHUTS UP THEN RUN ON BACK IN.
WE'LL SEE IF WE CAN'T CUT THIS INTO SOMETHING TOMORROW.

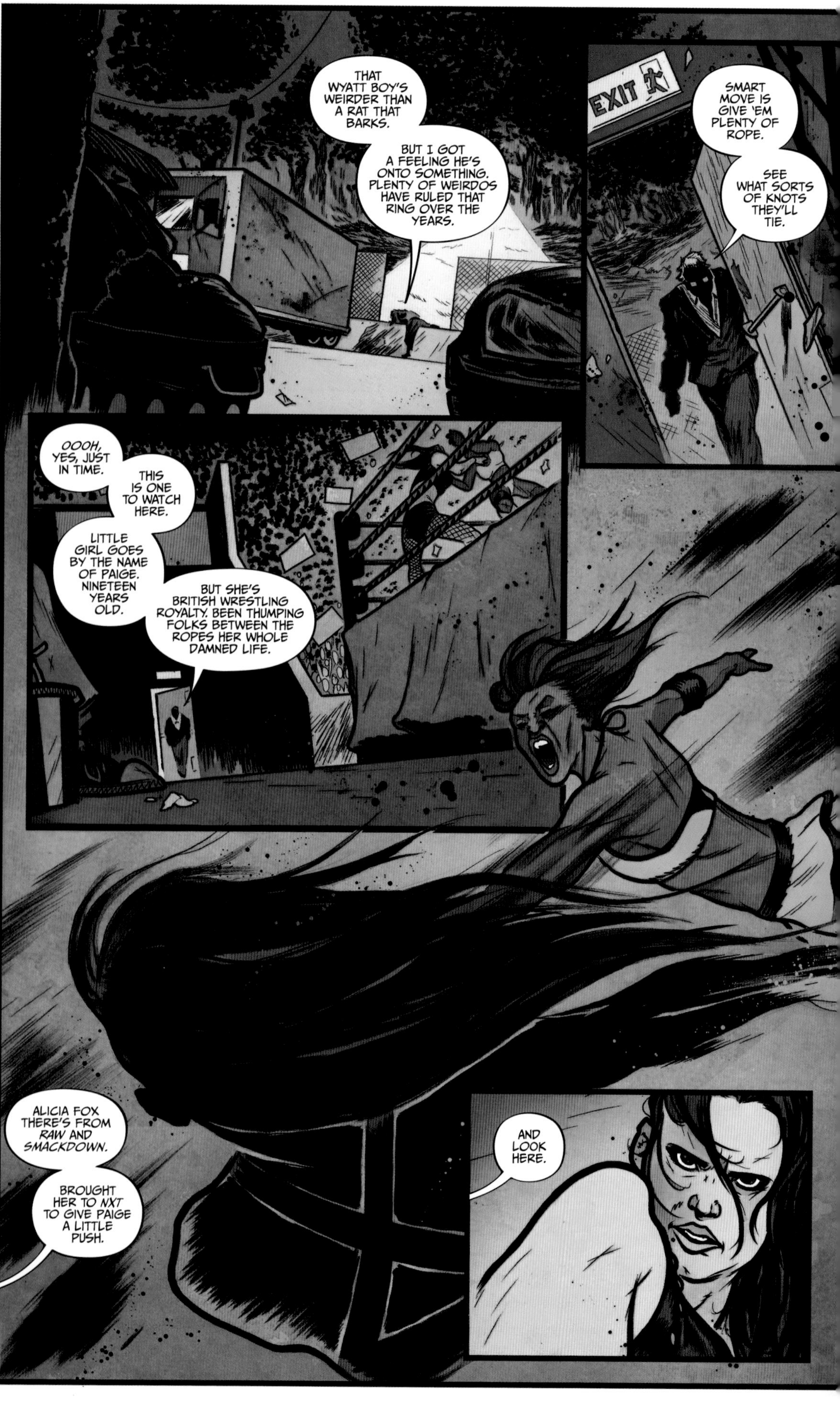
THAT WYATT BOY'S WEIRDER THAN A RAT THAT BARKS.
BUT I GOT A FEELING HE'S ONTO SOMETHING. PLENTY OF WEIRDOS HAVE RULED THAT RING OVER THE YEARS.
EXIT
SMART MOVE IS GIVE 'EM PLENTY OF ROPE.
SEE WHAT SORTS OF KNOTS THEY'LL TIE.
OOOH, YES, JUST IN TIME.
THIS IS ONE TO WATCH HERE.
LITTLE GIRL GOES BY THE NAME OF PAIGE. NINETEEN YEARS OLD.
BUT SHE'S BRITISH WRESTLING ROYALTY. BEEN THUMPING FOLKS BETWEEN THE ROPES HER WHOLE DAMNED LIFE.
ALICIA FOX THERE'S FROM *RAW* AND *SMACKDOWN*.
BROUGHT HER TO *NXT* TO GIVE PAIGE A LITTLE PUSH.
AND LOOK HERE.

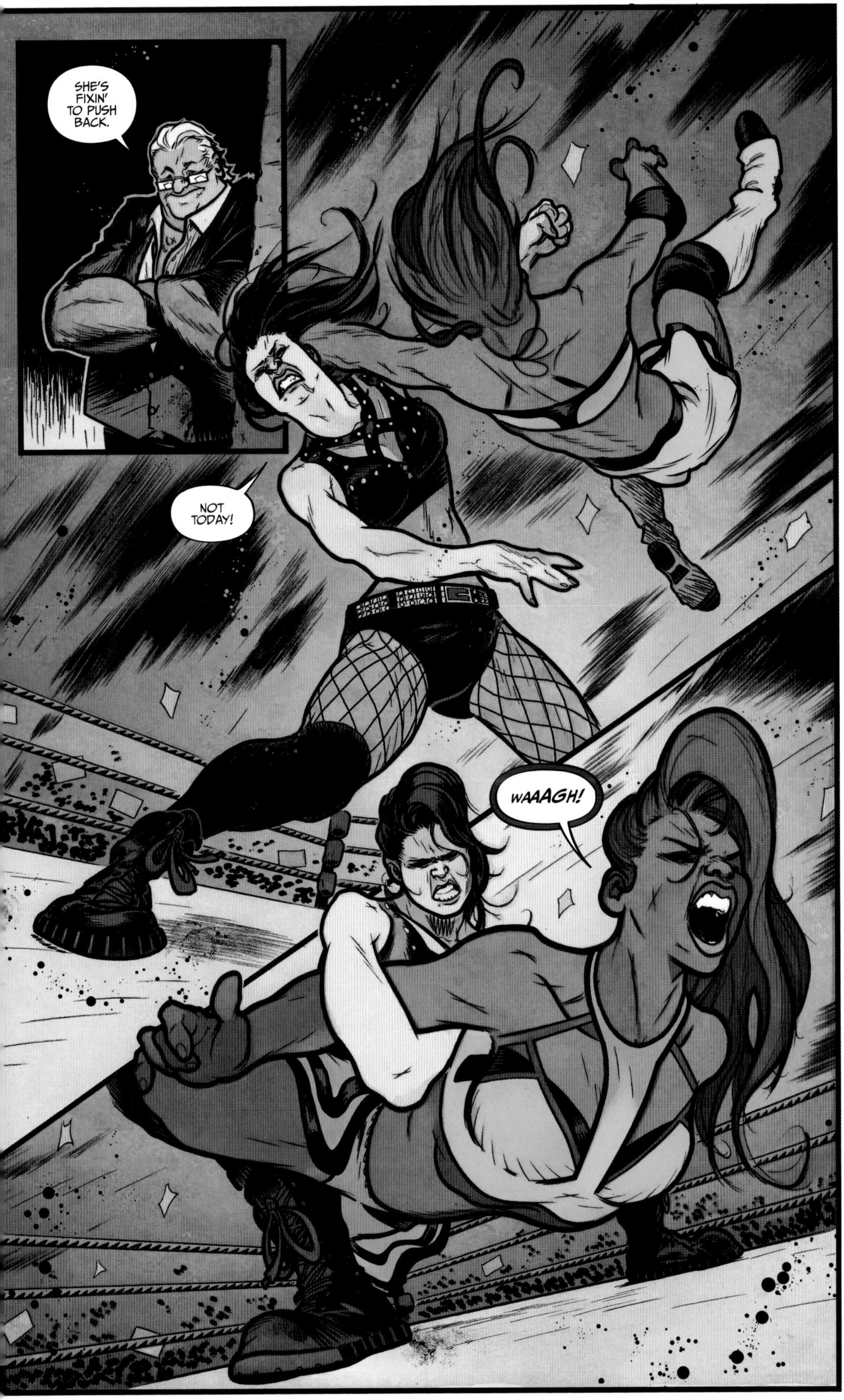
SHE'S FIXIN' TO PUSH BACK.
NOT TODAY!
WAAAGH!

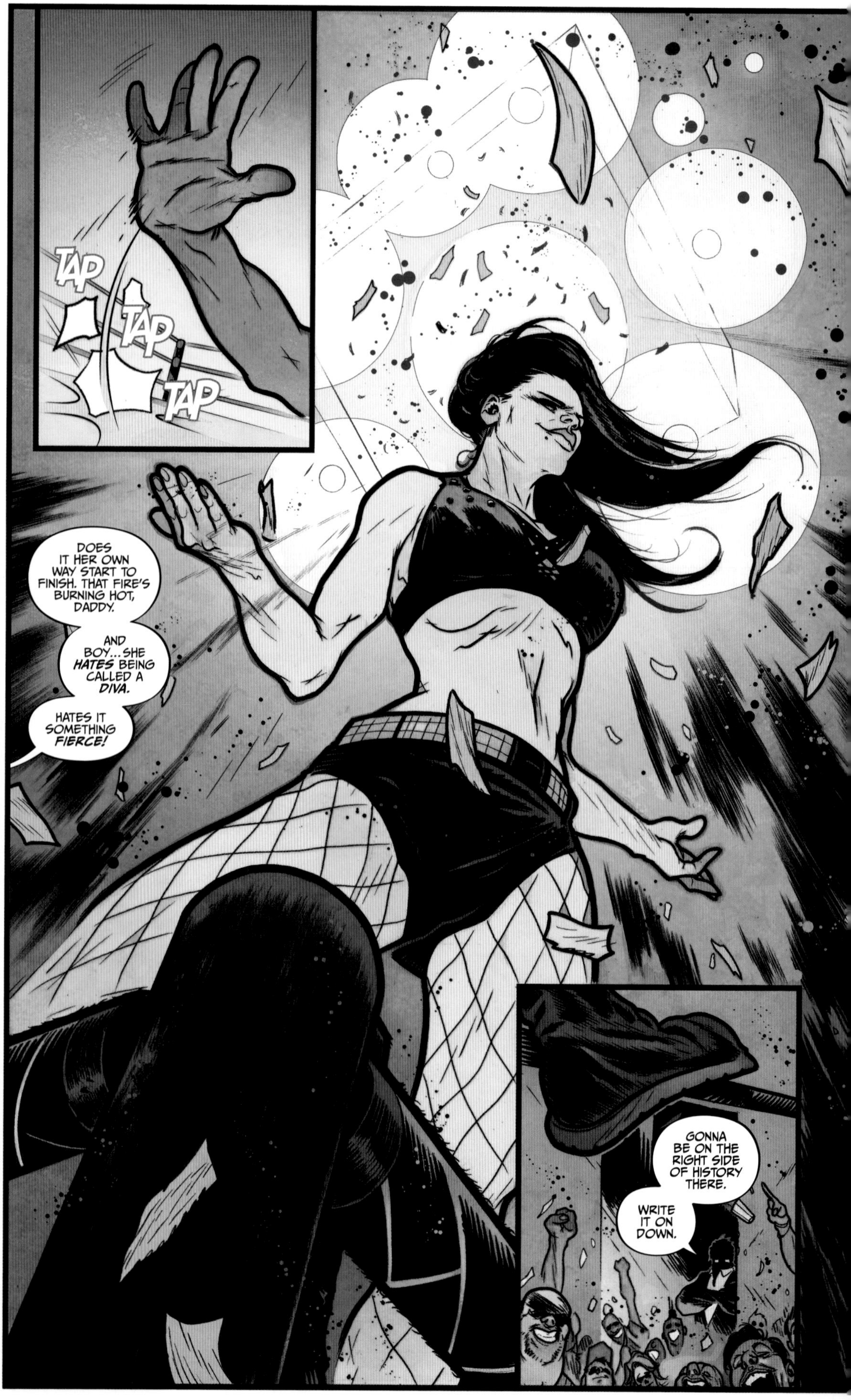
TAP
TAP
TAP
DOES IT HER OWN WAY START TO FINISH. THAT FIRE'S BURNING HOT, DADDY.
AND BOY...SHE *HATES* BEING CALLED A *DIVA.*
HATES IT SOMETHING *FIERCE!*
GONNA BE ON THE RIGHT SIDE OF HISTORY THERE.
WRITE IT ON DOWN.

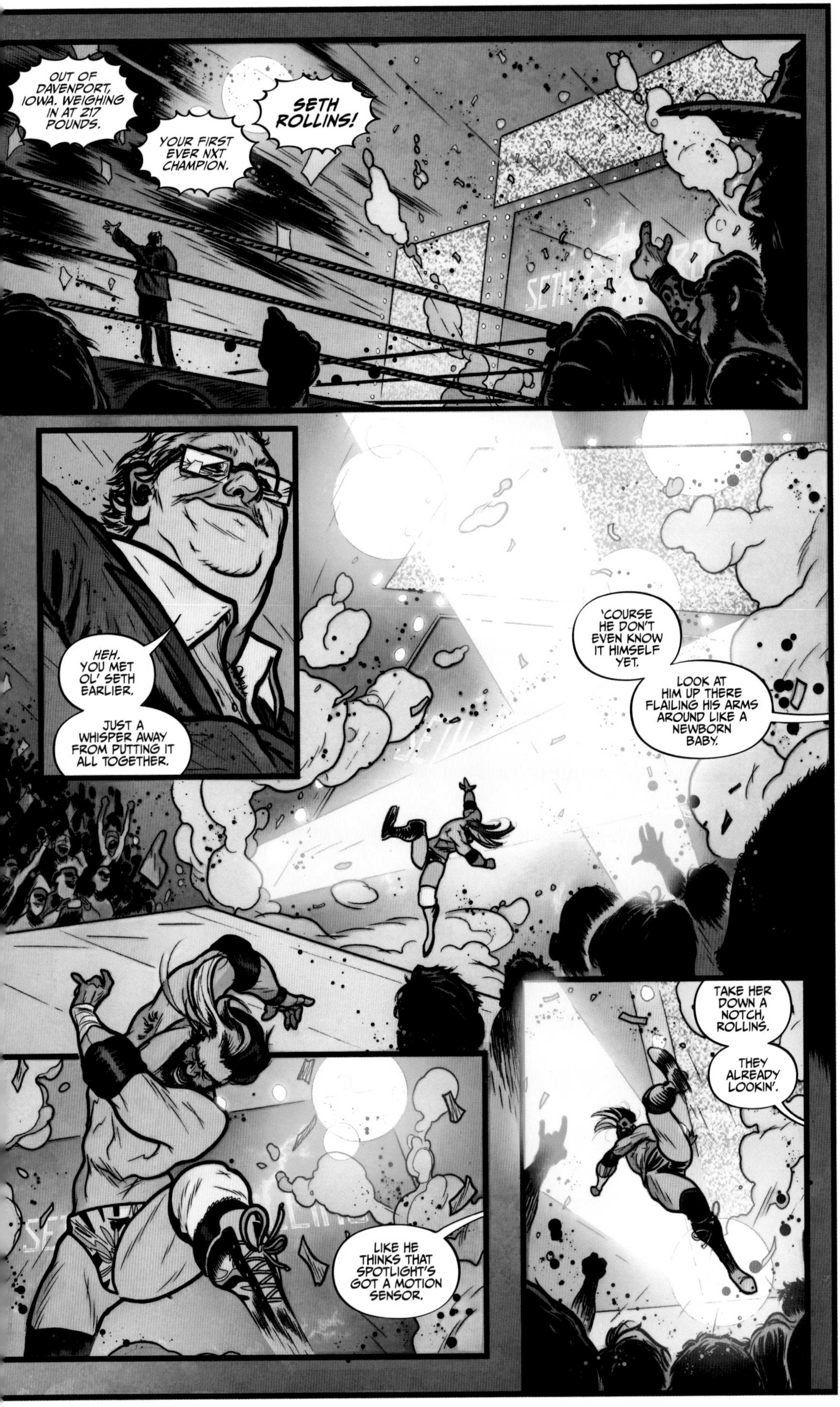

OUT OF DAVENPORT, IOWA. WEIGHING IN AT 217 POUNDS.
YOUR FIRST EVER NXT CHAMPION.
SETH ROLLINS!
HEH. YOU MET OL' SETH EARLIER.
JUST A WHISPER AWAY FROM PUTTING IT ALL TOGETHER.
'COURSE HE DON'T EVEN KNOW IT HIMSELF YET.
LOOK AT HIM UP THERE FLAILING HIS ARMS AROUND LIKE A NEWBORN BABY.
LIKE HE THINKS THAT SPOTLIGHT'S GOT A MOTION SENSOR.
TAKE HER DOWN A NOTCH, ROLLINS.
THEY ALREADY LOOKIN'.

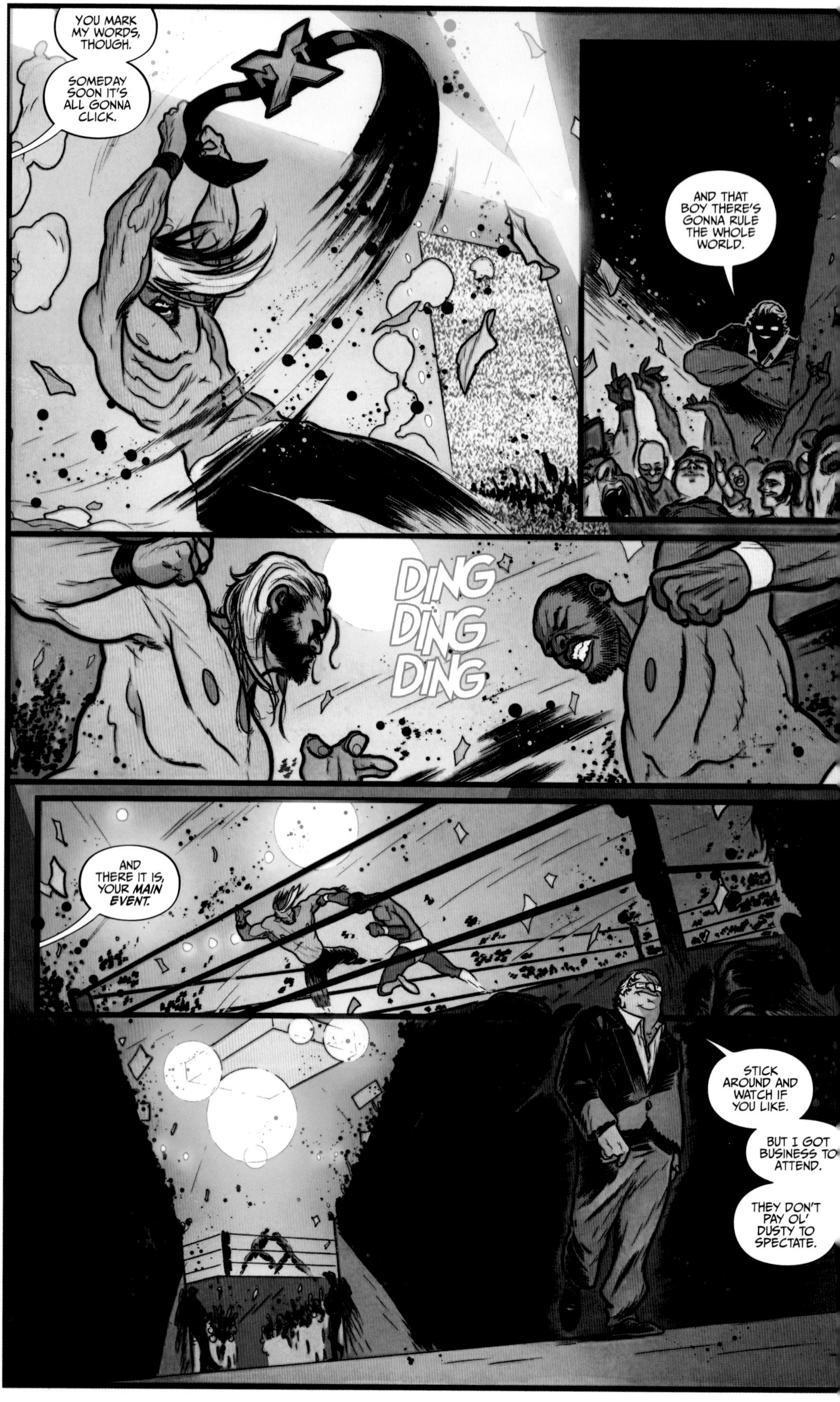
YOU MARK MY WORDS, THOUGH.
SOMEDAY SOON IT'S ALL GONNA CLICK.
AND THAT BOY THERE'S GONNA RULE THE WHOLE WORLD.
DING DING DING
AND THERE IT IS, YOUR *MAIN EVENT.*
STICK AROUND AND WATCH IF YOU LIKE.
BUT I GOT BUSINESS TO ATTEND.
THEY DON'T PAY OL' DUSTY TO SPECTATE.

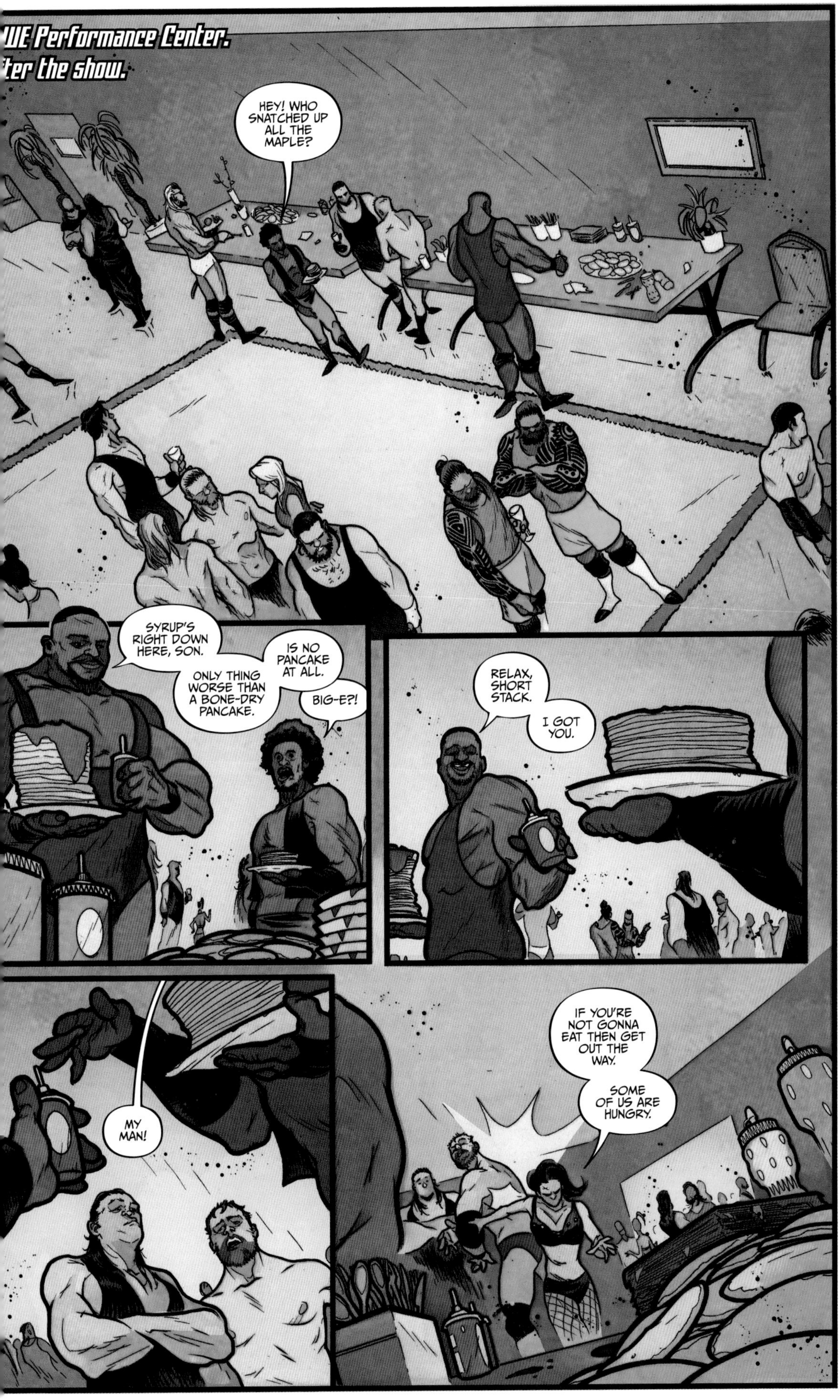
WE Performance Center.
ter the show.
HEY! WHO SNATCHED UP ALL THE MAPLE?
SYRUP'S RIGHT DOWN HERE, SON.
ONLY THING WORSE THAN A BONE-DRY PANCAKE.
IS NO PANCAKE AT ALL.
BIG-E?!
RELAX, SHORT STACK.
I GOT YOU.
MY MAN!
IF YOU'RE NOT GONNA EAT THEN GET OUT THE WAY.
SOME OF US ARE HUNGRY.

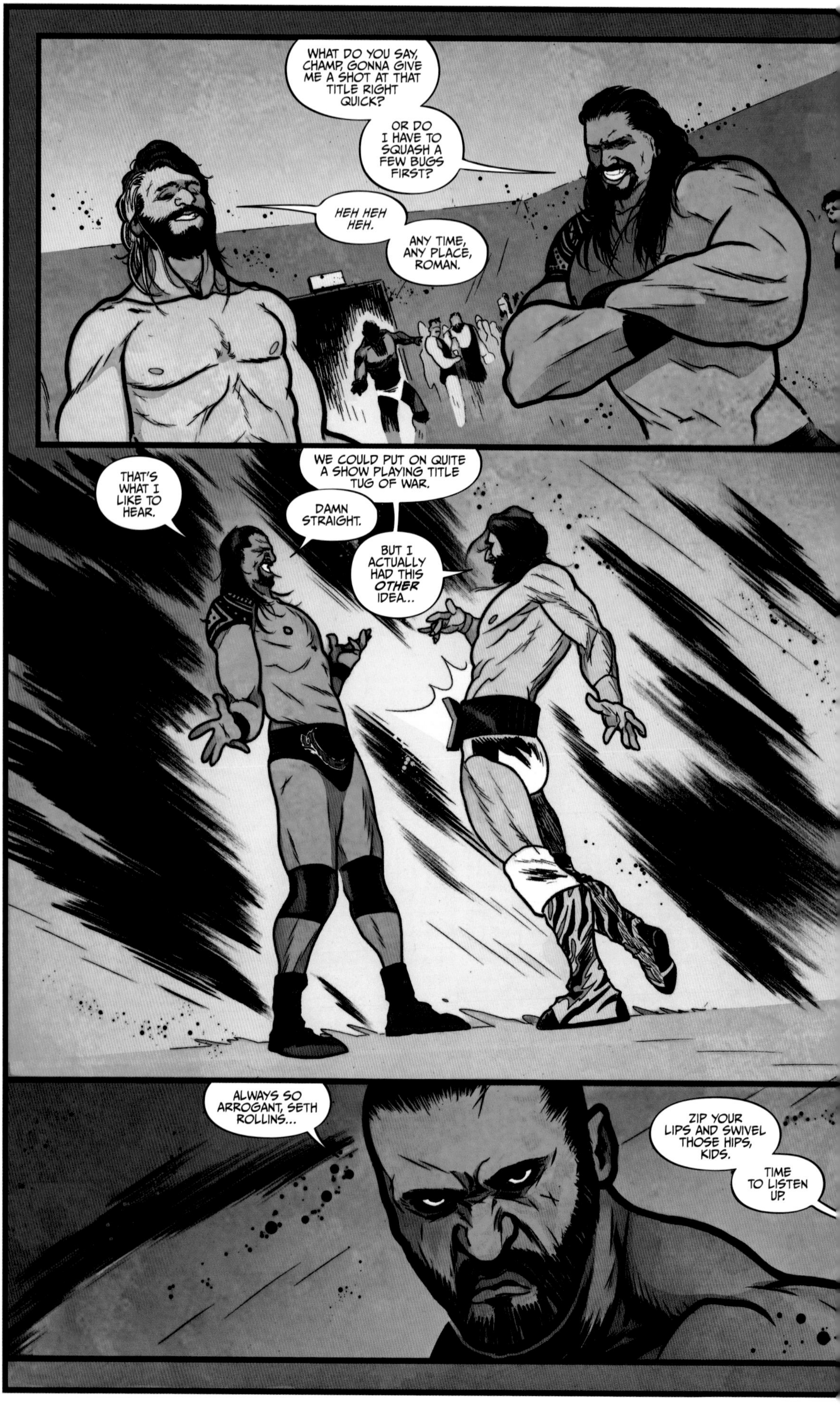
WHAT DO YOU SAY, CHAMP, GONNA GIVE ME A SHOT AT THAT TITLE RIGHT QUICK?
OR DO I HAVE TO SQUASH A FEW BUGS FIRST?
HEH HEH HEH.
ANY TIME, ANY PLACE, ROMAN.
THAT'S WHAT I LIKE TO HEAR.
WE COULD PUT ON QUITE A SHOW PLAYING TITLE TUG OF WAR.
DAMN STRAIGHT.
BUT I ACTUALLY HAD THIS *OTHER* IDEA...
ALWAYS SO ARROGANT, SETH ROLLINS...
ZIP YOUR LIPS AND SWIVEL THOSE HIPS, KIDS.
TIME TO LISTEN UP.

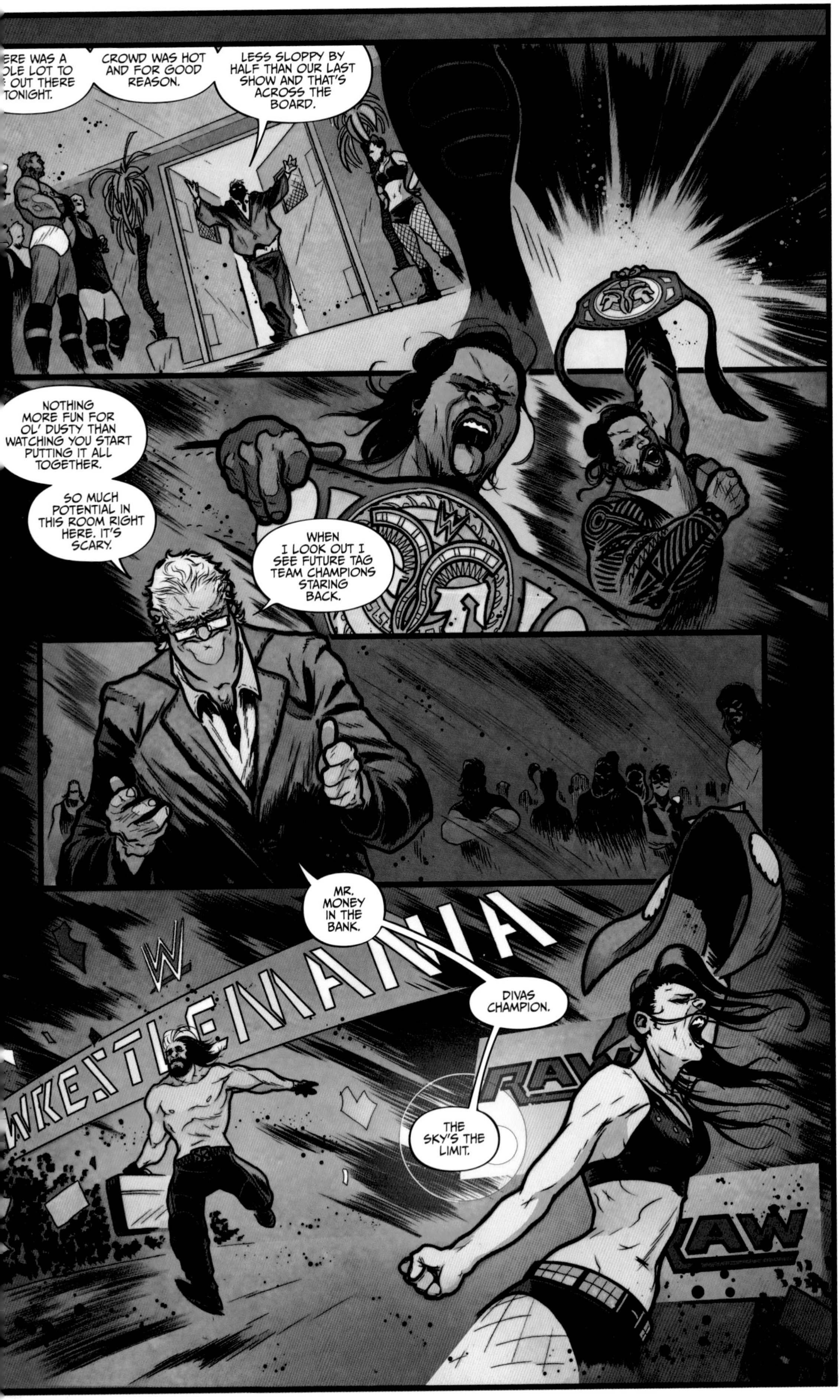
ERE WAS A
OLE LOT TO
OUT THERE
TONIGHT.
CROWD WAS HOT AND FOR GOOD REASON.
LESS SLOPPY BY HALF THAN OUR LAST SHOW AND THAT'S ACROSS THE BOARD.
NOTHING MORE FUN FOR OL' DUSTY THAN WATCHING YOU START PUTTING IT ALL TOGETHER.
SO MUCH POTENTIAL IN THIS ROOM RIGHT HERE. IT'S SCARY.
WHEN I LOOK OUT I SEE FUTURE TAG TEAM CHAMPIONS STARING BACK.
MR. MONEY IN THE BANK.
DIVAS CHAMPION.
THE SKY'S THE LIMIT.
WRESTLEMANIA
RAW

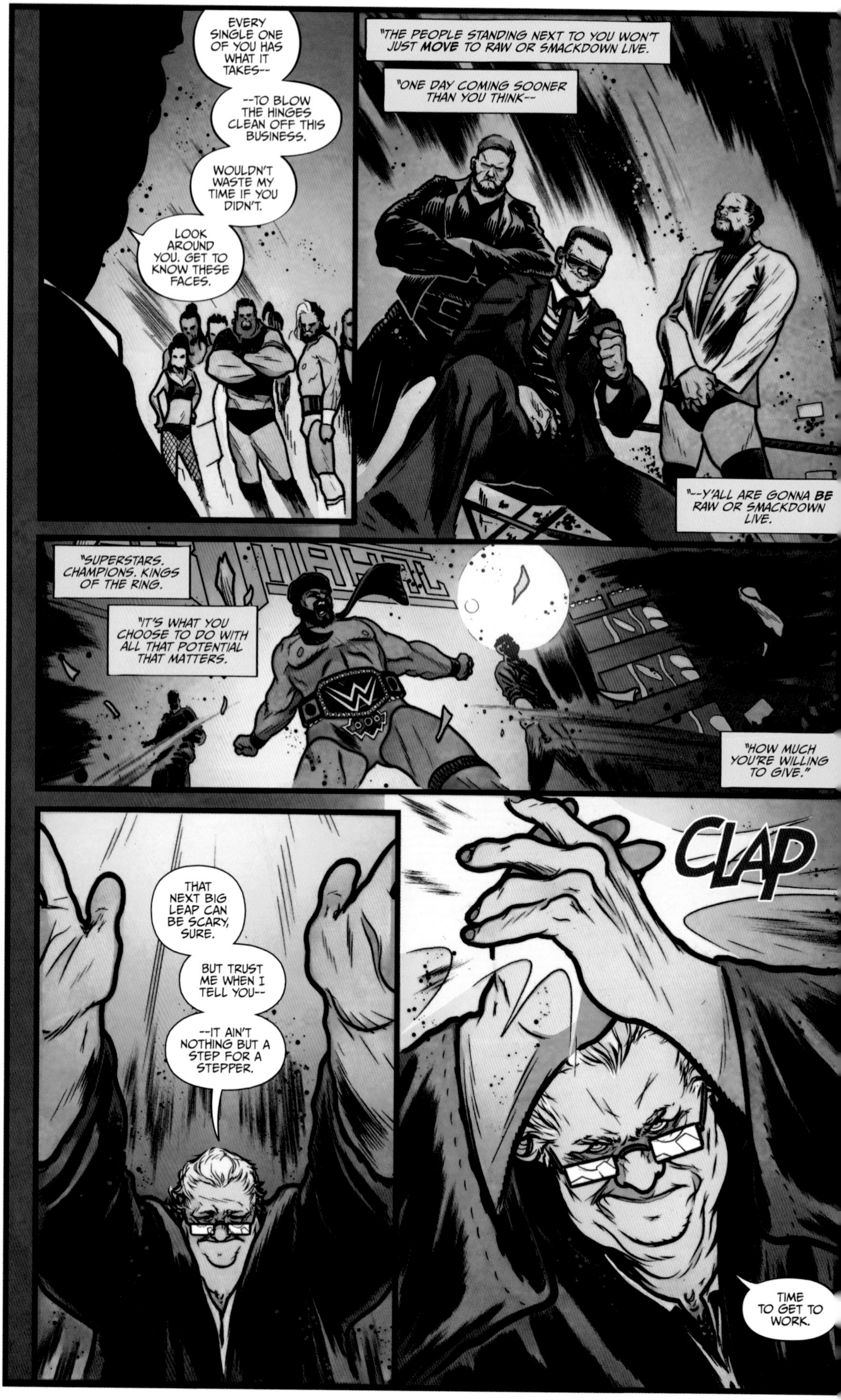
EVERY SINGLE ONE OF YOU HAS WHAT IT TAKES--
--TO BLOW THE HINGES CLEAN OFF THIS BUSINESS.
WOULDN'T WASTE MY TIME IF YOU DIDN'T.
LOOK AROUND YOU. GET TO KNOW THESE FACES.
"THE PEOPLE STANDING NEXT TO YOU WON'T JUST MOVE TO RAW OR SMACKDOWN LIVE.
"ONE DAY COMING SOONER THAN YOU THINK--
"--Y'ALL ARE GONNA BE RAW OR SMACKDOWN LIVE.
"SUPERSTARS. CHAMPIONS. KINGS OF THE RING.
"IT'S WHAT YOU CHOOSE TO DO WITH ALL THAT POTENTIAL THAT MATTERS.
"HOW MUCH YOU'RE WILLING TO GIVE."
THAT NEXT BIG LEAP CAN BE SCARY, SURE.
BUT TRUST ME WHEN I TELL YOU--
--IT AIN'T NOTHING BUT A STEP FOR A STEPPER.
CLAP
TIME TO GET TO WORK.

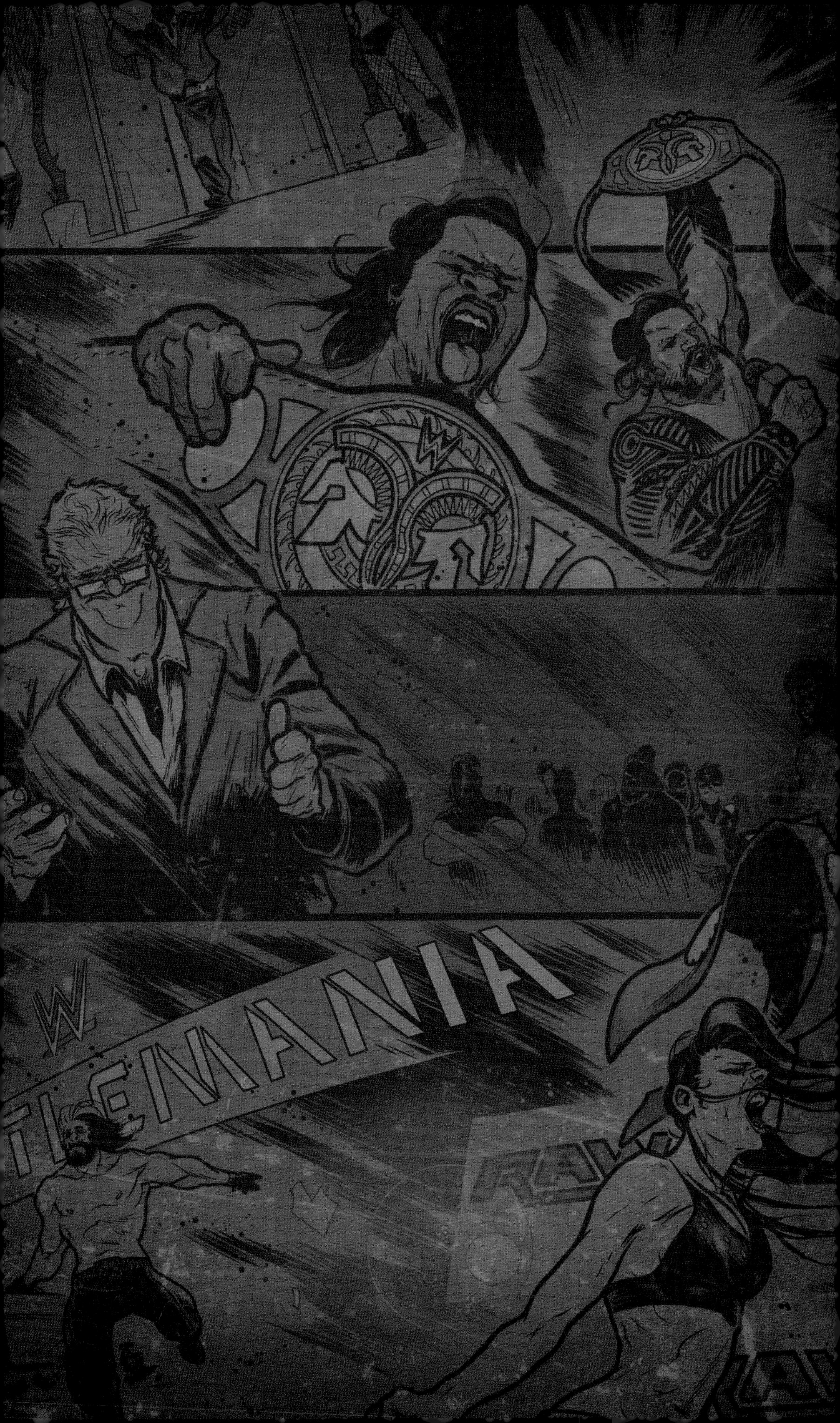

PROVING GROUND

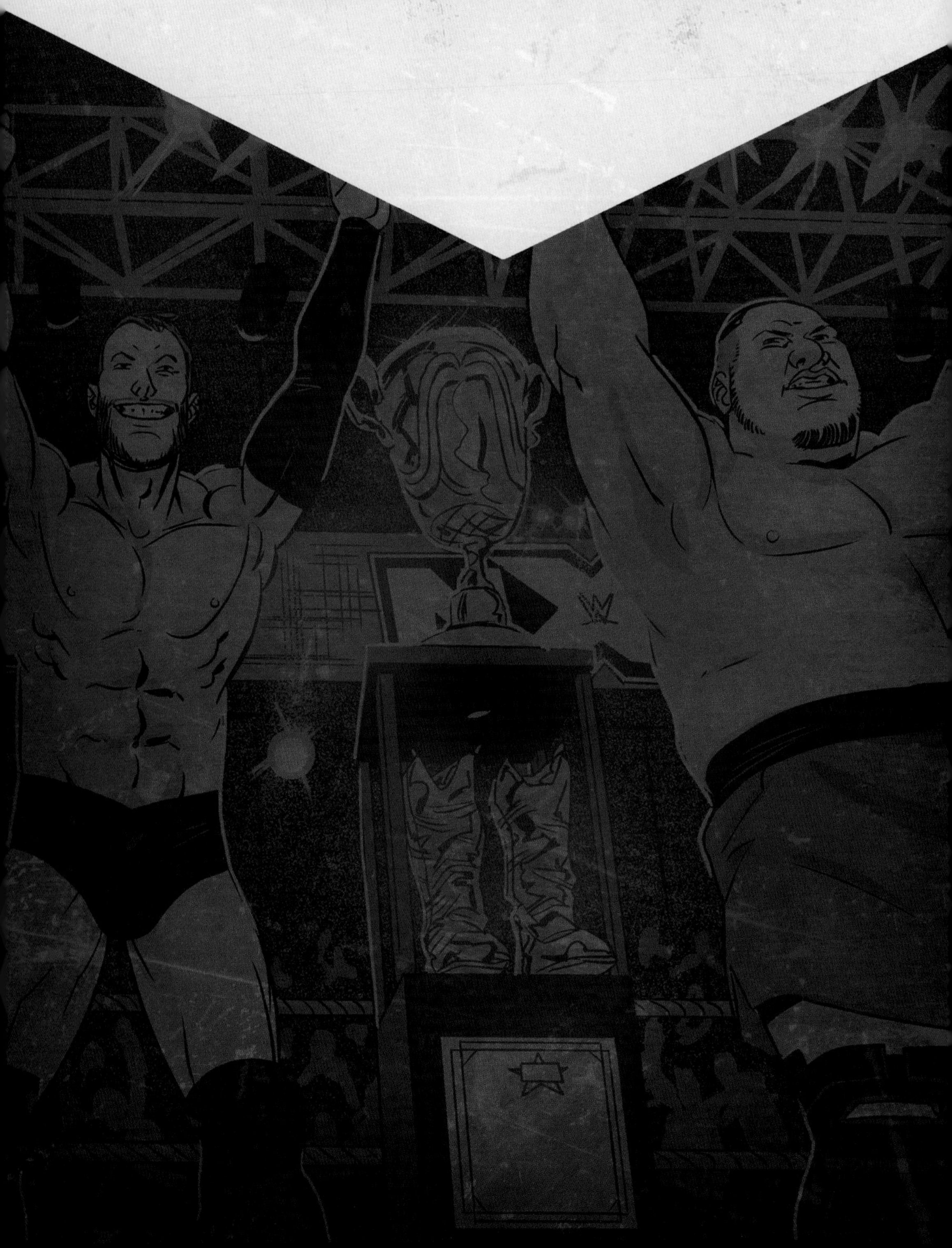

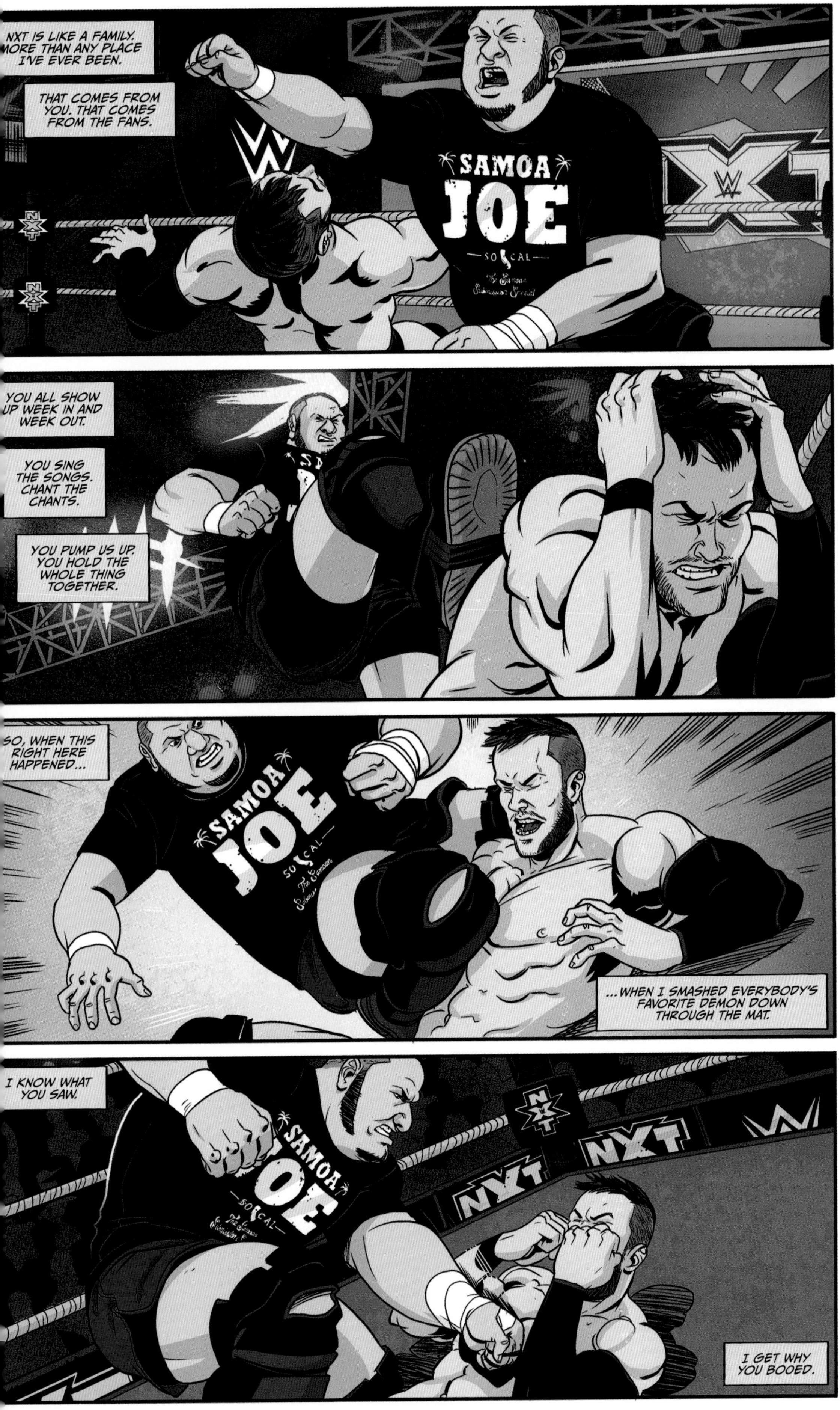
NXT IS LIKE A FAMILY. MORE THAN ANY PLACE I'VE EVER BEEN.
THAT COMES FROM YOU. THAT COMES FROM THE FANS.
YOU ALL SHOW UP WEEK IN AND WEEK OUT.
YOU SING THE SONGS. CHANT THE CHANTS.
YOU PUMP US UP. YOU HOLD THE WHOLE THING TOGETHER.
SO, WHEN THIS RIGHT HERE HAPPENED...
...WHEN I SMASHED EVERYBODY'S FAVORITE DEMON DOWN THROUGH THE MAT.
I KNOW WHAT YOU SAW.
I GET WHY YOU BOOED.

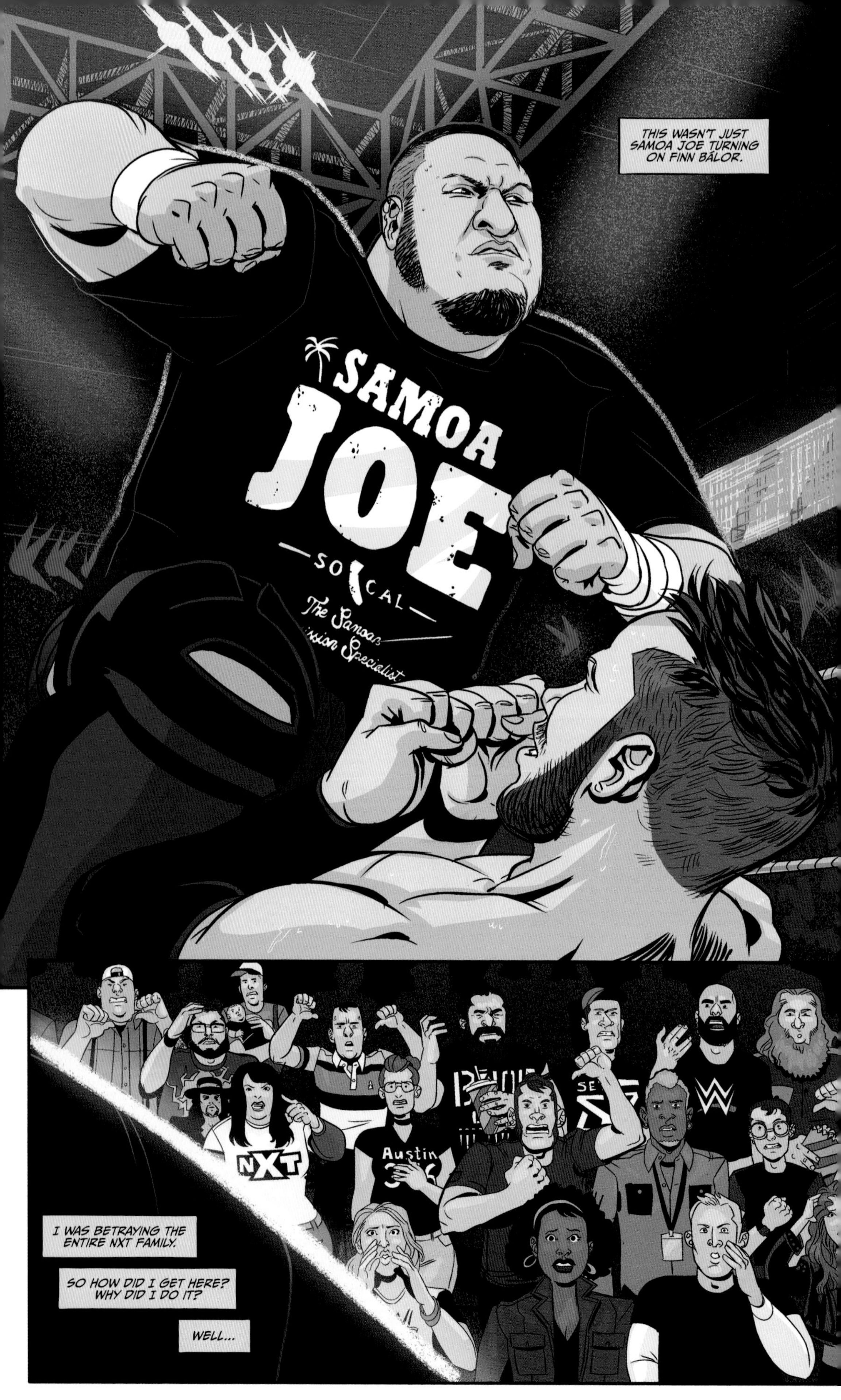
THIS WASN'T JUST SAMOA JOE TURNING ON FINN BÁLOR.
SAMOA JOE
SO CAL
NXT
Austin
I WAS BETRAYING THE ENTIRE NXT FAMILY.
SO HOW DID I GET HERE? WHY DID I DO IT?
WELL...

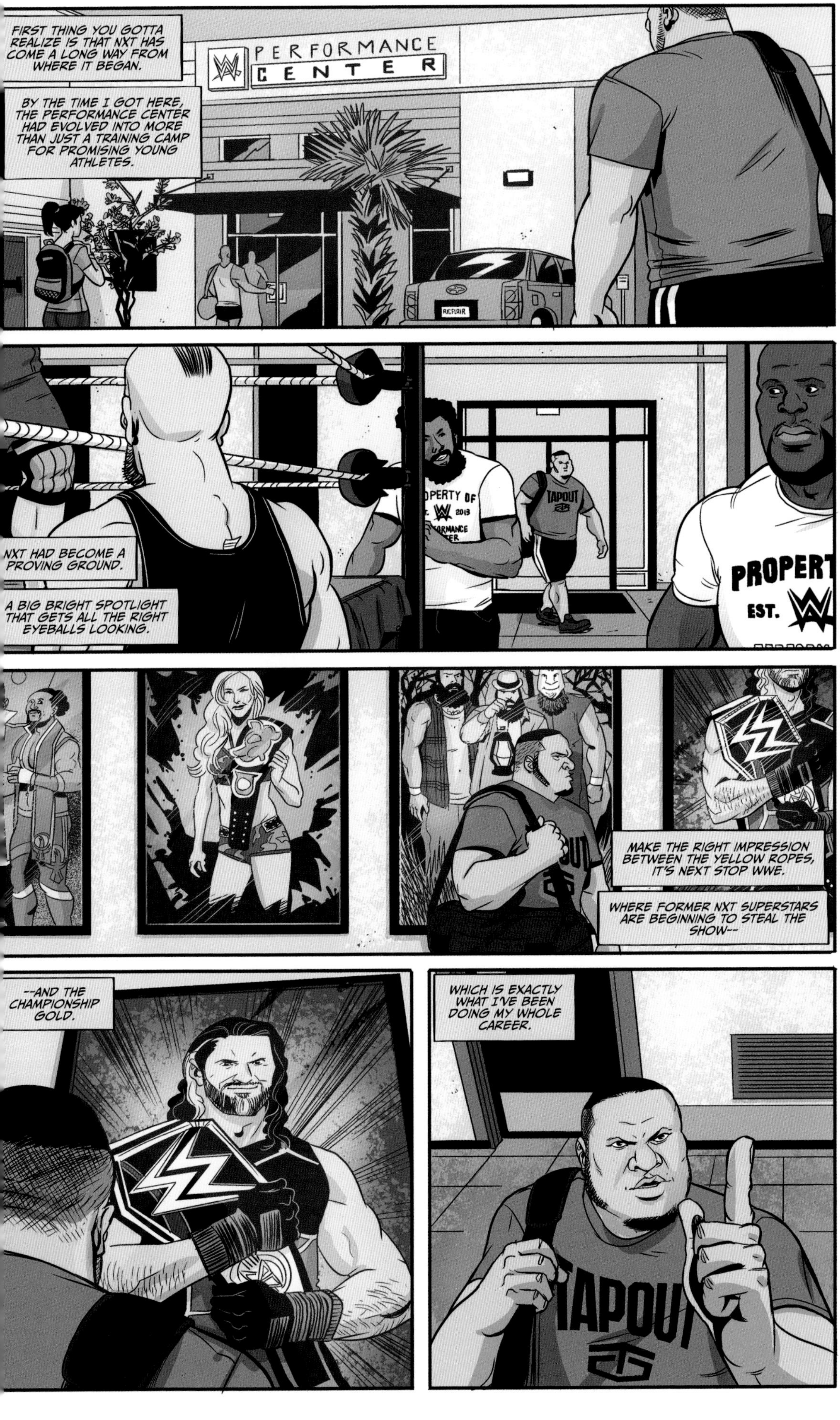
FIRST THING YOU GOTTA REALIZE IS THAT NXT HAS COME A LONG WAY FROM WHERE IT BEGAN.
PERFORMANCE CENTER
BY THE TIME I GOT HERE, THE PERFORMANCE CENTER HAD EVOLVED INTO MORE THAN JUST A TRAINING CAMP FOR PROMISING YOUNG ATHLETES.
RICFLAIR
NXT HAD BECOME A PROVING GROUND.
A BIG BRIGHT SPOTLIGHT THAT GETS ALL THE RIGHT EYEBALLS LOOKING.
TAPOUT
PROPERT
EST.
MAKE THE RIGHT IMPRESSION BETWEEN THE YELLOW ROPES, IT'S NEXT STOP WWE.
WHERE FORMER NXT SUPERSTARS ARE BEGINNING TO STEAL THE SHOW--
--AND THE CHAMPIONSHIP GOLD.
WHICH IS EXACTLY WHAT I'VE BEEN DOING MY WHOLE CAREER.
TAPOUT

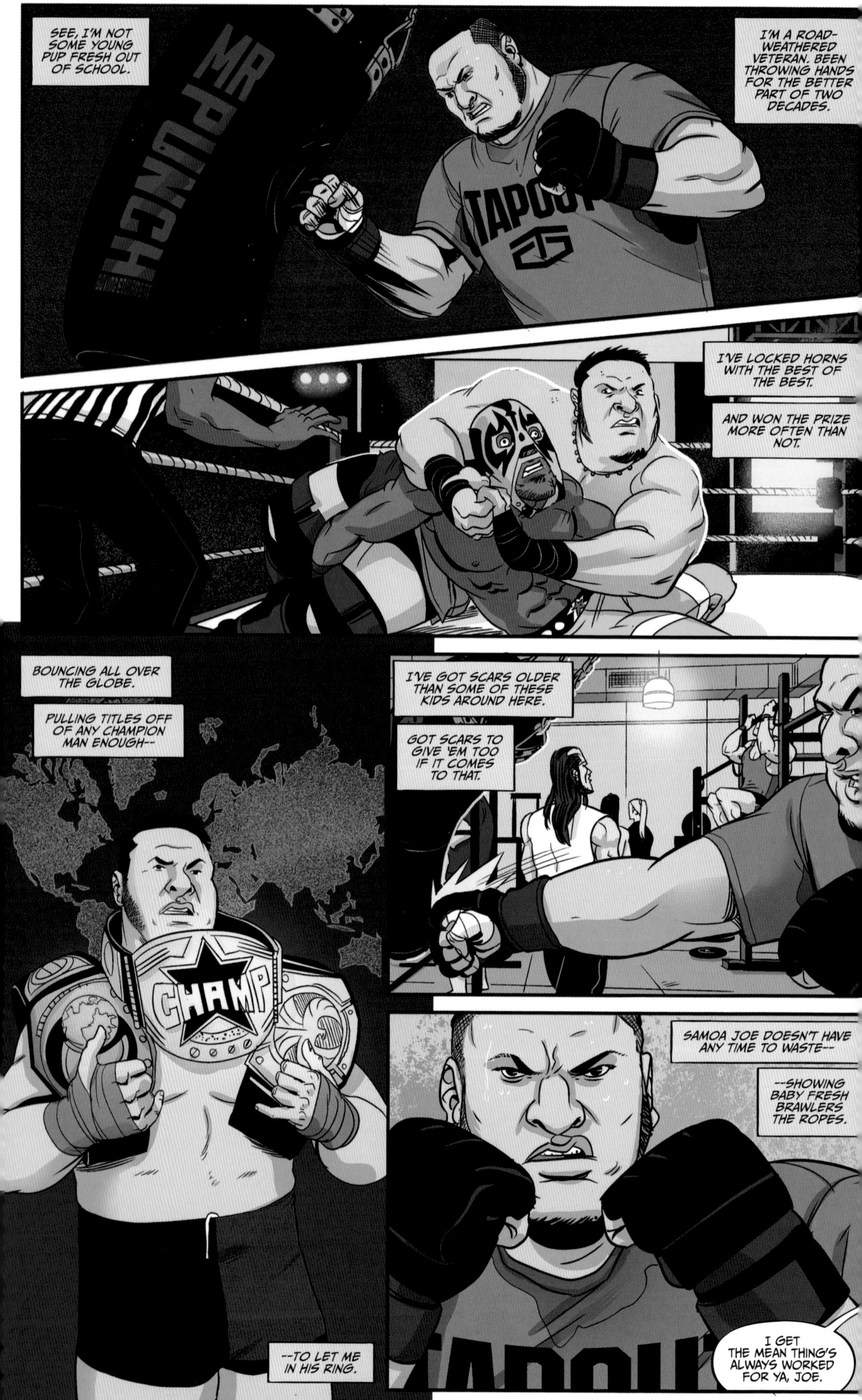
SEE, I'M NOT SOME YOUNG PUP FRESH OUT OF SCHOOL.
MR PUNCH
BOXING EQUIPMENT
I'M A ROAD-WEATHERED VETERAN. BEEN THROWING HANDS FOR THE BETTER PART OF TWO DECADES.
TAPOUT
I'VE LOCKED HORNS WITH THE BEST OF THE BEST.
AND WON THE PRIZE MORE OFTEN THAN NOT.
BOUNCING ALL OVER THE GLOBE.
PULLING TITLES OFF OF ANY CHAMPION MAN ENOUGH--
CHAMP
--TO LET ME IN HIS RING.
I'VE GOT SCARS OLDER THAN SOME OF THESE KIDS AROUND HERE.
GOT SCARS TO GIVE 'EM TOO IF IT COMES TO THAT.
SAMOA JOE DOESN'T HAVE ANY TIME TO WASTE--
--SHOWING BABY FRESH BRAWLERS THE ROPES.
I GET THE MEAN THING'S ALWAYS WORKED FOR YA, JOE.

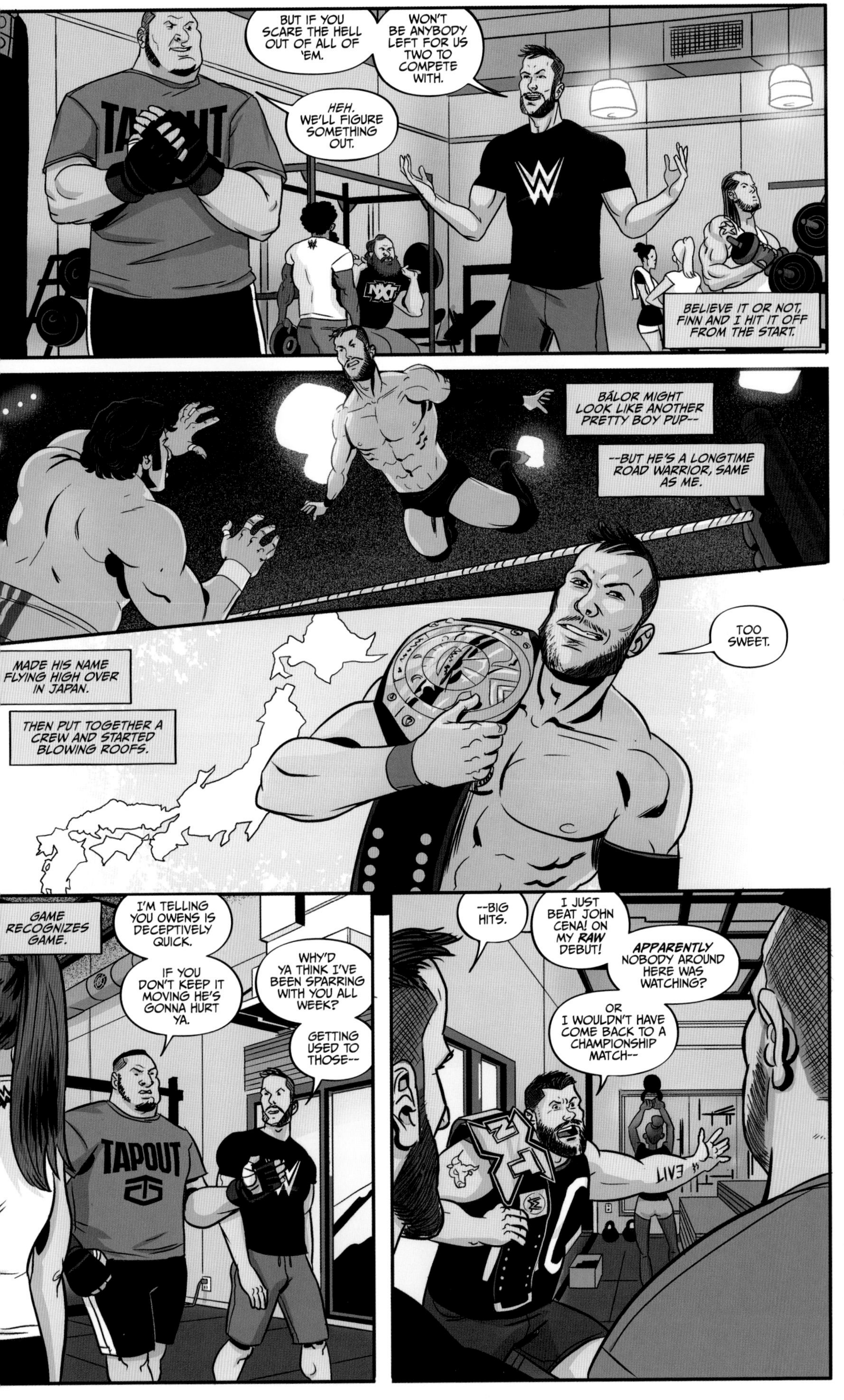
BUT IF YOU SCARE THE HELL OUT OF ALL OF 'EM.
WON'T BE ANYBODY LEFT FOR US TWO TO COMPETE WITH.
HEH. WE'LL FIGURE SOMETHING OUT.
TAPOUT
NXT
BELIEVE IT OR NOT, FINN AND I HIT IT OFF FROM THE START.
BÁLOR MIGHT LOOK LIKE ANOTHER PRETTY BOY PUP--
--BUT HE'S A LONGTIME ROAD WARRIOR, SAME AS ME.
TOO SWEET.
MADE HIS NAME FLYING HIGH OVER IN JAPAN.
THEN PUT TOGETHER A CREW AND STARTED BLOWING ROOFS.
GAME RECOGNIZES GAME.
I'M TELLING YOU OWENS IS DECEPTIVELY QUICK.
IF YOU DON'T KEEP IT MOVING HE'S GONNA HURT YA.
WHY'D YA THINK I'VE BEEN SPARRING WITH YOU ALL WEEK?
GETTING USED TO THOSE--
TAPOUT
--BIG HITS.
I JUST BEAT JOHN CENA! ON MY RAW DEBUT!
APPARENTLY NOBODY AROUND HERE WAS WATCHING?
OR I WOULDN'T HAVE COME BACK TO A CHAMPIONSHIP MATCH--

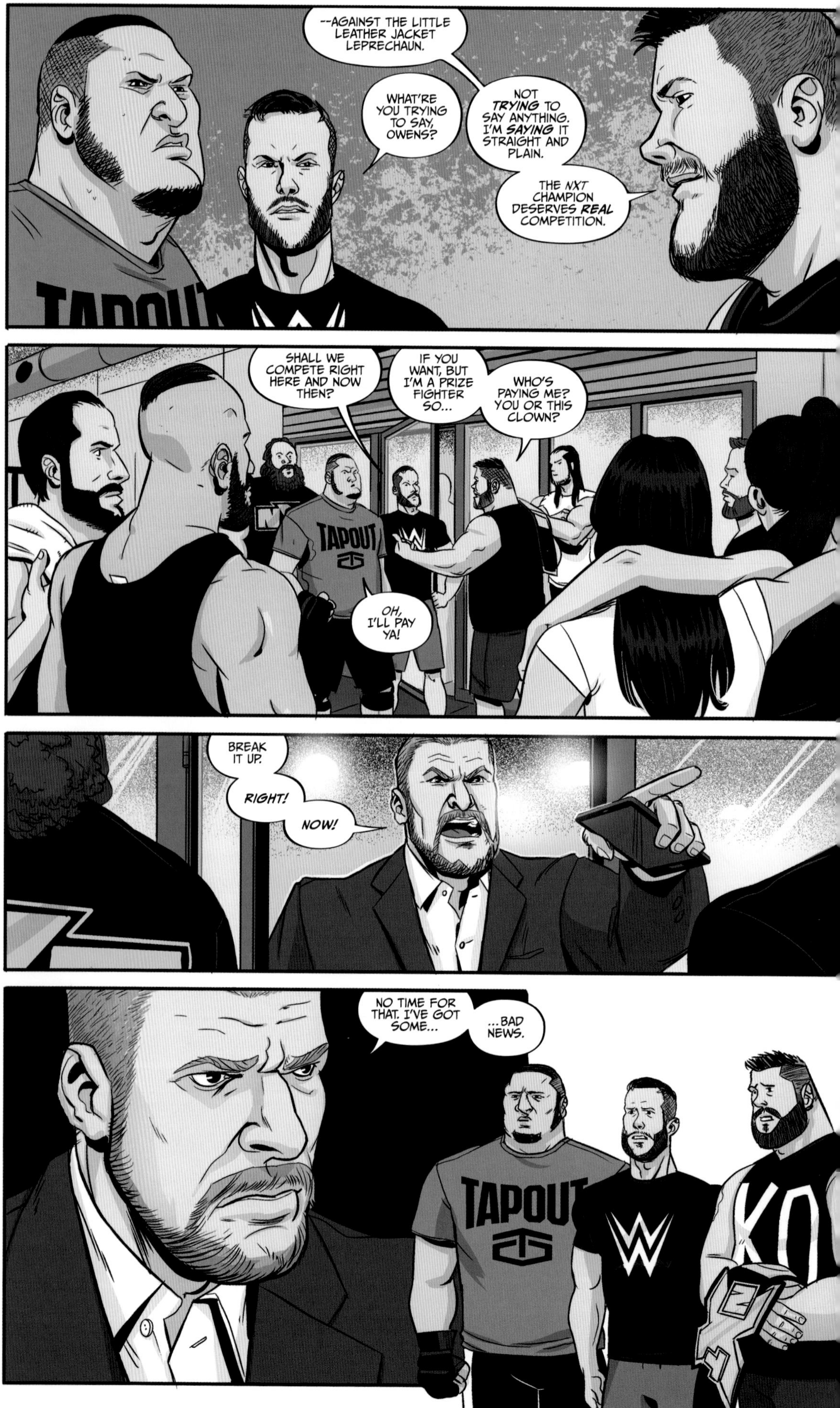
--AGAINST THE LITTLE LEATHER JACKET LEPRECHAUN.
WHAT'RE YOU TRYING TO SAY, OWENS?
NOT TRYING TO SAY ANYTHING. I'M SAYING IT STRAIGHT AND PLAIN.
THE NXT CHAMPION DESERVES REAL COMPETITION.
SHALL WE COMPETE RIGHT HERE AND NOW THEN?
IF YOU WANT, BUT I'M A PRIZE FIGHTER SO...
WHO'S PAYING ME? YOU OR THIS CLOWN?
OH, I'LL PAY YA!
TAPOUT
BREAK IT UP.
RIGHT!
NOW!
NO TIME FOR THAT. I'VE GOT SOME...
...BAD NEWS.
TAPOUT

In Memory of
DUSTY RHODES
1945 - 2015

THIS WEEK THIS INDUSTRY LOST A LEGEND.

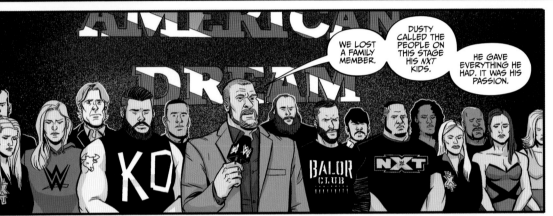

WE LOST A FAMILY MEMBER.

DUSTY CALLED THE PEOPLE ON THIS STAGE HIS *NXT* KIDS.

HE GAVE EVERYTHING HE HAD. IT WAS HIS PASSION.

AND ALL OF YOU WERE HIS *NXT* FAMILY.

SO PLEASE, AS A FAMILY, STAND WITH ME NOW--

--TO HONOR THE PASSING OF THE AMERICAN DREAM, DUSTY RHODES.

DING DING

DING DING DING

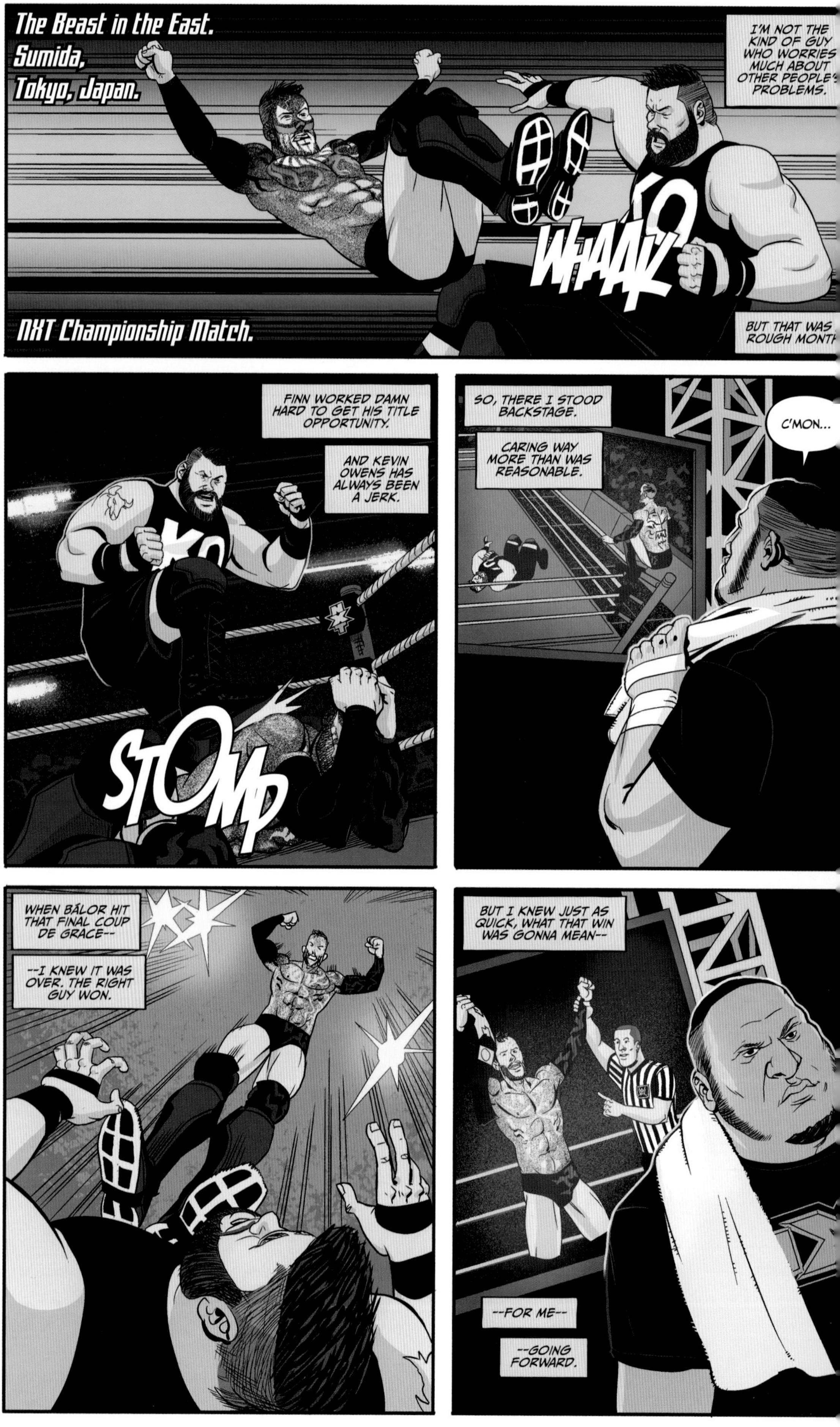

The Beast in the East.
Sumida,
Tokyo, Japan.
I'M NOT THE KIND OF GUY WHO WORRIES MUCH ABOUT OTHER PEOPLE'S PROBLEMS.
WHAAK
NXT Championship Match.
BUT THAT WAS A ROUGH MONTH
FINN WORKED DAMN HARD TO GET HIS TITLE OPPORTUNITY.
AND KEVIN OWENS HAS ALWAYS BEEN A JERK.
STOMP
SO, THERE I STOOD BACKSTAGE.
CARING WAY MORE THAN WAS REASONABLE.
C'MON...
WHEN BÁLOR HIT THAT FINAL COUP DE GRACE--
--I KNEW IT WAS OVER. THE RIGHT GUY WON.
BUT I KNEW JUST AS QUICK, WHAT THAT WIN WAS GONNA MEAN--
--FOR ME--
--GOING FORWARD.

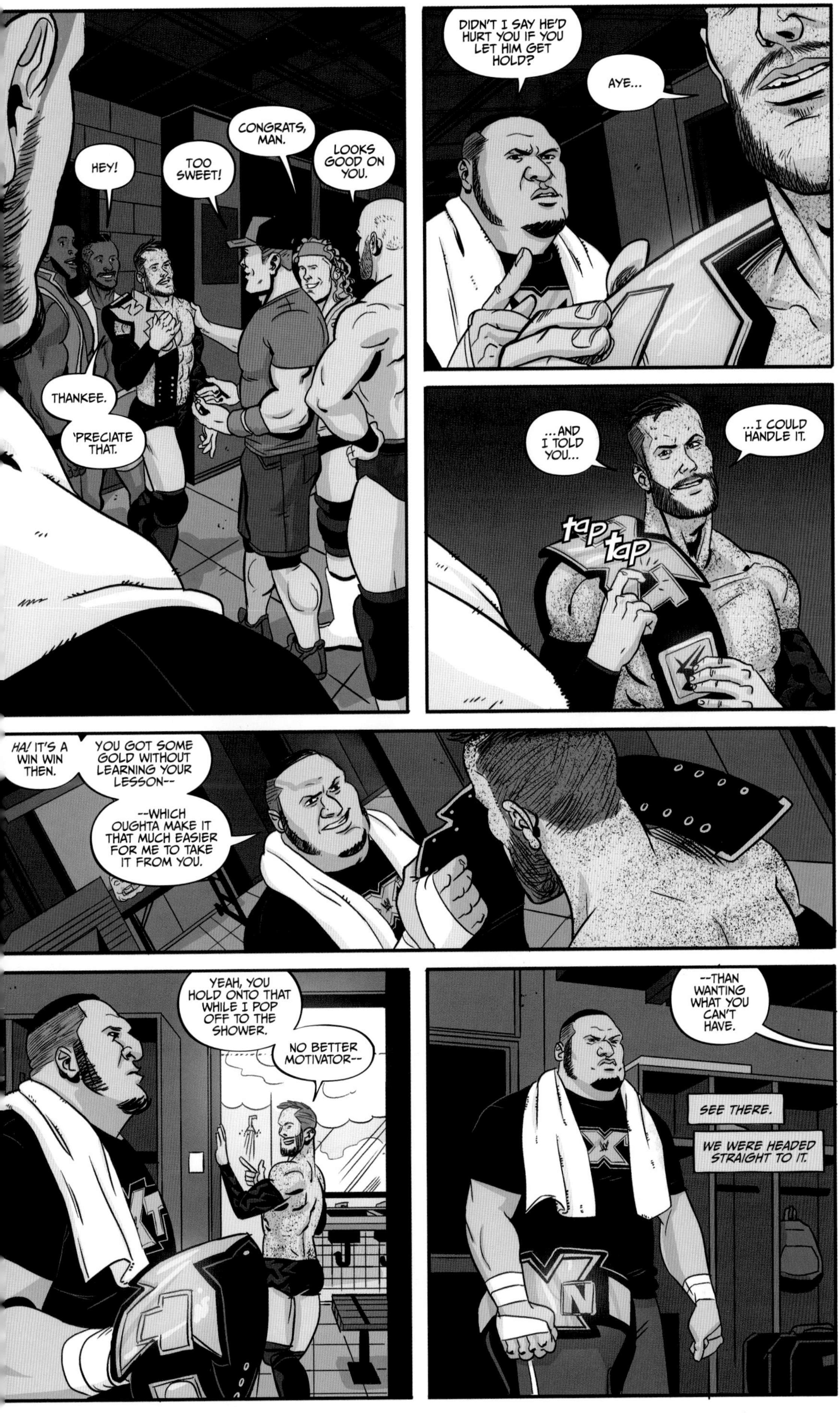
HEY!
TOO SWEET!
CONGRATS, MAN.
LOOKS GOOD ON YOU.
THANKEE.
'PRECIATE THAT.
DIDN'T I SAY HE'D HURT YOU IF YOU LET HIM GET HOLD?
AYE...
...AND I TOLD YOU...
...I COULD HANDLE IT.
tap tap
HA! IT'S A WIN WIN THEN.
YOU GOT SOME GOLD WITHOUT LEARNING YOUR LESSON--
--WHICH OUGHTA MAKE IT THAT MUCH EASIER FOR ME TO TAKE IT FROM YOU.
YEAH, YOU HOLD ONTO THAT WHILE I POP OFF TO THE SHOWER.
NO BETTER MOTIVATOR--
--THAN WANTING WHAT YOU CAN'T HAVE.
SEE THERE.
WE WERE HEADED STRAIGHT TO IT.

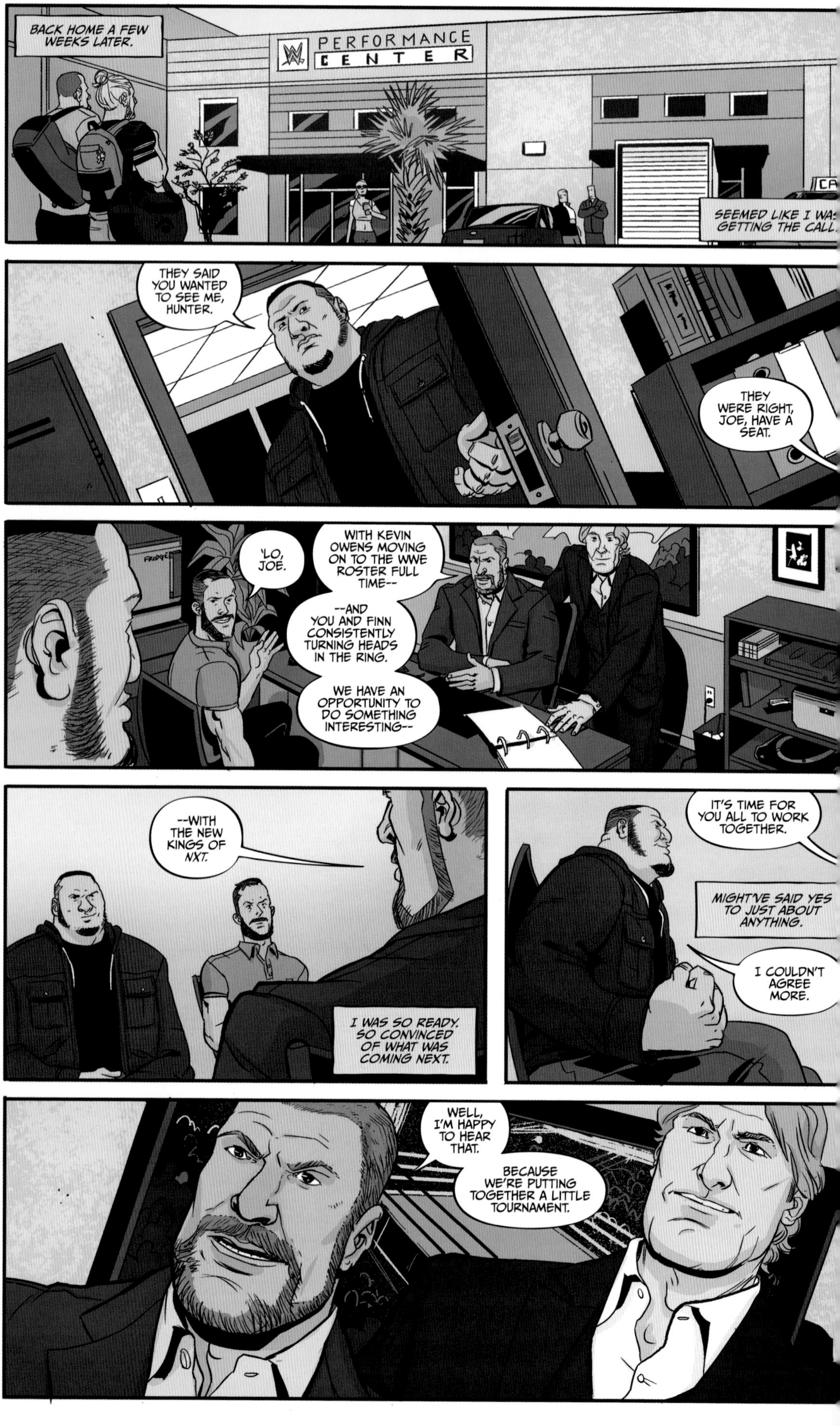

BACK HOME A FEW WEEKS LATER.
PERFORMANCE CENTER
SEEMED LIKE I WAS GETTING THE CALL.
THEY SAID YOU WANTED TO SEE ME, HUNTER.
THEY WERE RIGHT, JOE, HAVE A SEAT.
FRIDGE
'LO, JOE.
WITH KEVIN OWENS MOVING ON TO THE WWE ROSTER FULL TIME--
--AND YOU AND FINN CONSISTENTLY TURNING HEADS IN THE RING.
WE HAVE AN OPPORTUNITY TO DO SOMETHING INTERESTING--
--WITH THE NEW KINGS OF NXT.
I WAS SO READY. SO CONVINCED OF WHAT WAS COMING NEXT.
IT'S TIME FOR YOU ALL TO WORK TOGETHER.
MIGHT'VE SAID YES TO JUST ABOUT ANYTHING.
I COULDN'T AGREE MORE.
WELL, I'M HAPPY TO HEAR THAT.
BECAUSE WE'RE PUTTING TOGETHER A LITTLE TOURNAMENT.

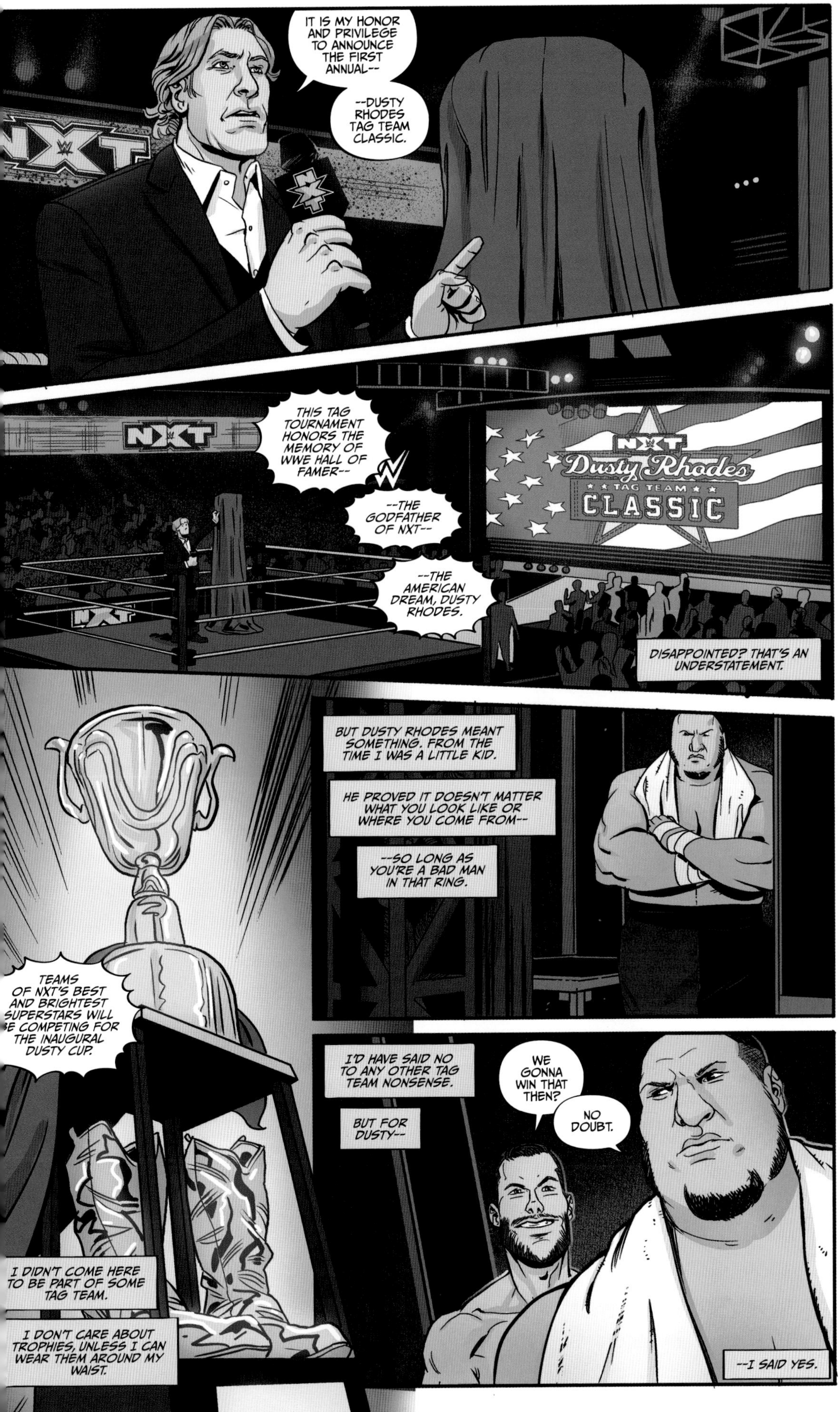
IT IS MY HONOR AND PRIVILEGE TO ANNOUNCE THE FIRST ANNUAL--
--DUSTY RHODES TAG TEAM CLASSIC.
NXT
THIS TAG TOURNAMENT HONORS THE MEMORY OF WWE HALL OF FAMER--
--THE GODFATHER OF NXT--
--THE AMERICAN DREAM, DUSTY RHODES.
NXT Dusty Rhodes TAG TEAM CLASSIC
DISAPPOINTED? THAT'S AN UNDERSTATEMENT.
BUT DUSTY RHODES MEANT SOMETHING. FROM THE TIME I WAS A LITTLE KID.
HE PROVED IT DOESN'T MATTER WHAT YOU LOOK LIKE OR WHERE YOU COME FROM--
--SO LONG AS YOU'RE A BAD MAN IN THAT RING.
TEAMS OF NXT'S BEST AND BRIGHTEST SUPERSTARS WILL BE COMPETING FOR THE INAUGURAL DUSTY CUP.
I DIDN'T COME HERE TO BE PART OF SOME TAG TEAM.
I DON'T CARE ABOUT TROPHIES, UNLESS I CAN WEAR THEM AROUND MY WAIST.
I'D HAVE SAID NO TO ANY OTHER TAG TEAM NONSENSE.
BUT FOR DUSTY--
WE GONNA WIN THAT THEN?
NO DOUBT.
--I SAID YES.

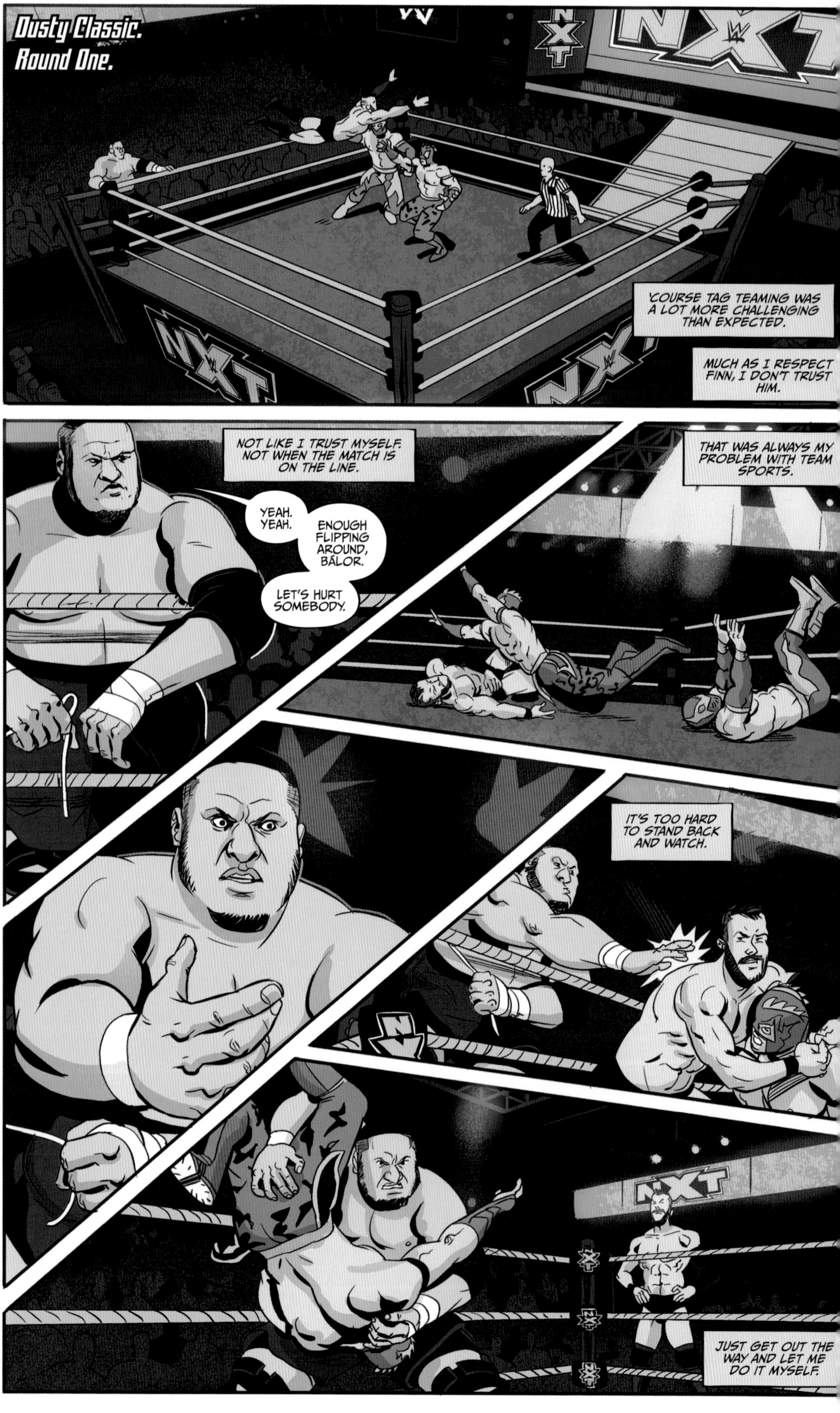
Dusty Classic.
Round One.
'COURSE TAG TEAMING WAS A LOT MORE CHALLENGING THAN EXPECTED.
MUCH AS I RESPECT FINN, I DON'T TRUST HIM.
NOT LIKE I TRUST MYSELF. NOT WHEN THE MATCH IS ON THE LINE.
YEAH. YEAH.
ENOUGH FLIPPING AROUND, BÁLOR.
LET'S HURT SOMEBODY.
THAT WAS ALWAYS MY PROBLEM WITH TEAM SPORTS.
IT'S TOO HARD TO STAND BACK AND WATCH.
JUST GET OUT THE WAY AND LET ME DO IT MYSELF.

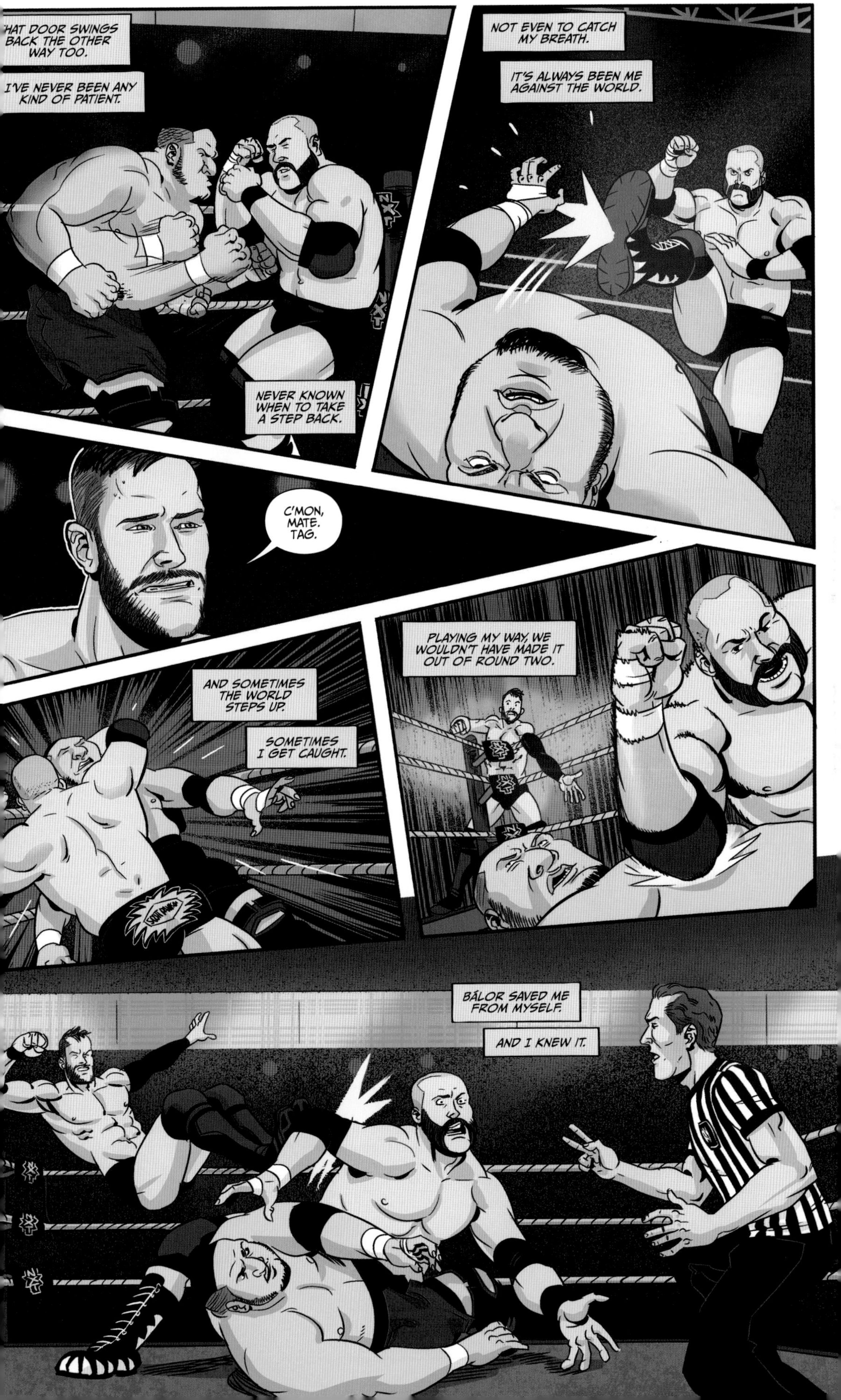
THAT DOOR SWINGS BACK THE OTHER WAY TOO.
I'VE NEVER BEEN ANY KIND OF PATIENT.
NEVER KNOWN WHEN TO TAKE A STEP BACK.
NOT EVEN TO CATCH MY BREATH.
IT'S ALWAYS BEEN ME AGAINST THE WORLD.
C'MON, MATE. TAG.
AND SOMETIMES THE WORLD STEPS UP.
SOMETIMES I GET CAUGHT.
PLAYING MY WAY, WE WOULDN'T HAVE MADE IT OUT OF ROUND TWO.
BÁLOR SAVED ME FROM MYSELF.
AND I KNEW IT.

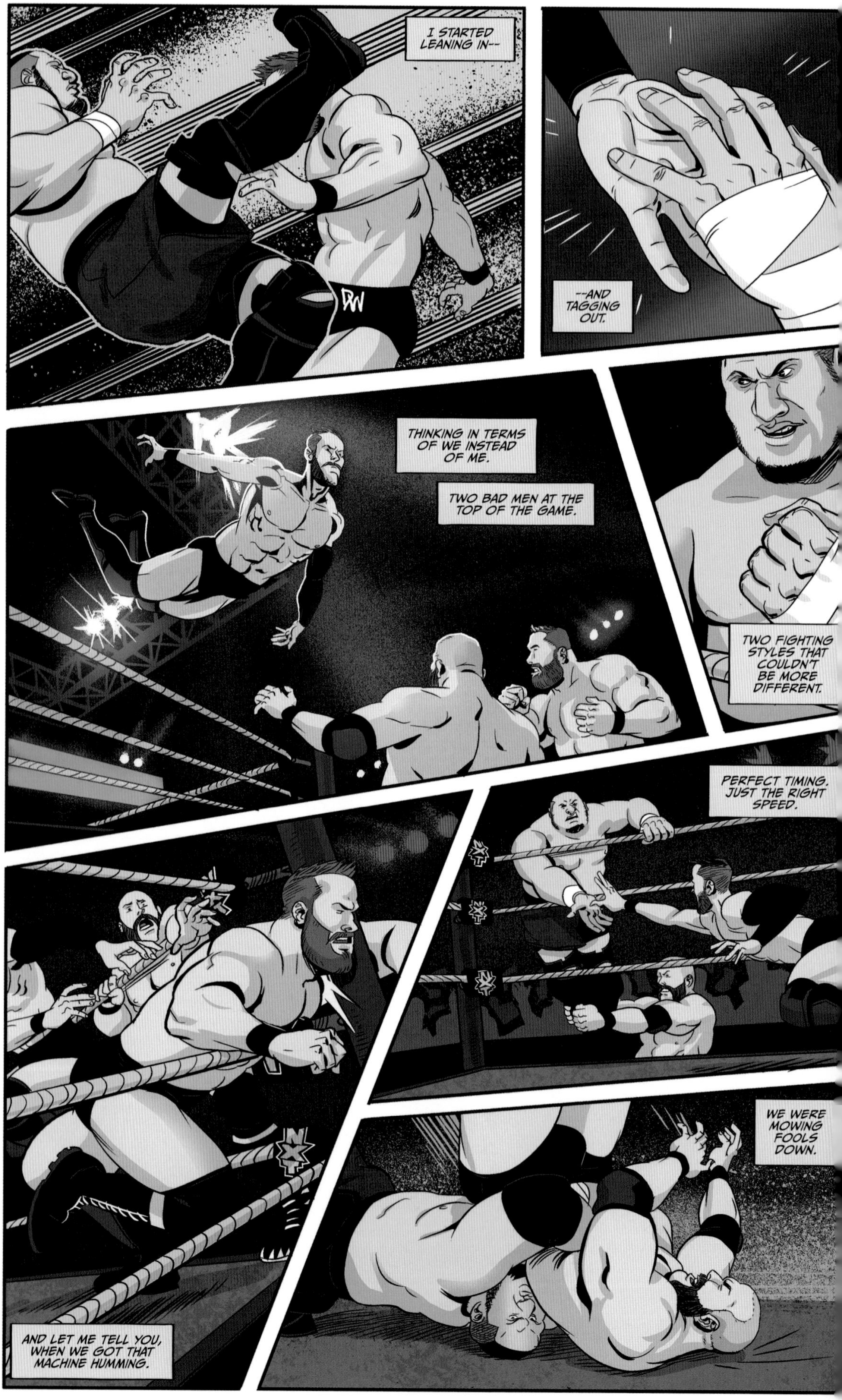
I STARTED LEANING IN--
--AND TAGGING OUT.
THINKING IN TERMS OF WE INSTEAD OF ME.
TWO BAD MEN AT THE TOP OF THE GAME.
TWO FIGHTING STYLES THAT COULDN'T BE MORE DIFFERENT.
PERFECT TIMING. JUST THE RIGHT SPEED.
AND LET ME TELL YOU, WHEN WE GOT THAT MACHINE HUMMING.
WE WERE MOWING FOOLS DOWN.

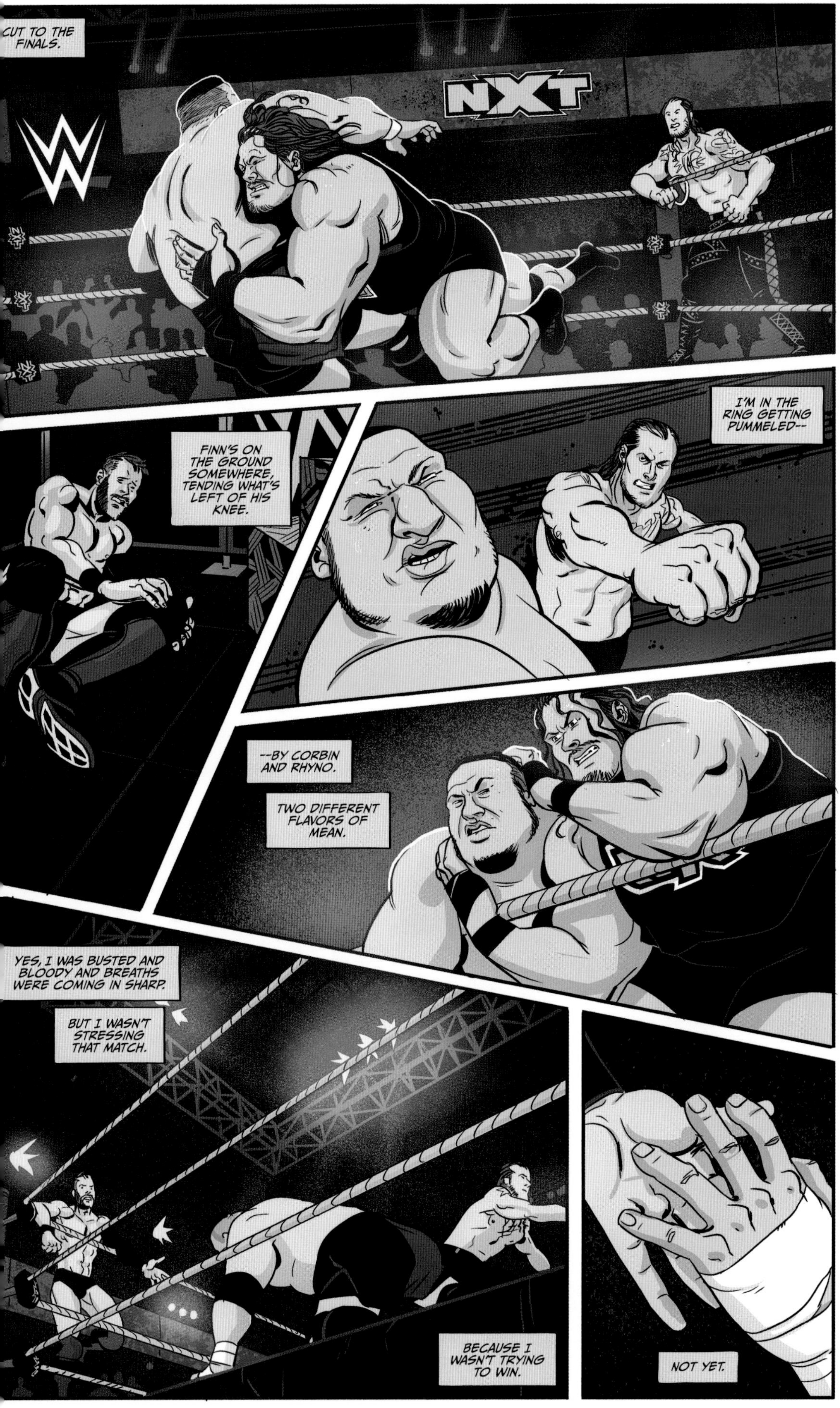
CUT TO THE FINALS.
NXT
FINN'S ON THE GROUND SOMEWHERE, TENDING WHAT'S LEFT OF HIS KNEE.
I'M IN THE RING GETTING PUMMELED--
--BY CORBIN AND RHYNO.
TWO DIFFERENT FLAVORS OF MEAN.
YES, I WAS BUSTED AND BLOODY AND BREATHS WERE COMING IN SHARP.
BUT I WASN'T STRESSING THAT MATCH.
BECAUSE I WASN'T TRYING TO WIN.
NOT YET.

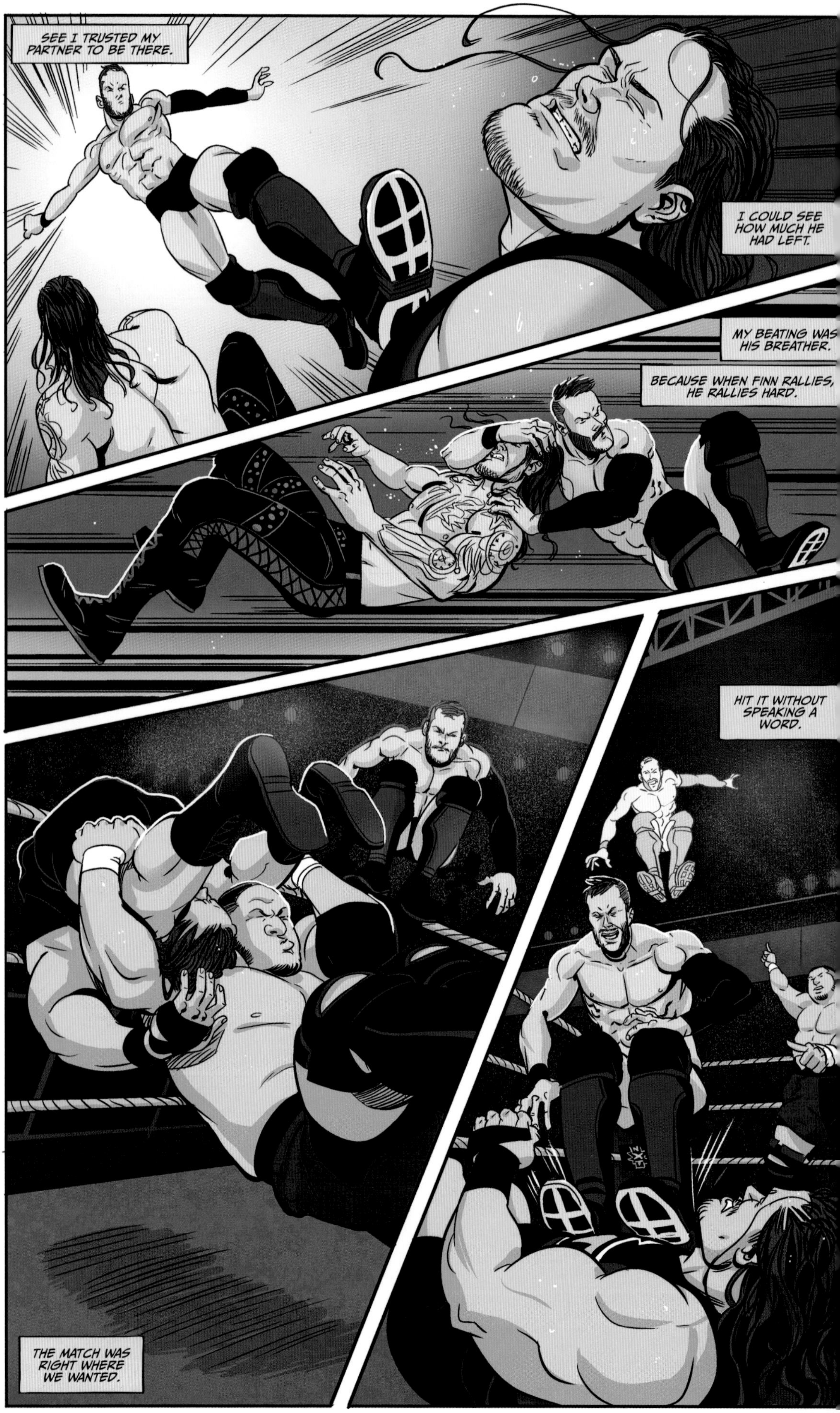
SEE I TRUSTED MY PARTNER TO BE THERE.
I COULD SEE HOW MUCH HE HAD LEFT.
MY BEATING WAS HIS BREATHER.
BECAUSE WHEN FINN RALLIES, HE RALLIES HARD.
THE MATCH WAS RIGHT WHERE WE WANTED.
HIT IT WITHOUT SPEAKING A WORD.

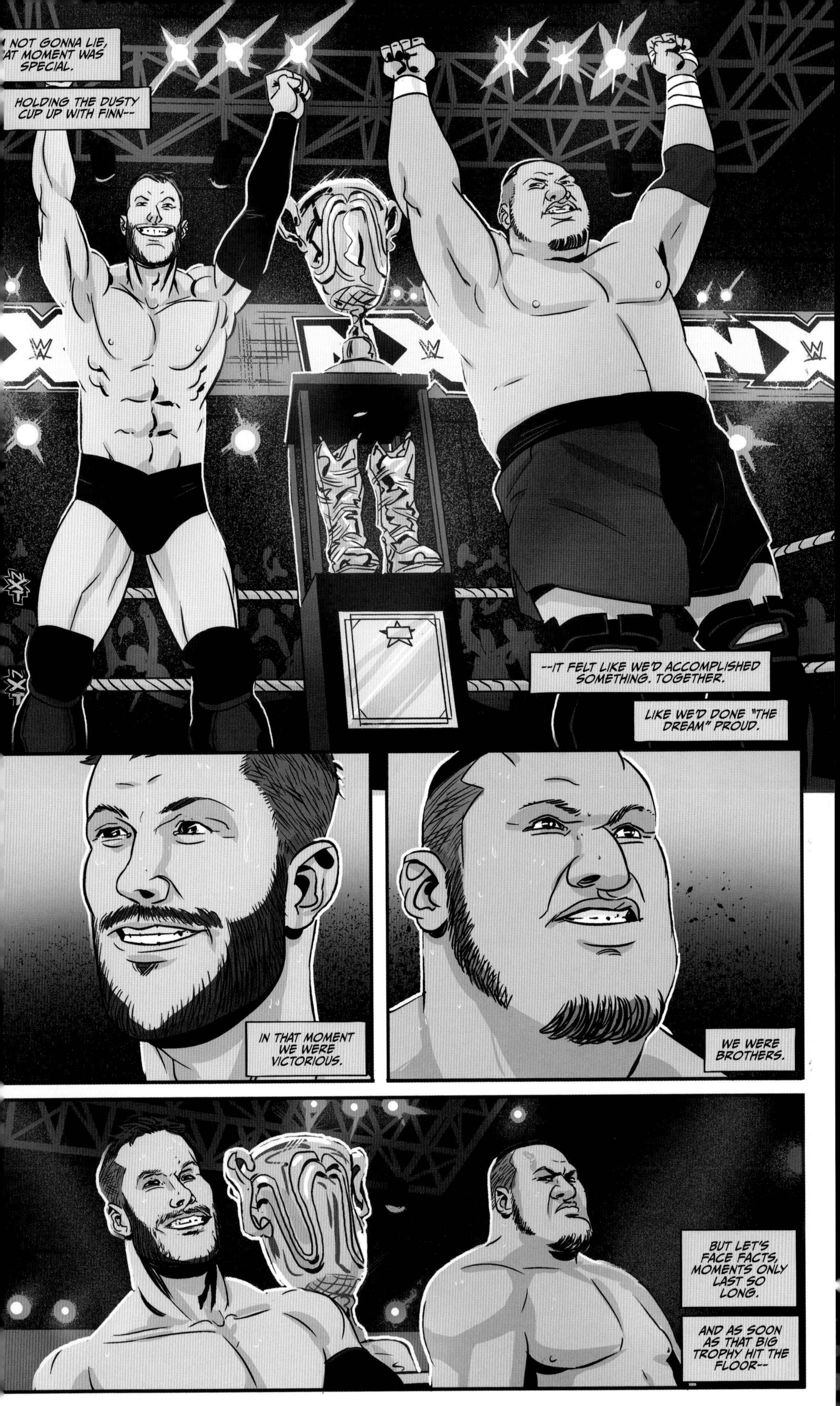
NOT GONNA LIE, AT MOMENT WAS SPECIAL.
HOLDING THE DUSTY CUP UP WITH FINN--
--IT FELT LIKE WE'D ACCOMPLISHED SOMETHING. TOGETHER.
LIKE WE'D DONE "THE DREAM" PROUD.
IN THAT MOMENT WE WERE VICTORIOUS.
WE WERE BROTHERS.
BUT LET'S FACE FACTS, MOMENTS ONLY LAST SO LONG.
AND AS SOON AS THAT BIG TROPHY HIT THE FLOOR--

--IT WAS TIME TO GET BACK TO WORK.

MR. REGAL, CAN I HAVE A WORD.

ANYTHING FOR YOU, JOE.

THAT WAS QUITE A MATCH JUST THERE, BY THE WAY.

YOU AND BÁLOR MAKE QUITE A TEAM.

WE DO, BUT NOW THAT'S DONE. WHICH MEANS WE CAN START TALKING ABOUT A CHAMPIONSHIP.

HEH. NOT EVEN A SHOWER FIRST. I LIKE THAT.

DON'T SEE ANY REASON TO MINCE WORDS.

I TOLD YOU THE DAY I SIGNED THAT I'M HERE TO COMPETE FOR THE *NXT* TITLE.

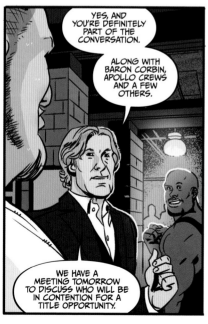

YES, AND YOU'RE DEFINITELY PART OF THE CONVERSATION.

ALONG WITH BARON CORBIN, APOLLO CREWS AND A FEW OTHERS.

WE HAVE A MEETING TOMORROW TO DISCUSS WHO WILL BE IN CONTENTION FOR A TITLE OPPORTUNITY.

A MEETING?!

YES. BELIEVE IT OR NOT, THAT'S HOW WE DECIDE THESE THINGS.

WE TALK.

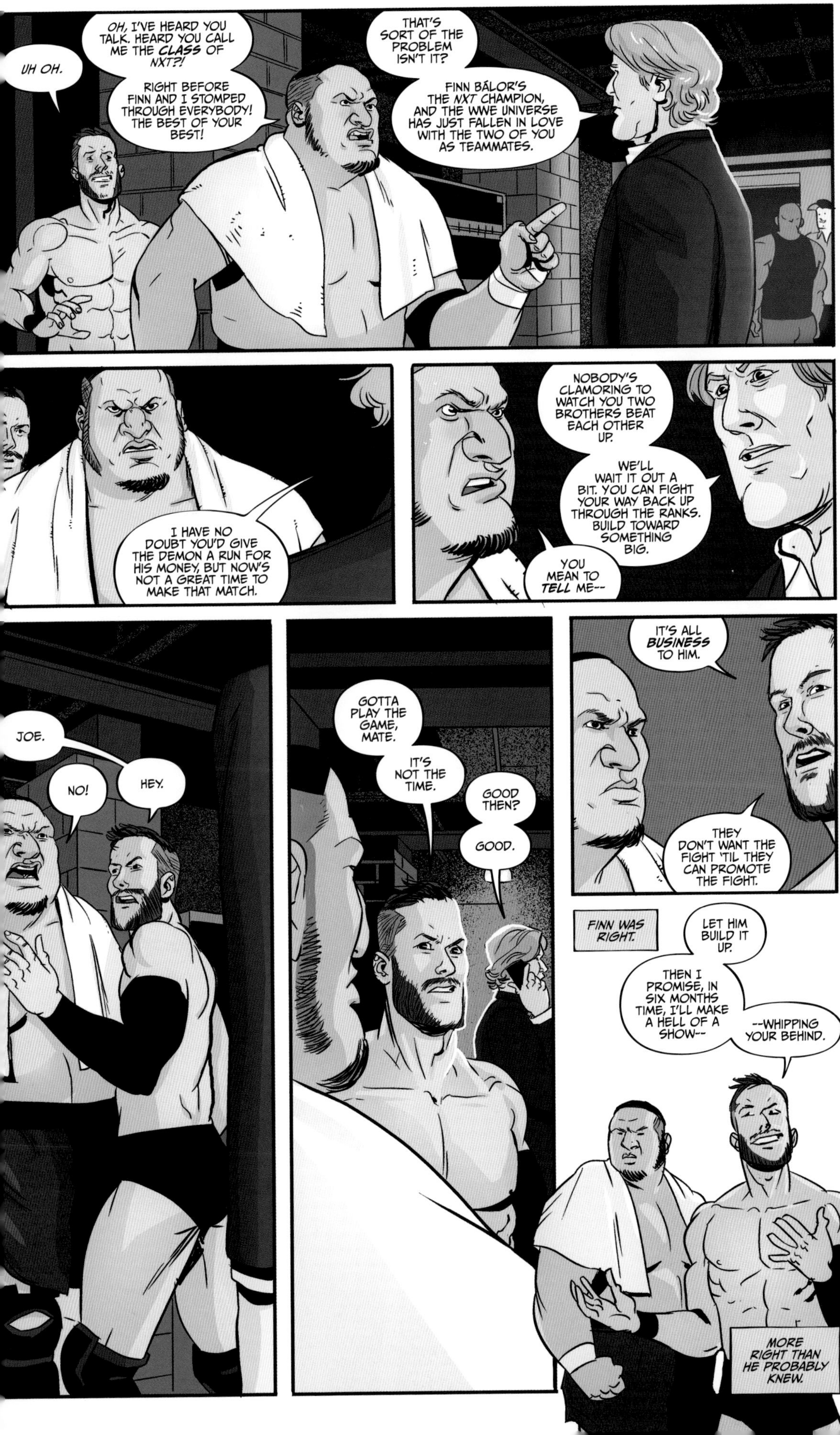
UH OH.
OH, I'VE HEARD YOU TALK. HEARD YOU CALL ME THE CLASS OF NXT?!
RIGHT BEFORE FINN AND I STOMPED THROUGH EVERYBODY! THE BEST OF YOUR BEST!
THAT'S SORT OF THE PROBLEM ISN'T IT?
FINN BÁLOR'S THE NXT CHAMPION, AND THE WWE UNIVERSE HAS JUST FALLEN IN LOVE WITH THE TWO OF YOU AS TEAMMATES.
I HAVE NO DOUBT YOU'D GIVE THE DEMON A RUN FOR HIS MONEY, BUT NOW'S NOT A GREAT TIME TO MAKE THAT MATCH.
NOBODY'S CLAMORING TO WATCH YOU TWO BROTHERS BEAT EACH OTHER UP.
WE'LL WAIT IT OUT A BIT. YOU CAN FIGHT YOUR WAY BACK UP THROUGH THE RANKS. BUILD TOWARD SOMETHING BIG.
YOU MEAN TO TELL ME--
JOE.
NO!
HEY.
GOTTA PLAY THE GAME, MATE.
IT'S NOT THE TIME.
GOOD THEN?
GOOD.
IT'S ALL BUSINESS TO HIM.
THEY DON'T WANT THE FIGHT 'TIL THEY CAN PROMOTE THE FIGHT.
FINN WAS RIGHT.
LET HIM BUILD IT UP.
THEN I PROMISE, IN SIX MONTHS TIME, I'LL MAKE A HELL OF A SHOW--
--WHIPPING YOUR BEHIND.
MORE RIGHT THAN HE PROBABLY KNEW.

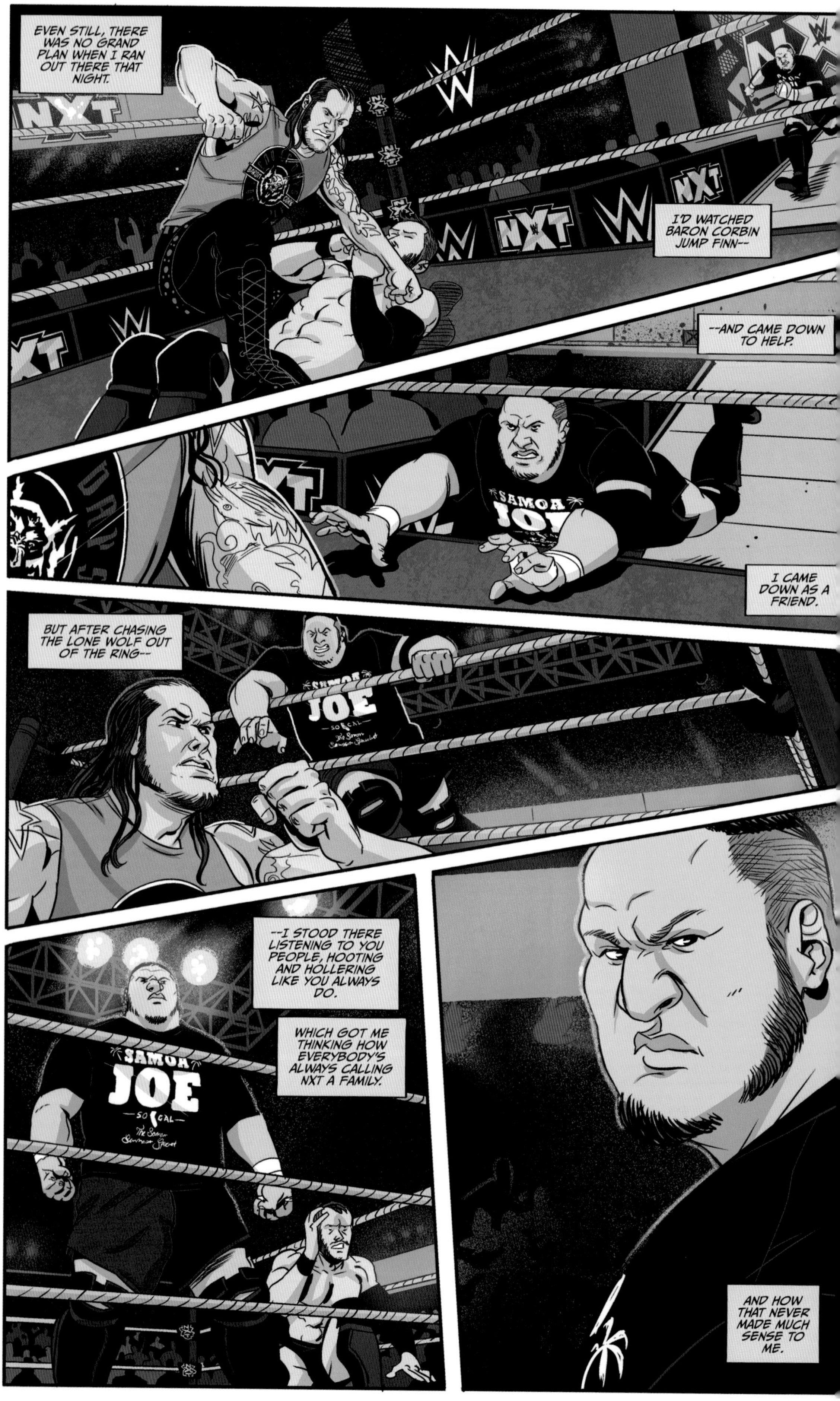
EVEN STILL, THERE WAS NO GRAND PLAN WHEN I RAN OUT THERE THAT NIGHT.
I'D WATCHED BARON CORBIN JUMP FINN--
--AND CAME DOWN TO HELP.
I CAME DOWN AS A FRIEND.
BUT AFTER CHASING THE LONE WOLF OUT OF THE RING--
--I STOOD THERE LISTENING TO YOU PEOPLE, HOOTING AND HOLLERING LIKE YOU ALWAYS DO.
WHICH GOT ME THINKING HOW EVERYBODY'S ALWAYS CALLING NXT A FAMILY.
AND HOW THAT NEVER MADE MUCH SENSE TO ME.

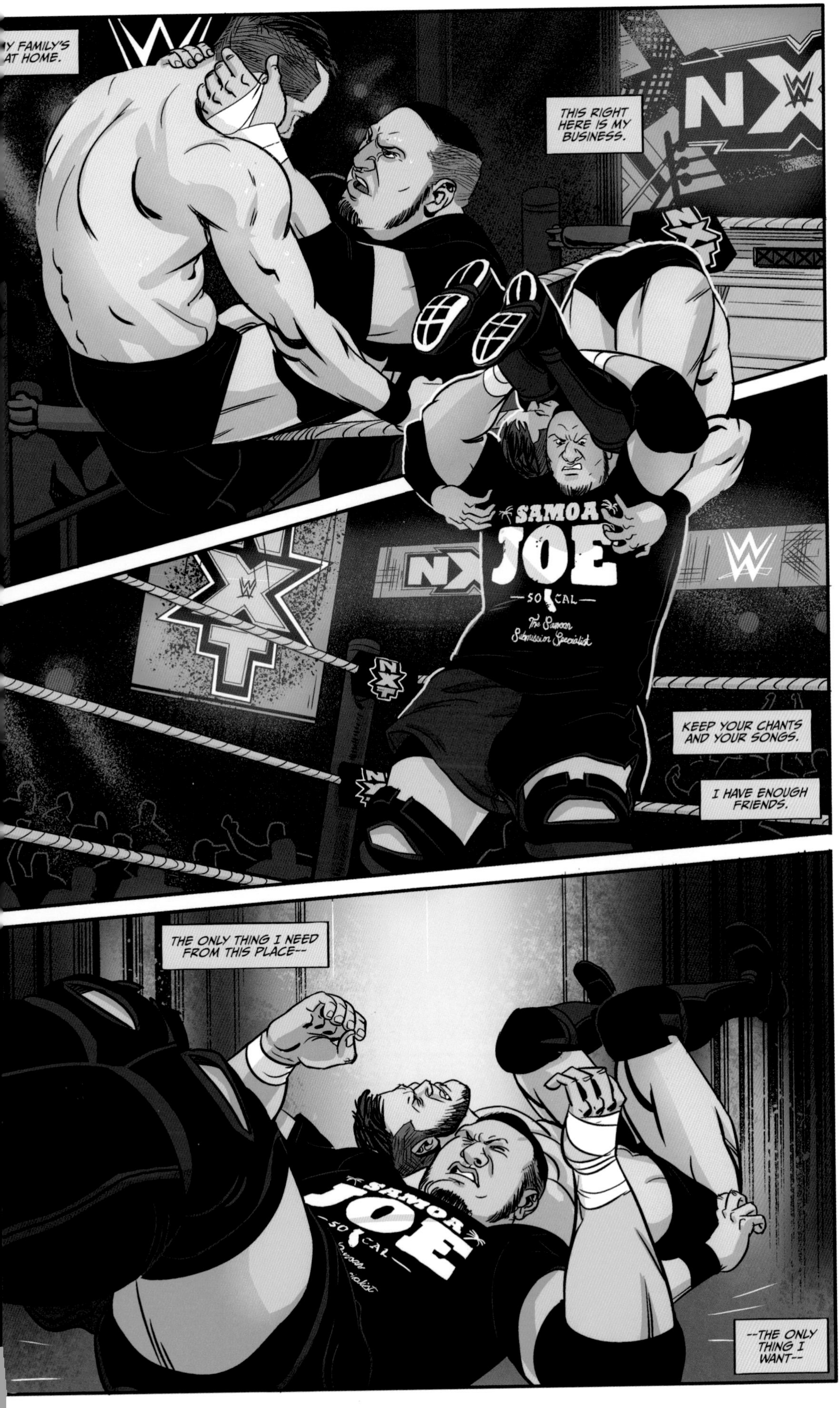
Y FAMILY'S AT HOME.
THIS RIGHT HERE IS MY BUSINESS.
SAMOA JOE
SO CAL
The Samoan Submission Specialist
KEEP YOUR CHANTS AND YOUR SONGS.
I HAVE ENOUGH FRIENDS.
THE ONLY THING I NEED FROM THIS PLACE--
SAMOA JOE
--THE ONLY THING I WANT--

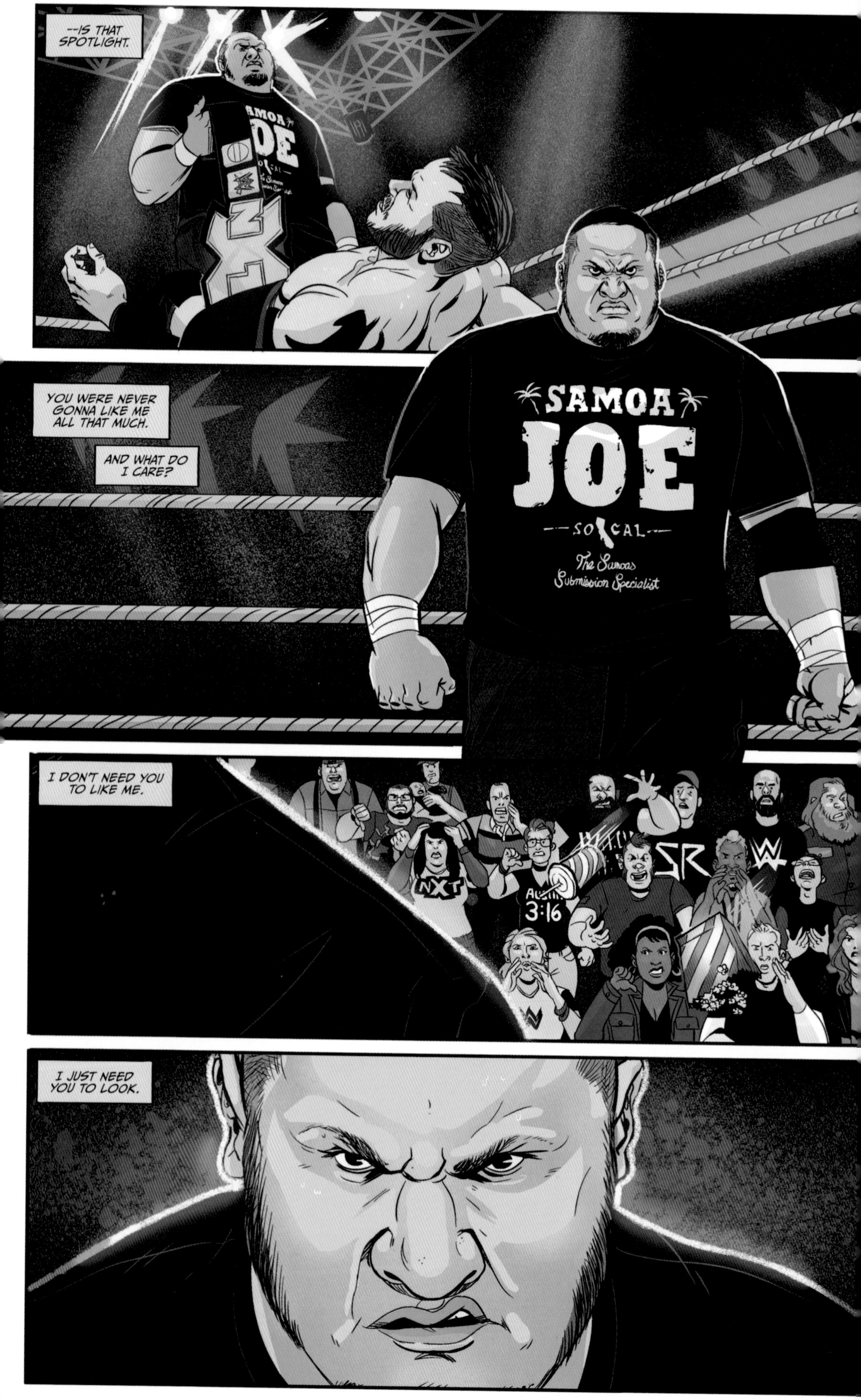
--IS THAT SPOTLIGHT.
SAMOA JOE
YOU WERE NEVER GONNA LIKE ME ALL THAT MUCH.
AND WHAT DO I CARE?
SAMOA JOE
SO CAL
The Samoan Submission Specialist
I DON'T NEED YOU TO LIKE ME.
NXT
AUSTIN 3:16
SR
I JUST NEED YOU TO LOOK.

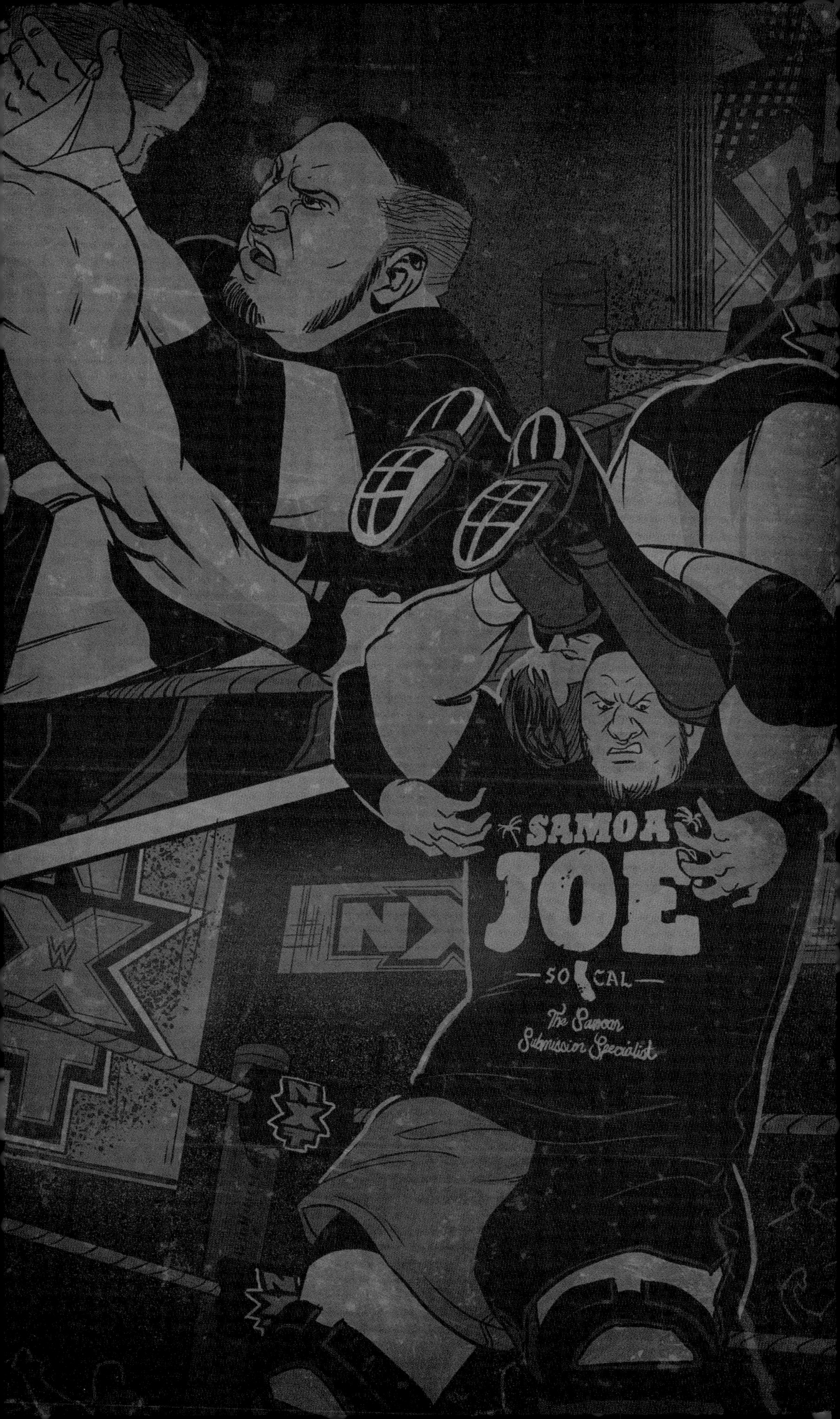
SAMOA
JOE
SO CAL
The Samoan
Submission Specialist

INTO THE FIRE

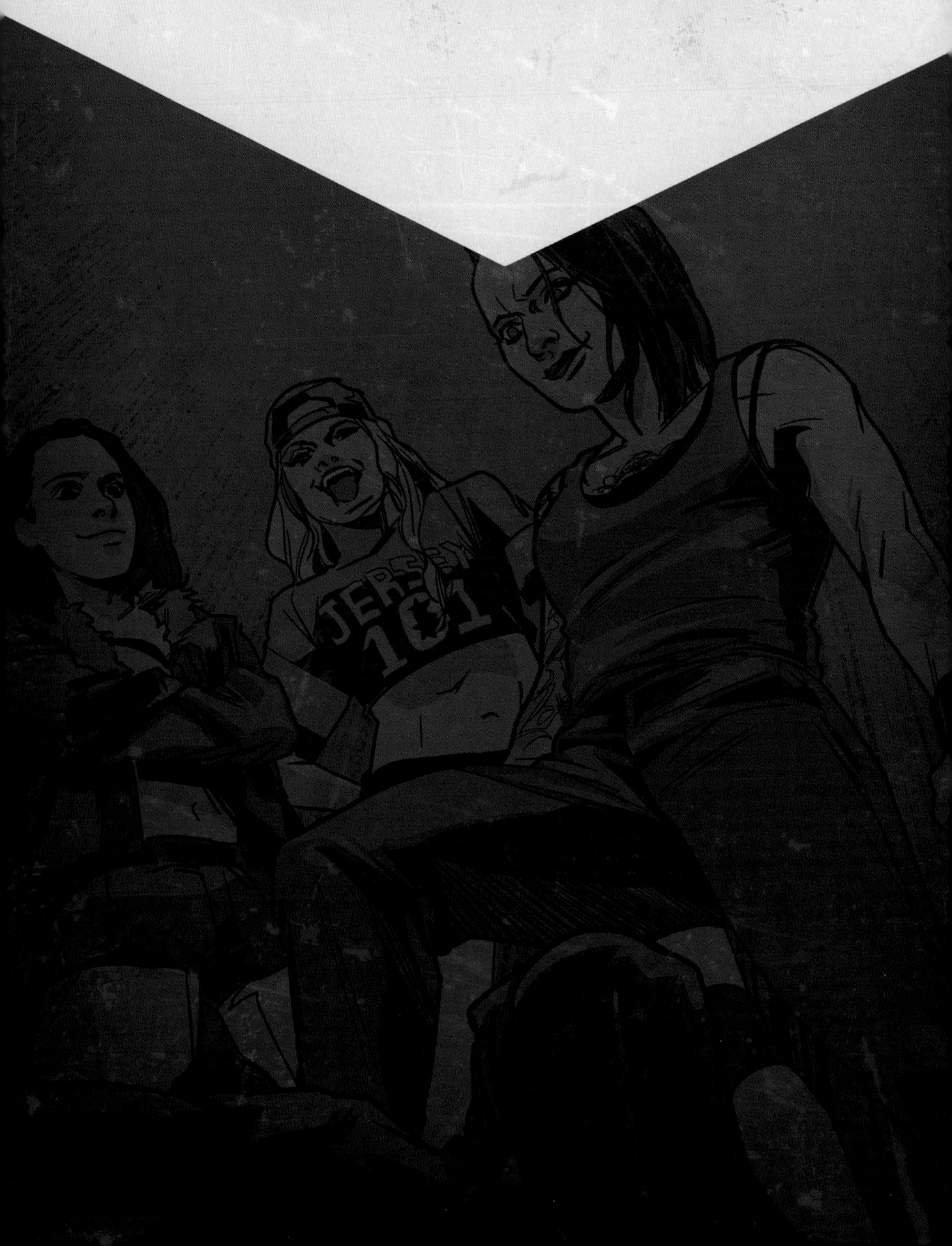

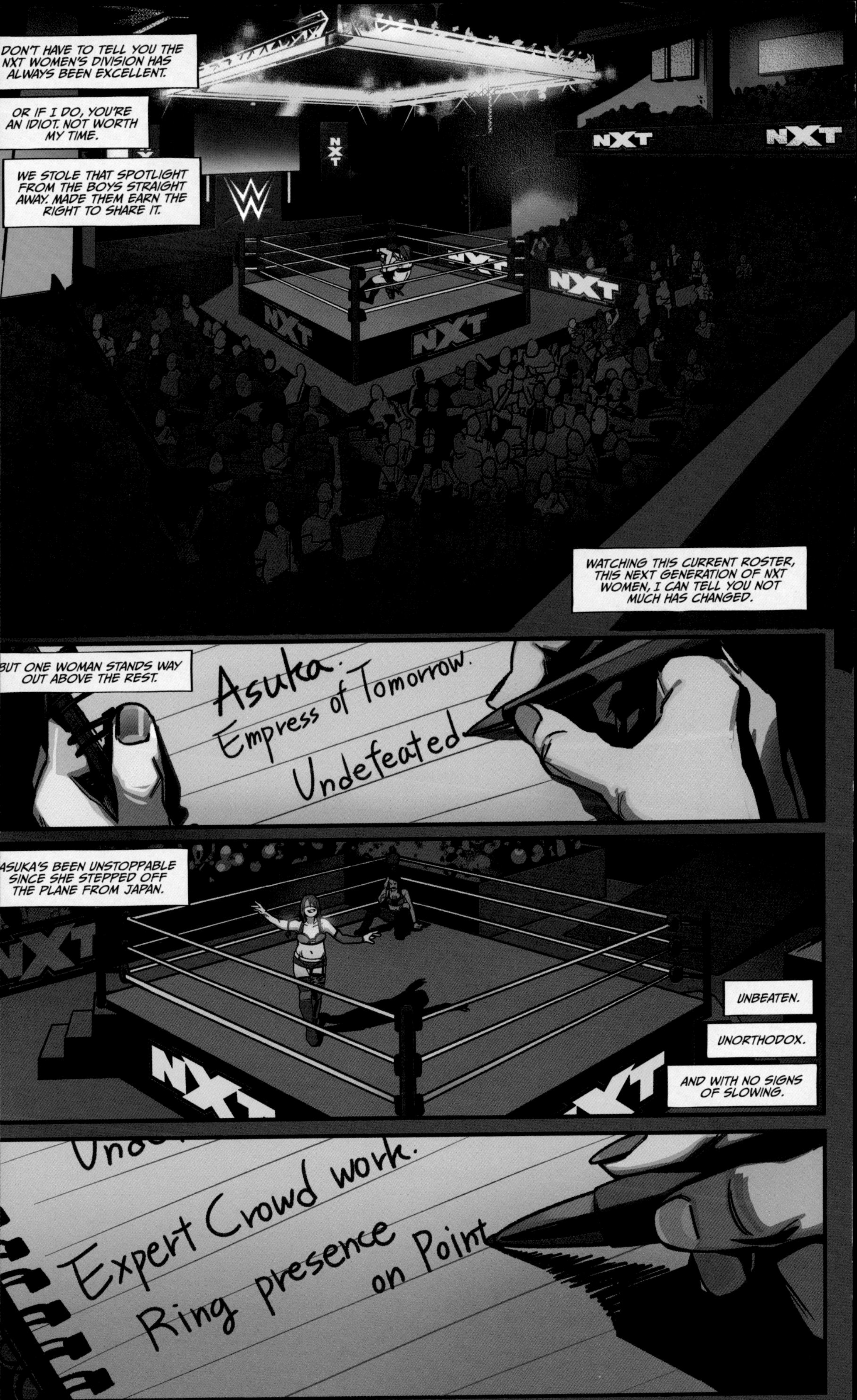

DON'T HAVE TO TELL YOU THE NXT WOMEN'S DIVISION HAS ALWAYS BEEN EXCELLENT.
OR IF I DO, YOU'RE AN IDIOT. NOT WORTH MY TIME.
WE STOLE THAT SPOTLIGHT FROM THE BOYS STRAIGHT AWAY. MADE THEM EARN THE RIGHT TO SHARE IT.
WATCHING THIS CURRENT ROSTER, THIS NEXT GENERATION OF NXT WOMEN, I CAN TELL YOU NOT MUCH HAS CHANGED.
BUT ONE WOMAN STANDS WAY OUT ABOVE THE REST.
Asuka.
Empress of Tomorrow.
Undefeated
ASUKA'S BEEN UNSTOPPABLE SINCE SHE STEPPED OFF THE PLANE FROM JAPAN.
UNBEATEN.
UNORTHODOX.
AND WITH NO SIGNS OF SLOWING.
Expert Crowd work.
Ring presence
on Point

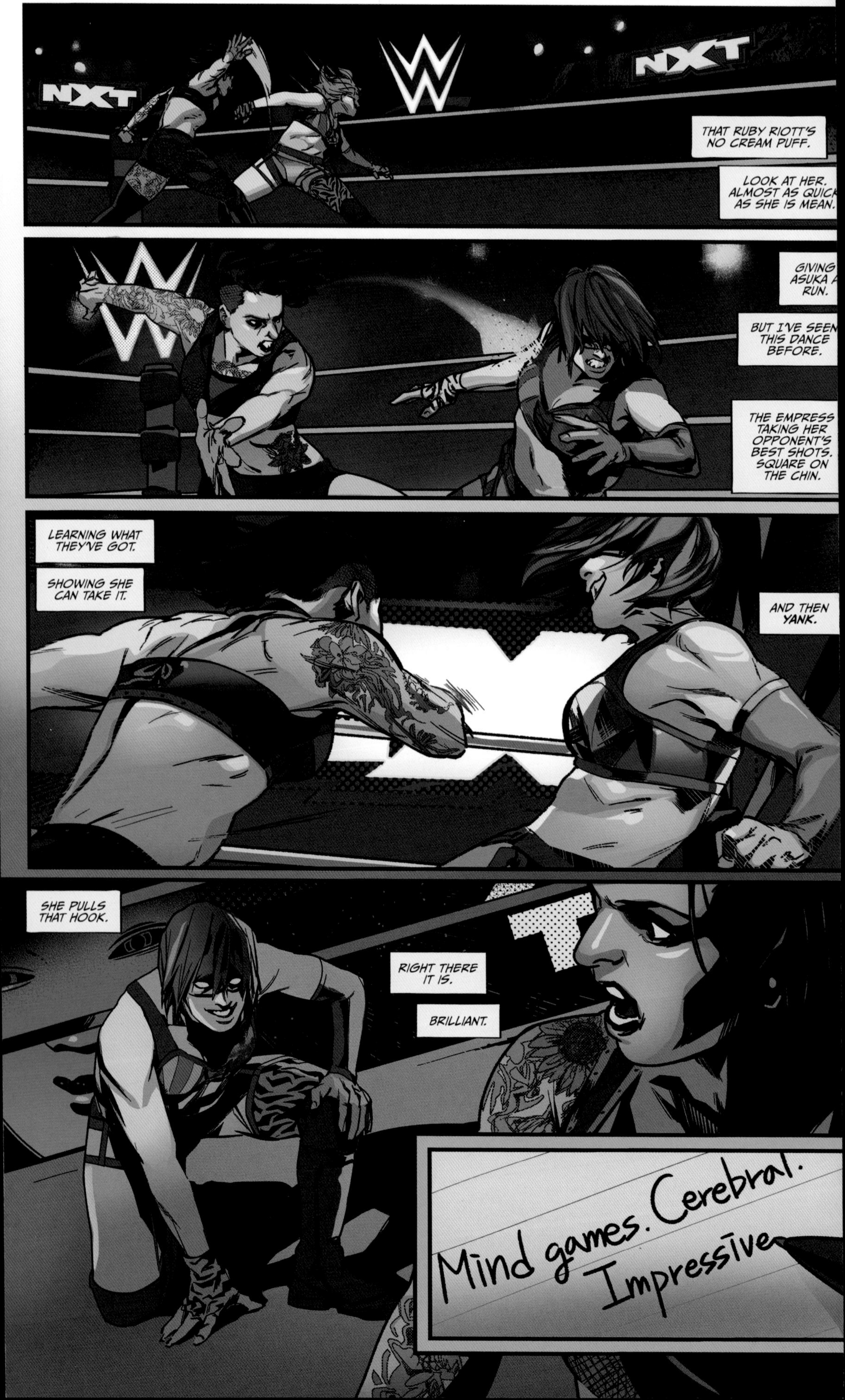
NXT
NXT
THAT RUBY RIOTT'S NO CREAM PUFF.
LOOK AT HER. ALMOST AS QUICK AS SHE IS MEAN.
GIVING ASUKA A RUN.
BUT I'VE SEEN THIS DANCE BEFORE.
THE EMPRESS TAKING HER OPPONENT'S BEST SHOTS. SQUARE ON THE CHIN.
LEARNING WHAT THEY'VE GOT.
SHOWING SHE CAN TAKE IT.
AND THEN YANK.
SHE PULLS THAT HOOK.
RIGHT THERE IT IS.
BRILLIANT.
Mind games. Cerebral.
Impressive

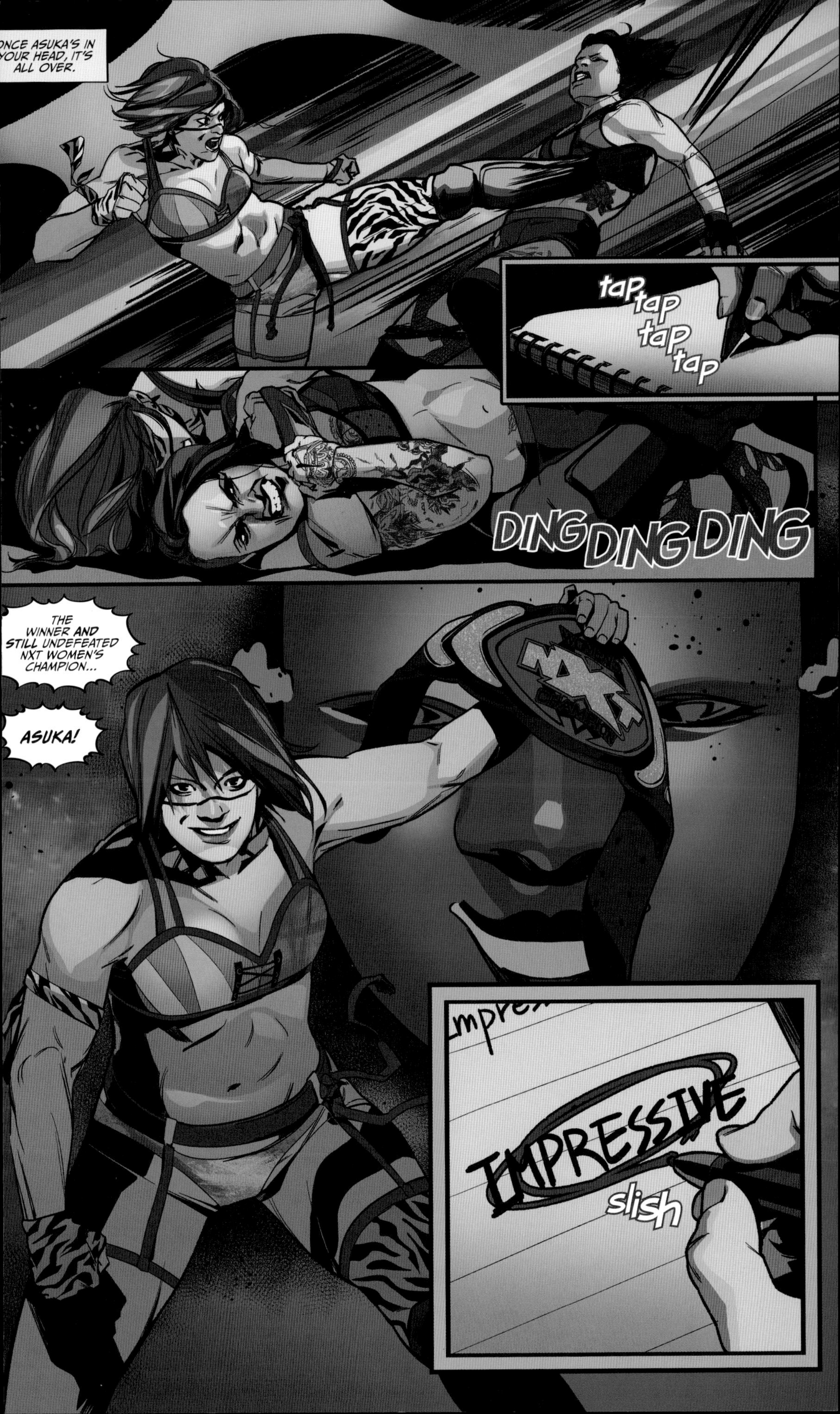
ONCE ASUKA'S IN YOUR HEAD, IT'S ALL OVER.
tap tap tap tap
DING DING DING
THE WINNER AND STILL UNDEFEATED NXT WOMEN'S CHAMPION...
ASUKA!
IMPRESSIVE
slish

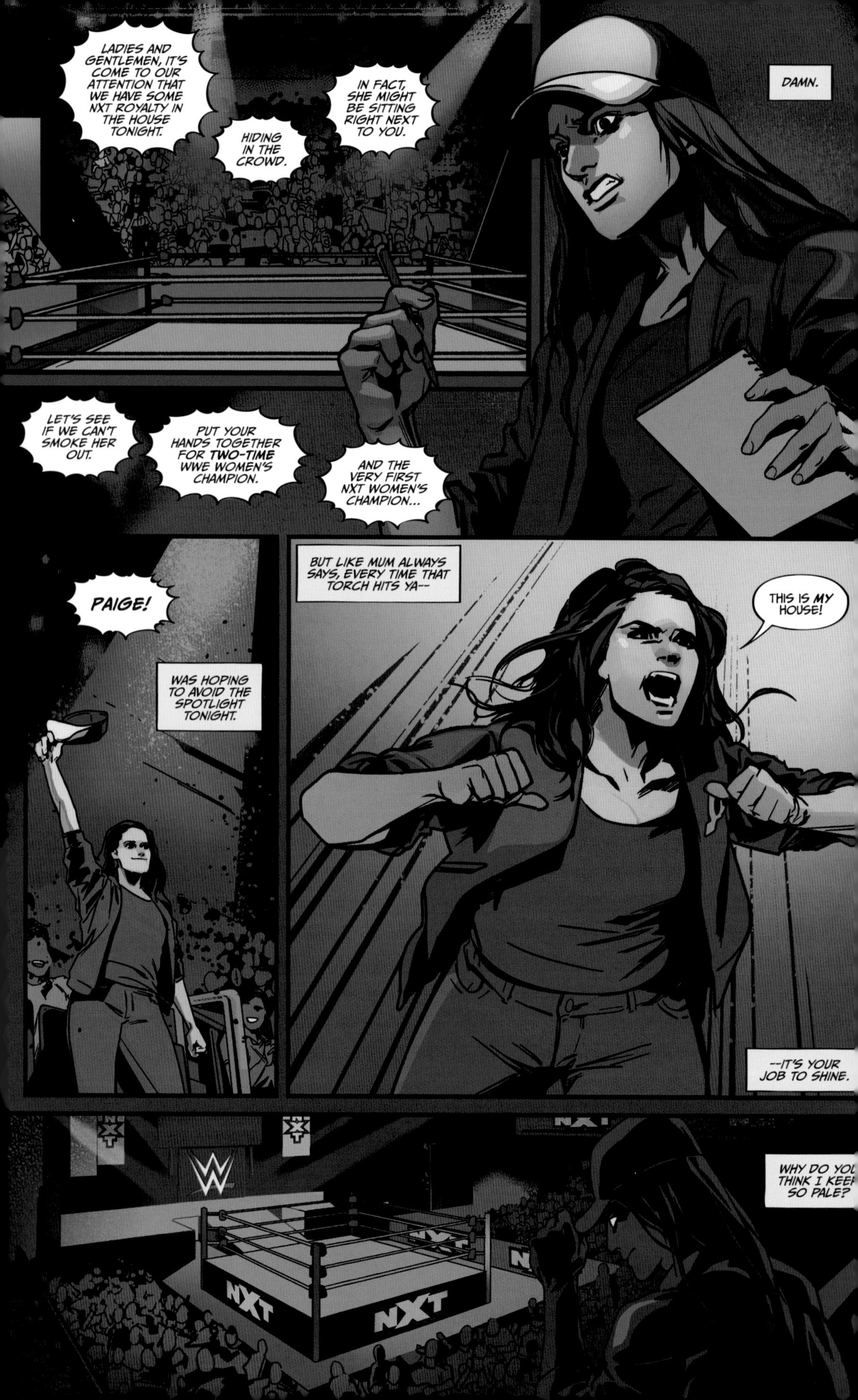
LADIES AND GENTLEMEN, IT'S COME TO OUR ATTENTION THAT WE HAVE SOME NXT ROYALTY IN THE HOUSE TONIGHT.
HIDING IN THE CROWD.
IN FACT, SHE MIGHT BE SITTING RIGHT NEXT TO YOU.
DAMN.
LET'S SEE IF WE CAN'T SMOKE HER OUT.
PUT YOUR HANDS TOGETHER FOR TWO-TIME WWE WOMEN'S CHAMPION.
AND THE VERY FIRST NXT WOMEN'S CHAMPION...
PAIGE!
WAS HOPING TO AVOID THE SPOTLIGHT TONIGHT.
BUT LIKE MUM ALWAYS SAYS, EVERY TIME THAT TORCH HITS YA--
THIS IS MY HOUSE!
--IT'S YOUR JOB TO SHINE.
NXT
NXT
NXT
WHY DO YOU THINK I KEEP SO PALE?

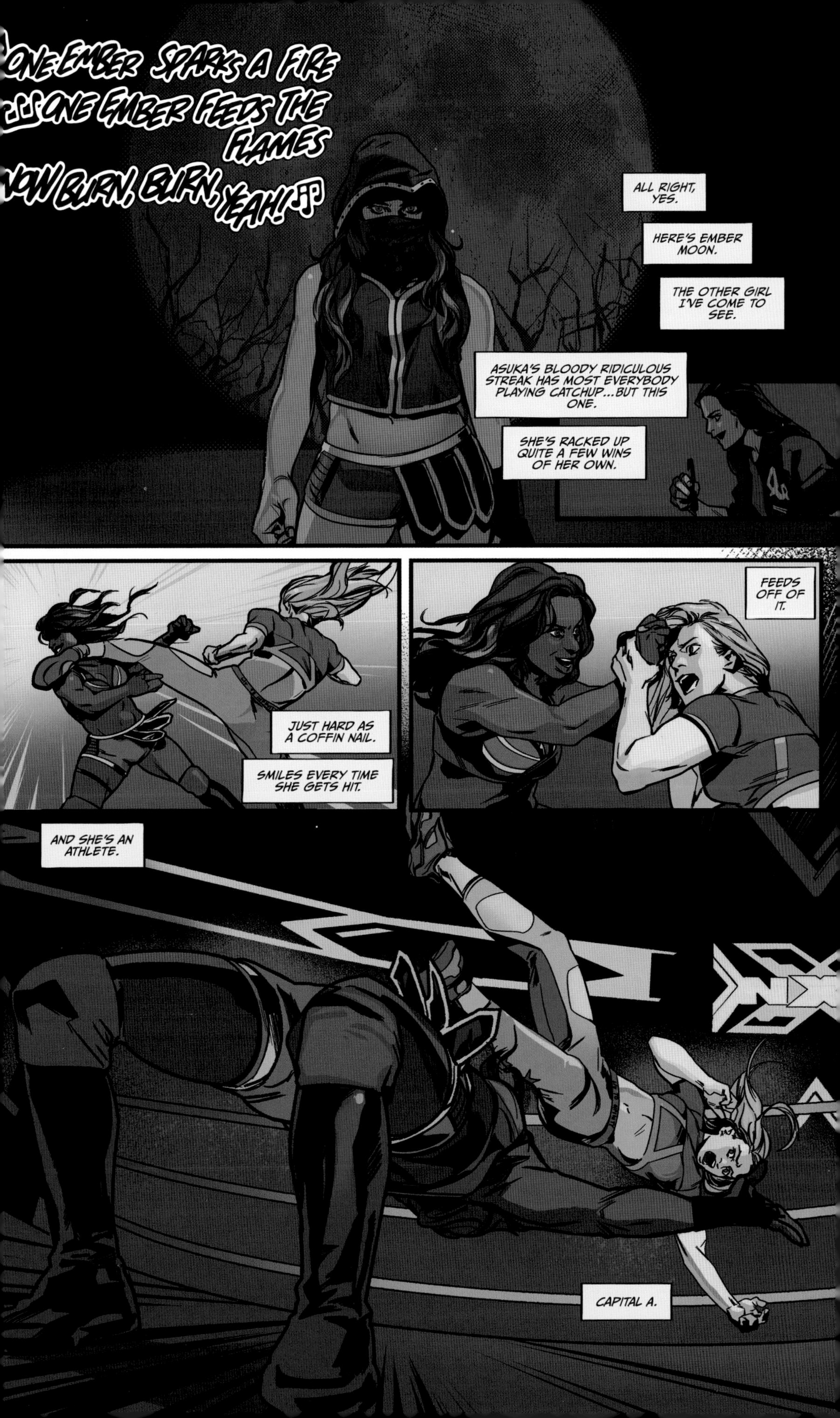
ONE EMBER SPARKS A FIRE
ONE EMBER FEEDS THE FLAMES
NOW BURN, BURN, YEAH!
ALL RIGHT, YES.
HERE'S EMBER MOON.
THE OTHER GIRL I'VE COME TO SEE.
ASUKA'S BLOODY RIDICULOUS STREAK HAS MOST EVERYBODY PLAYING CATCHUP...BUT THIS ONE.
SHE'S RACKED UP QUITE A FEW WINS OF HER OWN.
JUST HARD AS A COFFIN NAIL.
SMILES EVERY TIME SHE GETS HIT.
FEEDS OFF OF IT.
AND SHE'S AN ATHLETE.
CAPITAL A.

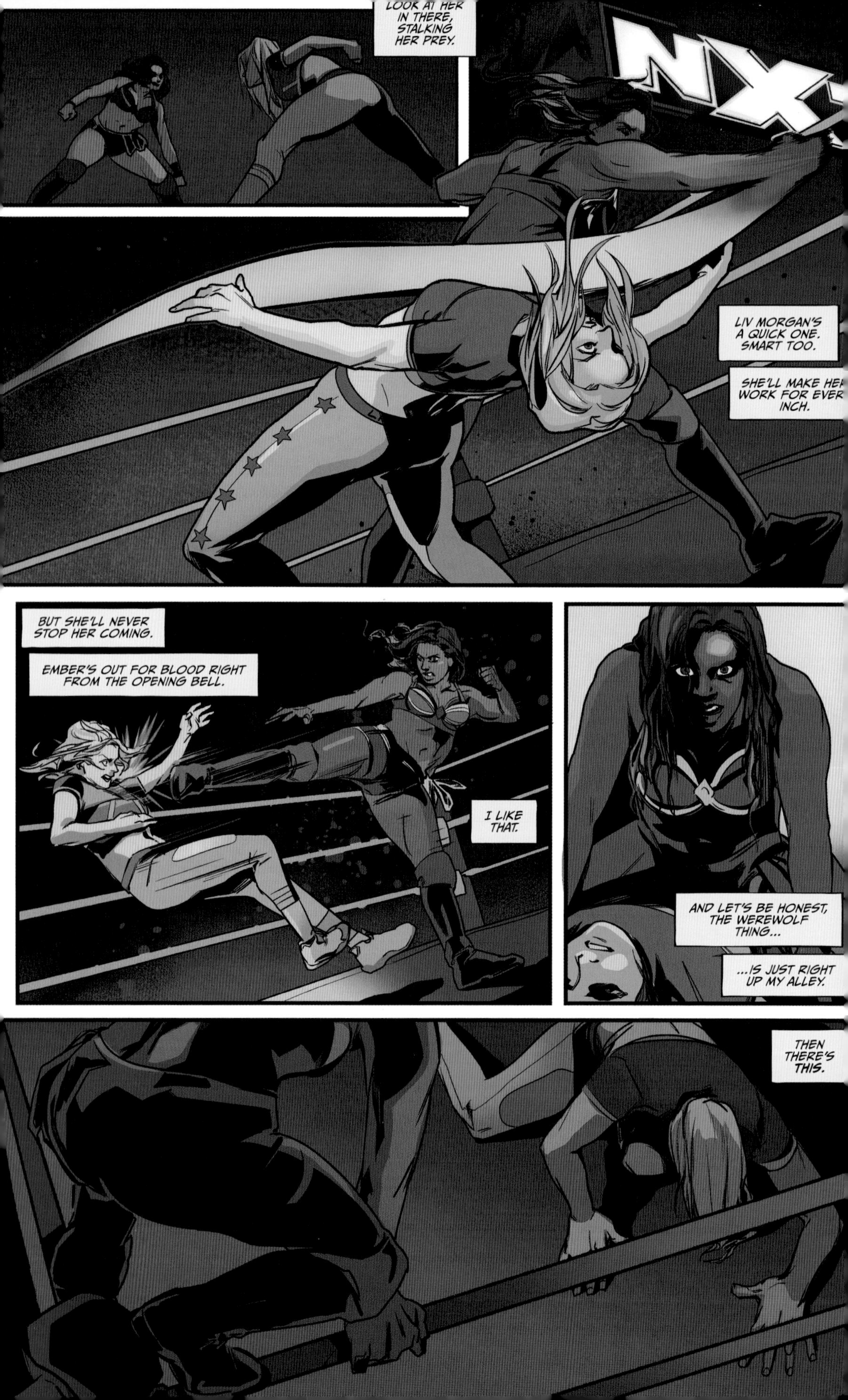
LOOK AT HER IN THERE, STALKING HER PREY.
NXT
LIV MORGAN'S A QUICK ONE. SMART TOO.
SHE'LL MAKE HER WORK FOR EVERY INCH.
BUT SHE'LL NEVER STOP HER COMING.
EMBER'S OUT FOR BLOOD RIGHT FROM THE OPENING BELL.
I LIKE THAT.
AND LET'S BE HONEST, THE WEREWOLF THING...
...IS JUST RIGHT UP MY ALLEY.
THEN THERE'S THIS.

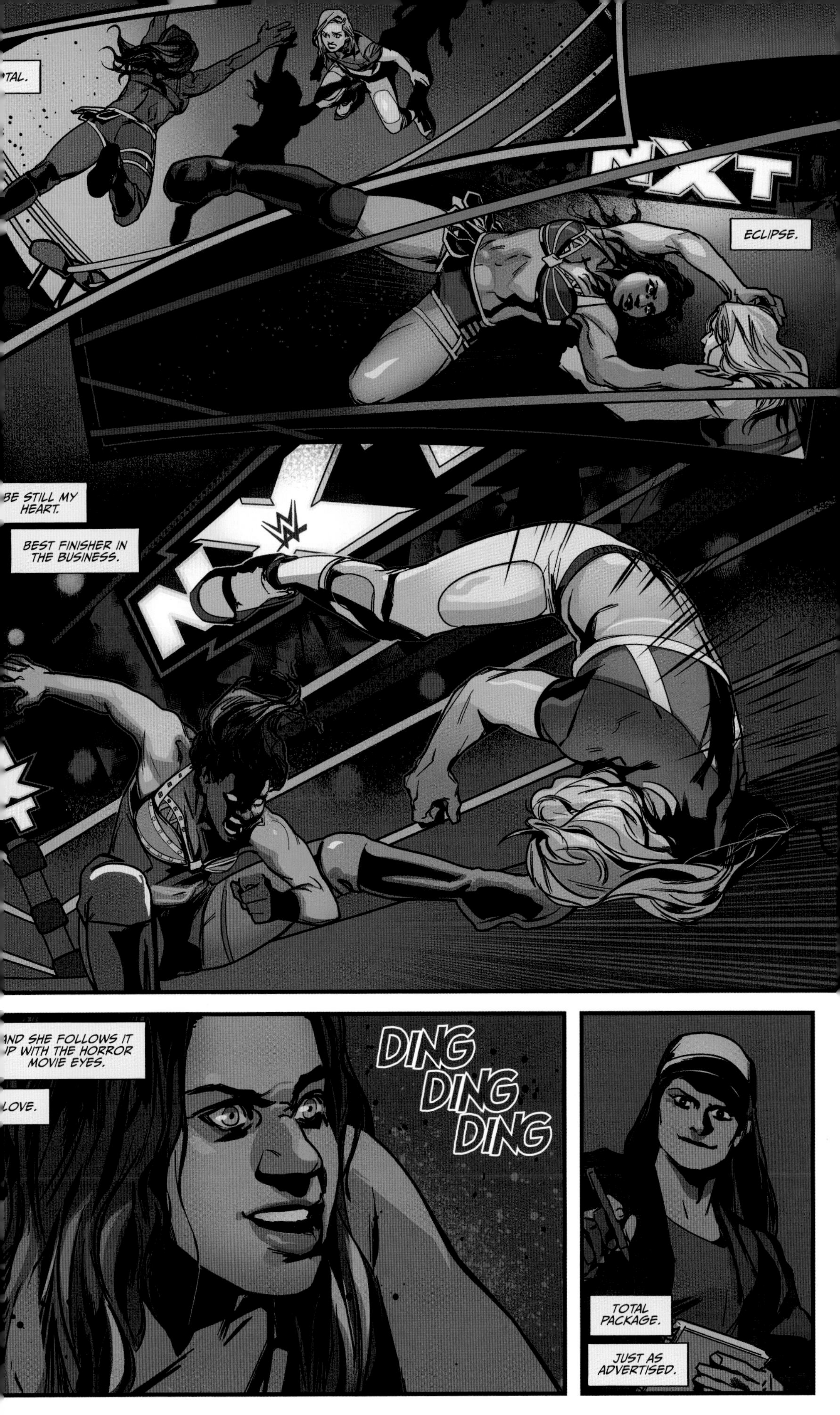
TAL.
ECLIPSE.
BE STILL MY HEART.
BEST FINISHER IN THE BUSINESS.
AND SHE FOLLOWS IT UP WITH THE HORROR MOVIE EYES.
LOVE.
DING DING DING
TOTAL PACKAGE.
JUST AS ADVERTISED.

EMPRESS. OF. TOMORROW.

SOUNDS LIKE A WOMAN WHO KEEPS HER EYES POINTED FORWARD. TOWARD THE FUTURE.

WHAT IF I TOLD YOU I'VE AN IDEA HOW TO JUMPSTART THAT.

HMM?

HOW TO MAKE SURE YOU STAY BURNING WHITE HOT. BLINDING BRIGHT.

I...

YOU'RE UNDEFEATED HERE IN *NXT*, YE HAVE BEEN FC MONTHS NOW.

WHAT MORE IS THERE TO PROVE?

AT THIS POINT MOVING TO *RAW* OR *SMACKDOWN LIVE*, THAT'S A FOREGONE CONCLUSION.

ONLY THING LEFT TO DECIDE IS *HOW*.

ALL BY YOURSELF? A LEAF ON THE WIND?

OR AS PART OF SOMETHING BIGGER.

IMAGINE THE TWO OF US WALKING DOWN THAT RAMP TOGETHER.

YOUR RAW DEBUT. MY BIG COMEBACK.

THERE'S NO BIGGER SPLASH THAN THAT.

WHAT DO YOU SAY?

I SAY...

...NO.

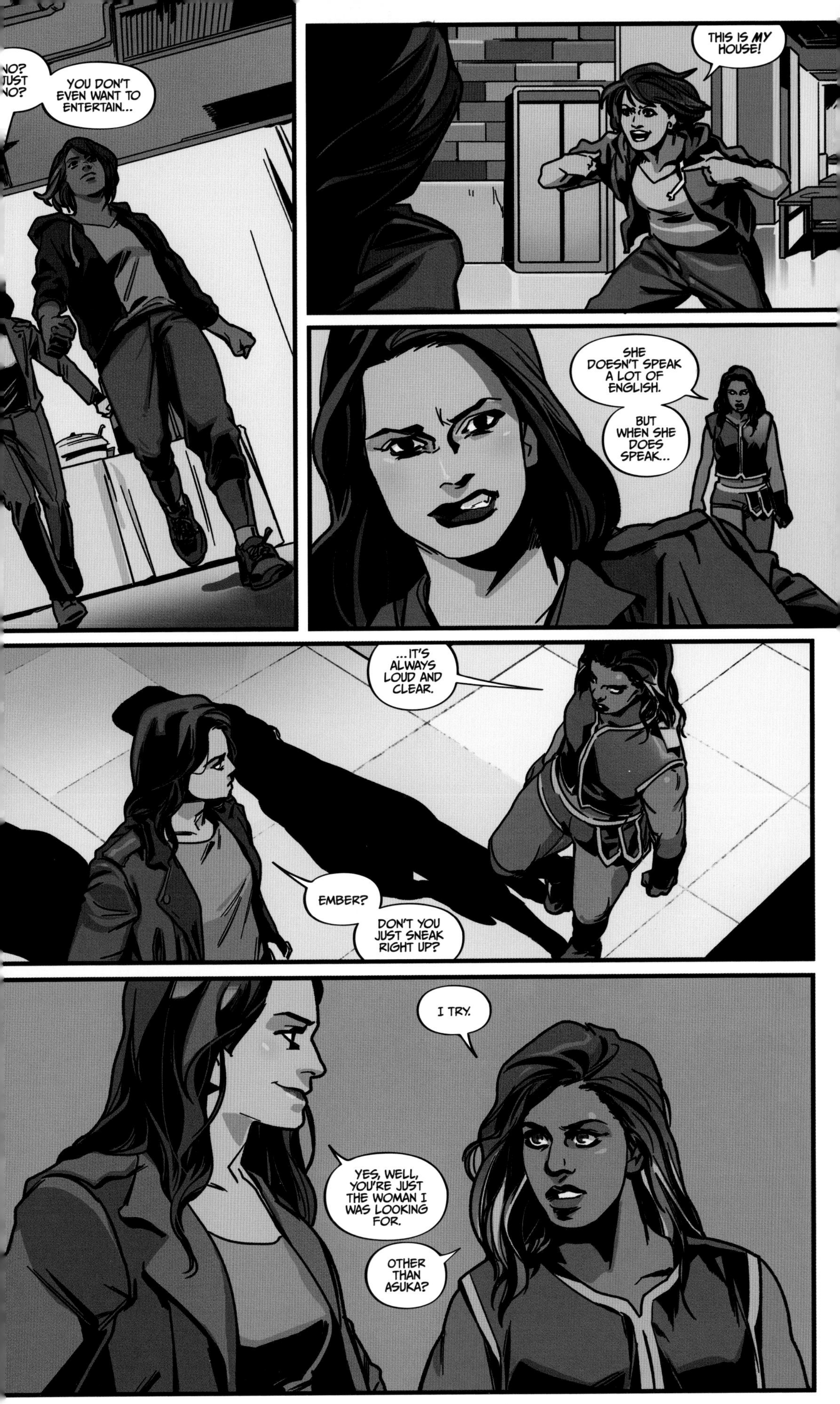
NO? JUST NO?
YOU DON'T EVEN WANT TO ENTERTAIN...
THIS IS MY HOUSE!
SHE DOESN'T SPEAK A LOT OF ENGLISH.
BUT WHEN SHE DOES SPEAK...
...IT'S ALWAYS LOUD AND CLEAR.
EMBER?
DON'T YOU JUST SNEAK RIGHT UP?
I TRY.
YES, WELL, YOU'RE JUST THE WOMAN I WAS LOOKING FOR.
OTHER THAN ASUKA?

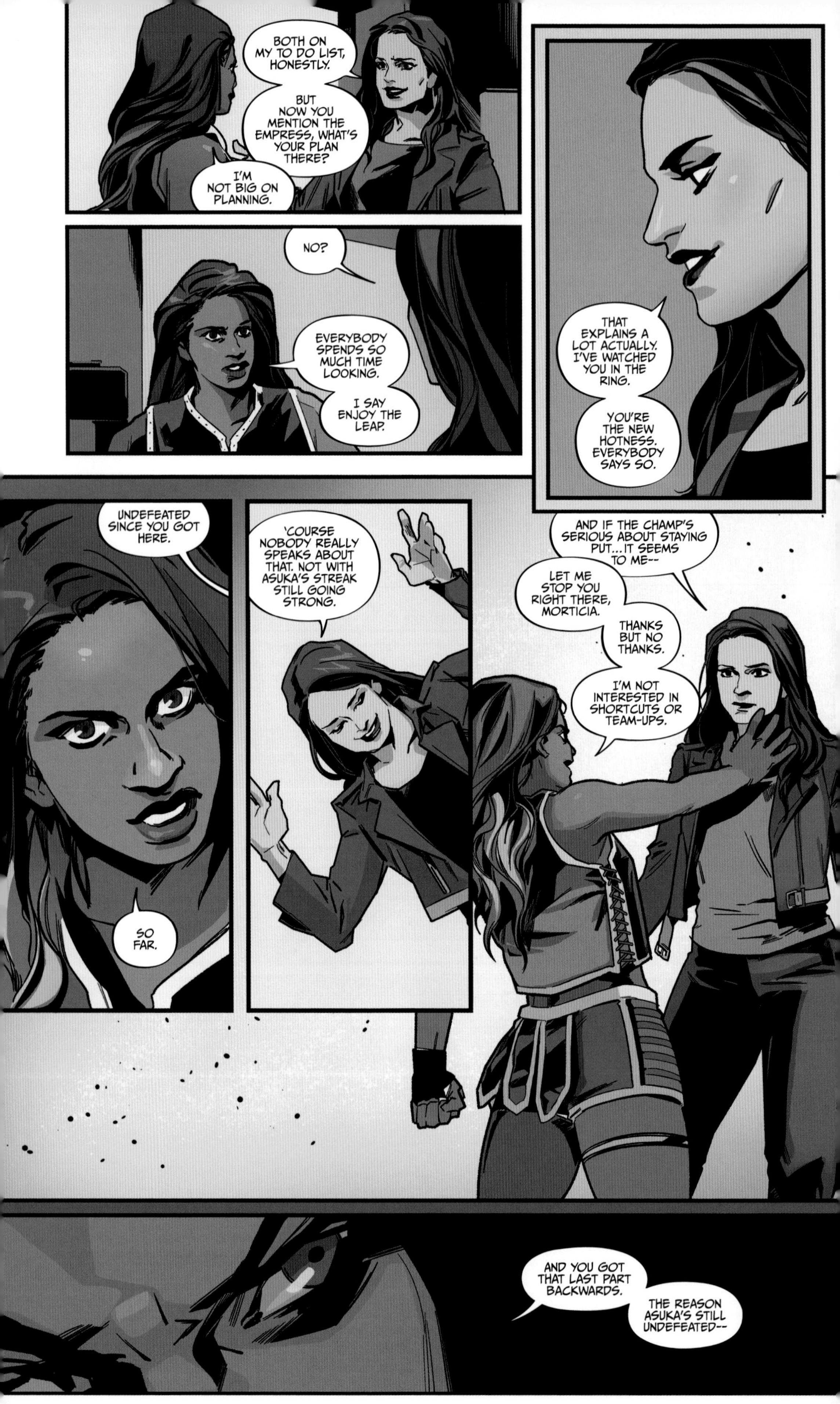
BOTH ON MY TO DO LIST, HONESTLY.
BUT NOW YOU MENTION THE EMPRESS, WHAT'S YOUR PLAN THERE?
I'M NOT BIG ON PLANNING.
NO?
EVERYBODY SPENDS SO MUCH TIME LOOKING.
I SAY ENJOY THE LEAP.
THAT EXPLAINS A LOT ACTUALLY. I'VE WATCHED YOU IN THE RING.
YOU'RE THE NEW HOTNESS. EVERYBODY SAYS SO.
UNDEFEATED SINCE YOU GOT HERE.
SO FAR.
'COURSE NOBODY REALLY SPEAKS ABOUT THAT. NOT WITH ASUKA'S STREAK STILL GOING STRONG.
AND IF THE CHAMP'S SERIOUS ABOUT STAYING PUT... IT SEEMS TO ME--
LET ME STOP YOU RIGHT THERE, MORTICIA.
THANKS BUT NO THANKS.
I'M NOT INTERESTED IN SHORTCUTS OR TEAM-UPS.
AND YOU GOT THAT LAST PART BACKWARDS.
THE REASON ASUKA'S STILL UNDEFEATED--

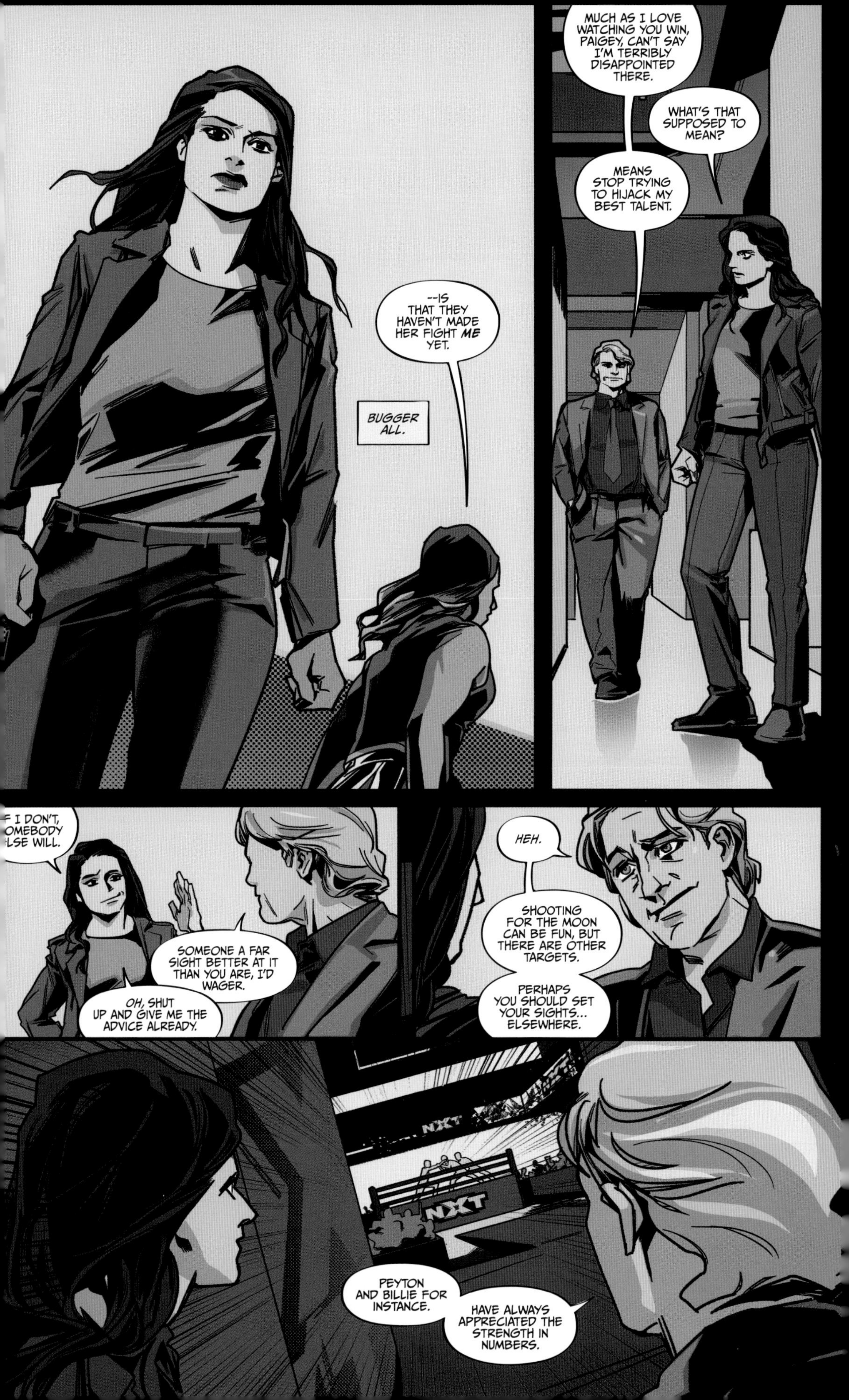
--IS THAT THEY HAVEN'T MADE HER FIGHT *ME* YET.
BUGGER ALL.
MUCH AS I LOVE WATCHING YOU WIN, PAIGEY, CAN'T SAY I'M TERRIBLY DISAPPOINTED THERE.
WHAT'S THAT SUPPOSED TO MEAN?
MEANS STOP TRYING TO HIJACK MY BEST TALENT.
F I DON'T, OMEBODY LSE WILL.
SOMEONE A FAR SIGHT BETTER AT IT THAN YOU ARE, I'D WAGER.
OH, SHUT UP AND GIVE ME THE ADVICE ALREADY.
HEH.
SHOOTING FOR THE MOON CAN BE FUN, BUT THERE ARE OTHER TARGETS.
PERHAPS YOU SHOULD SET YOUR SIGHTS... ELSEWHERE.
NXT
NXT
PEYTON AND BILLIE FOR INSTANCE.
HAVE ALWAYS APPRECIATED THE STRENGTH IN NUMBERS.

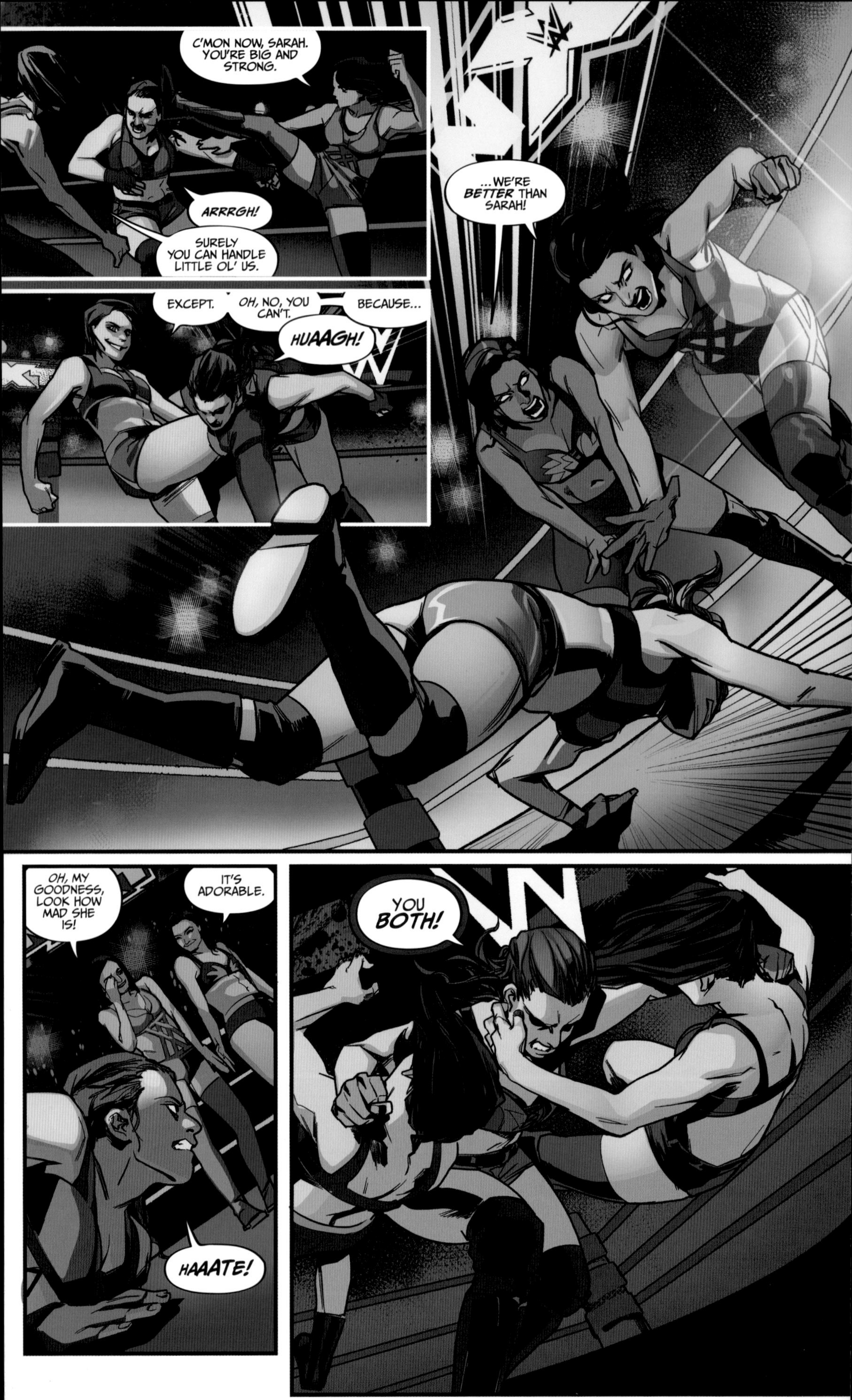

C'MON NOW, SARAH. YOU'RE BIG AND STRONG.
ARRRGH!
SURELY YOU CAN HANDLE LITTLE OL' US.
EXCEPT.
OH, NO, YOU CAN'T.
BECAUSE...
HUAAGH!
...WE'RE *BETTER* THAN SARAH!
OH, MY GOODNESS, LOOK HOW MAD SHE IS!
IT'S ADORABLE.
HAAATE!
YOU *BOTH!*

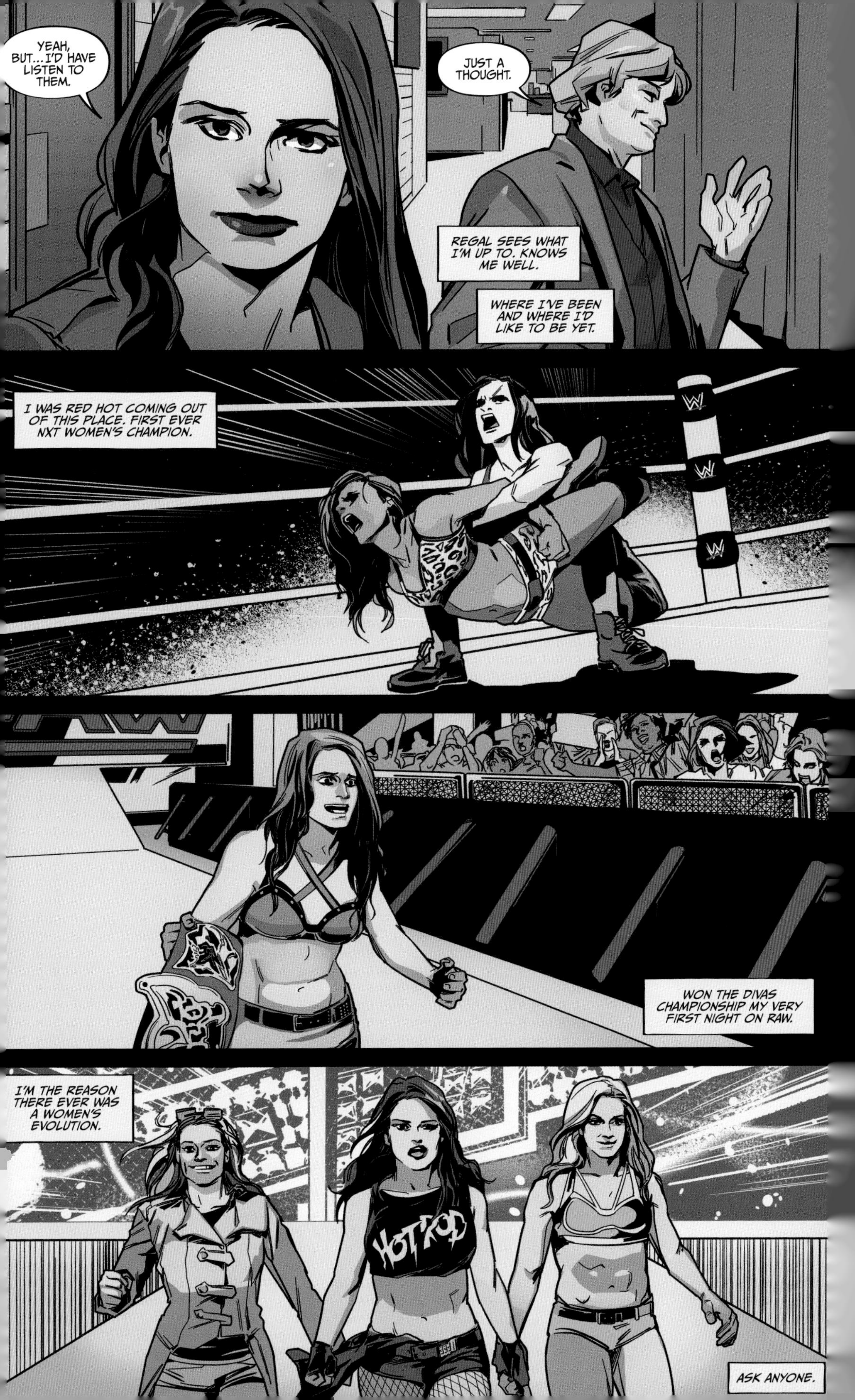
YEAH, BUT...I'D HAVE LISTEN TO THEM.
JUST A THOUGHT.
REGAL SEES WHAT I'M UP TO. KNOWS ME WELL.
WHERE I'VE BEEN AND WHERE I'D LIKE TO BE YET.
I WAS RED HOT COMING OUT OF THIS PLACE. FIRST EVER NXT WOMEN'S CHAMPION.
WON THE DIVAS CHAMPIONSHIP MY VERY FIRST NIGHT ON RAW.
I'M THE REASON THERE EVER WAS A WOMEN'S EVOLUTION.
HOT ROD
ASK ANYONE.

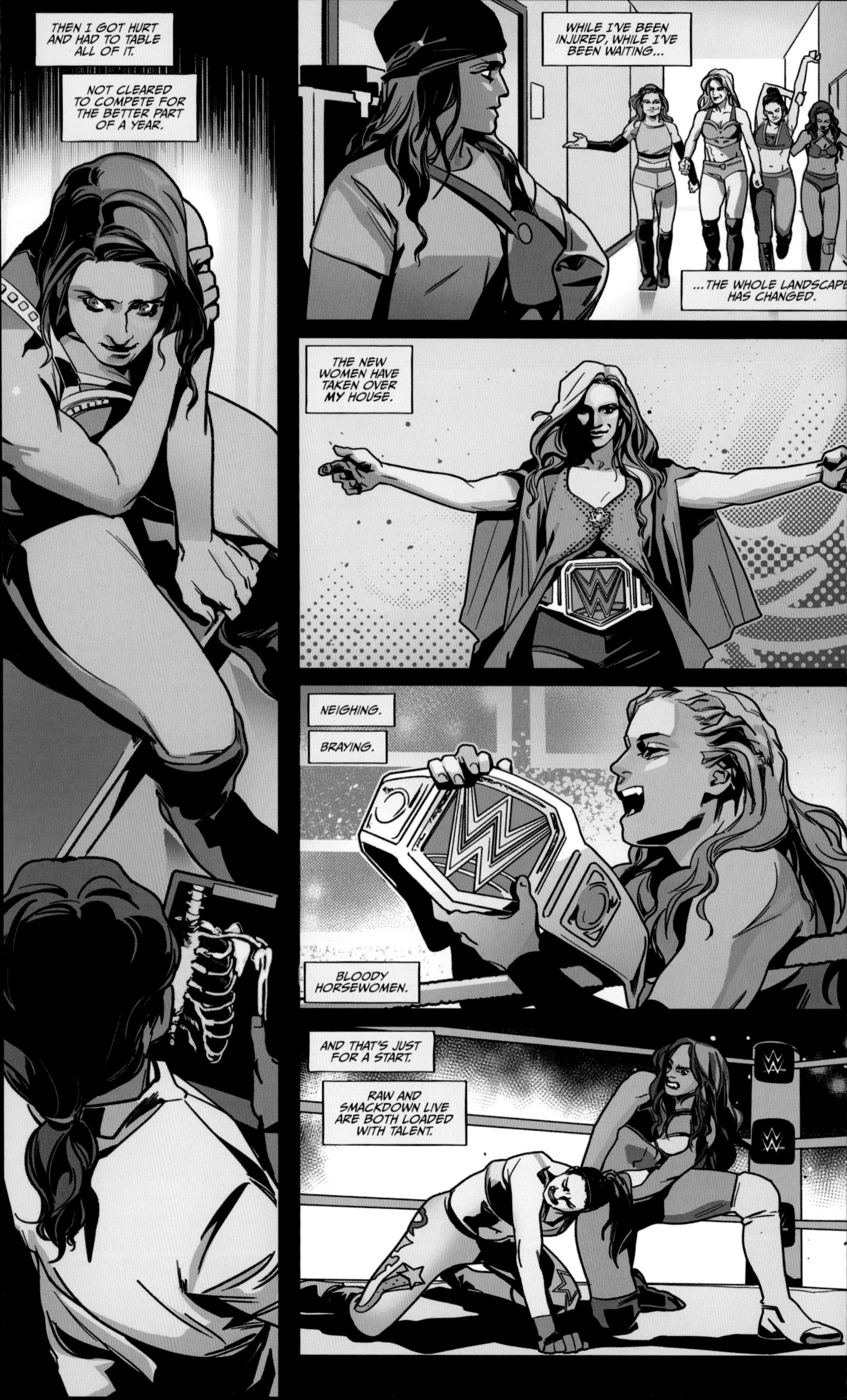
THEN I GOT HURT AND HAD TO TABLE ALL OF IT.
NOT CLEARED TO COMPETE FOR THE BETTER PART OF A YEAR.
WHILE I'VE BEEN INJURED, WHILE I'VE BEEN WAITING...
...THE WHOLE LANDSCAPE HAS CHANGED.
THE NEW WOMEN HAVE TAKEN OVER MY HOUSE.
NEIGHING.
BRAYING.
BLOODY HORSEWOMEN.
AND THAT'S JUST FOR A START.
RAW AND SMACKDOWN LIVE ARE BOTH LOADED WITH TALENT.

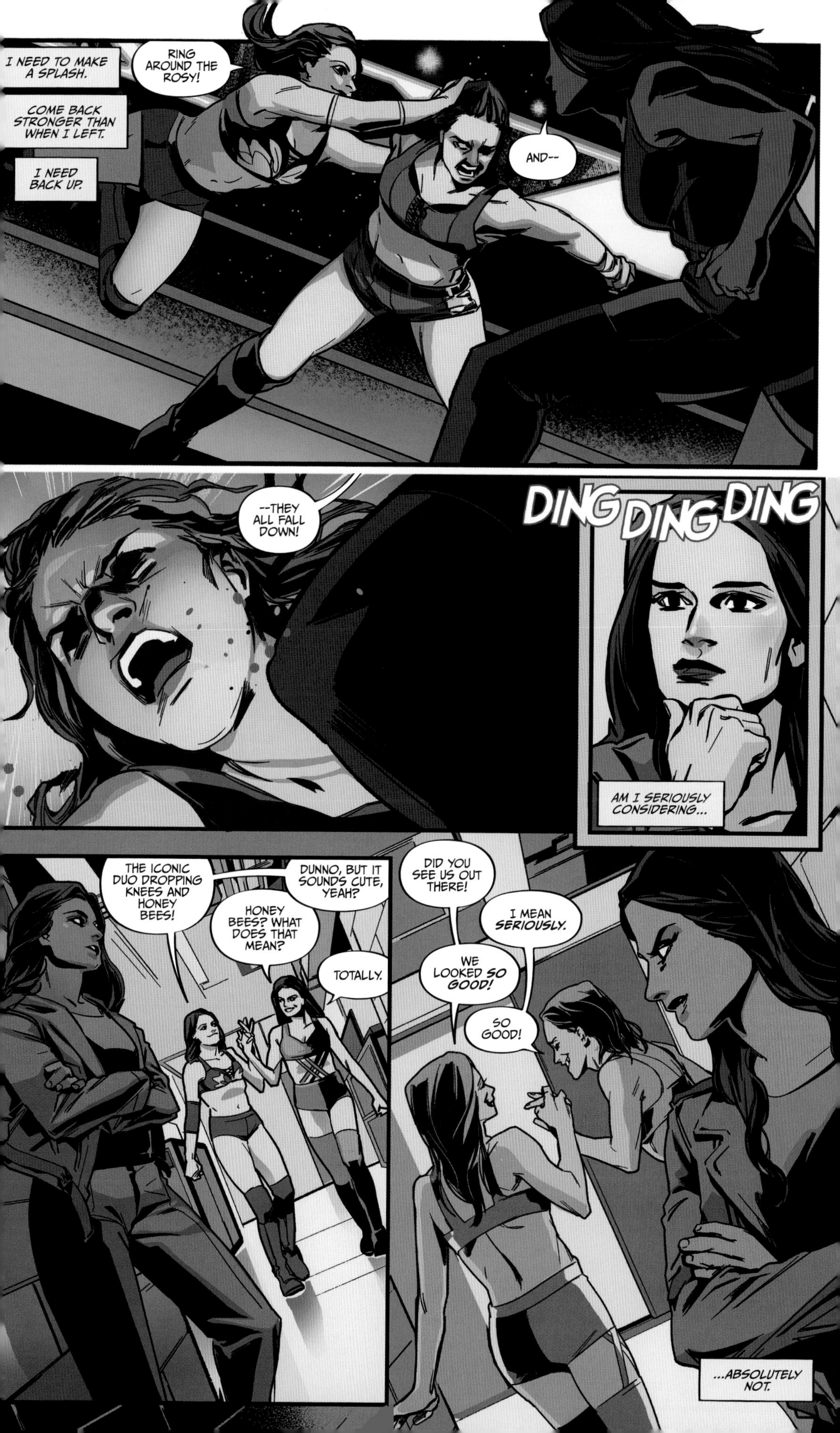

I NEED TO MAKE A SPLASH.
RING AROUND THE ROSY!
COME BACK STRONGER THAN WHEN I LEFT.
I NEED BACK UP.
AND--
--THEY ALL FALL DOWN!
DING DING DING
AM I SERIOUSLY CONSIDERING...
THE ICONIC DUO DROPPING KNEES AND HONEY BEES!
HONEY BEES? WHAT DOES THAT MEAN?
DUNNO, BUT IT SOUNDS CUTE, YEAH?
TOTALLY.
DID YOU SEE US OUT THERE!
I MEAN SERIOUSLY.
WE LOOKED SO GOOD!
SO GOOD!
...ABSOLUTELY NOT.

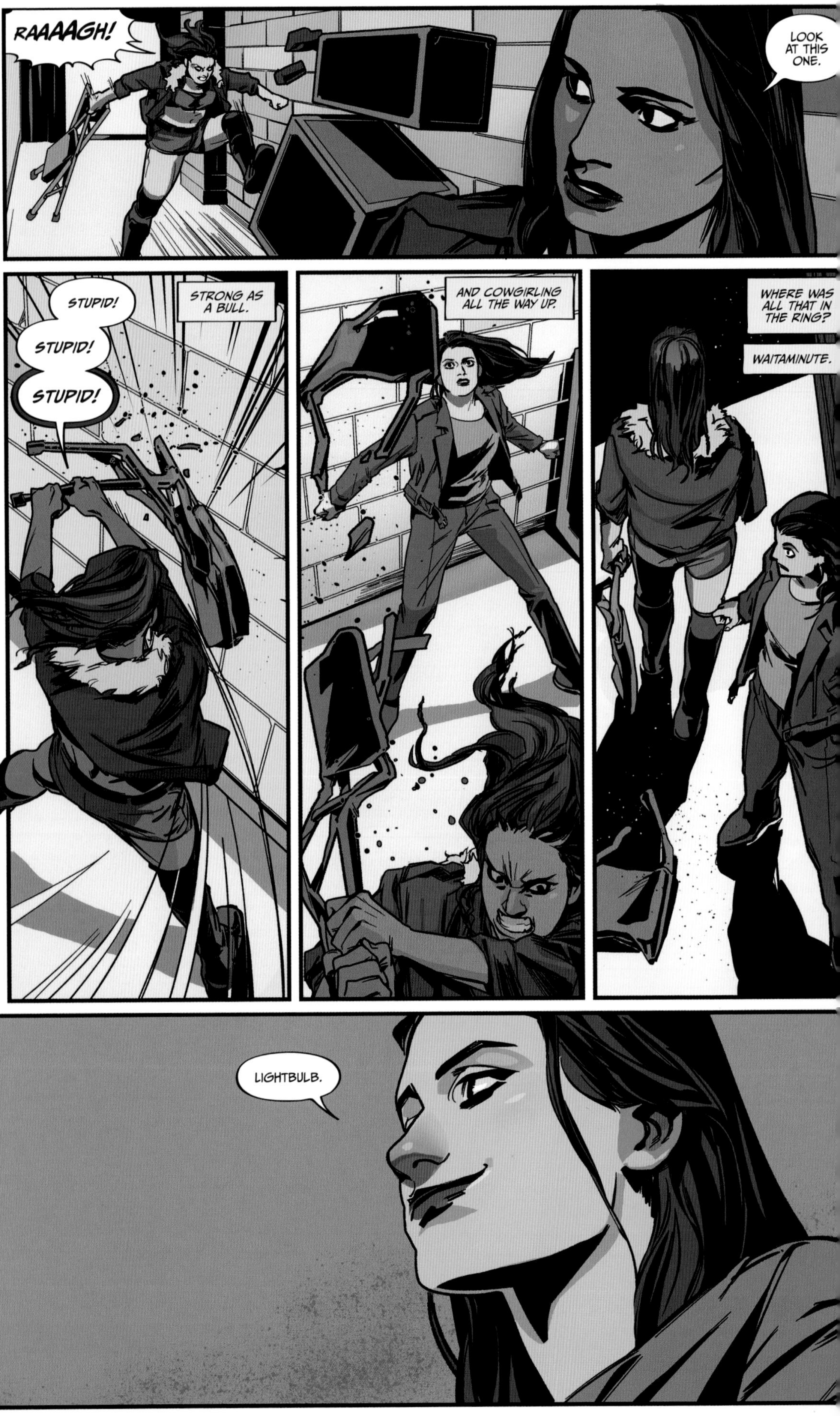
RAAAAGH!
LOOK AT THIS ONE.
STUPID!
STUPID!
STUPID!
STRONG AS A BULL.
AND COWGIRLING ALL THE WAY UP.
WHERE WAS ALL THAT IN THE RING?
WAITAMINUTE.
LIGHTBULB.

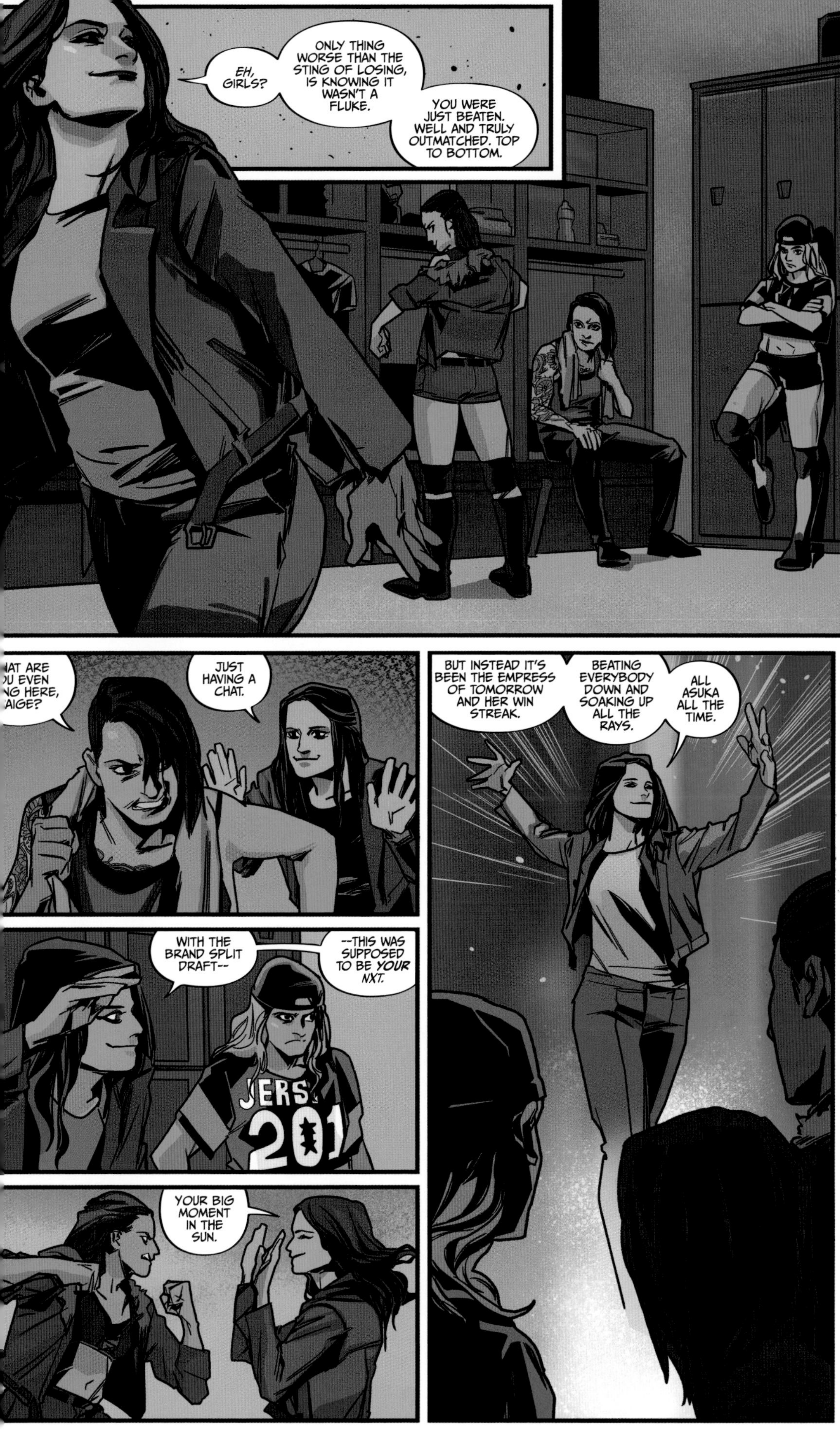
EH, GIRLS?
ONLY THING WORSE THAN THE STING OF LOSING, IS KNOWING IT WASN'T A FLUKE.
YOU WERE JUST BEATEN. WELL AND TRULY OUTMATCHED. TOP TO BOTTOM.
HAT ARE U EVEN NG HERE, AIGE?
JUST HAVING A CHAT.
WITH THE BRAND SPLIT DRAFT--
--THIS WAS SUPPOSED TO BE *YOUR* NXT.
YOUR BIG MOMENT IN THE SUN.
BUT INSTEAD IT'S BEEN THE EMPRESS OF TOMORROW AND HER WIN STREAK.
BEATING EVERYBODY DOWN AND SOAKING UP ALL THE RAYS.
ALL ASUKA ALL THE TIME.
JERS
201

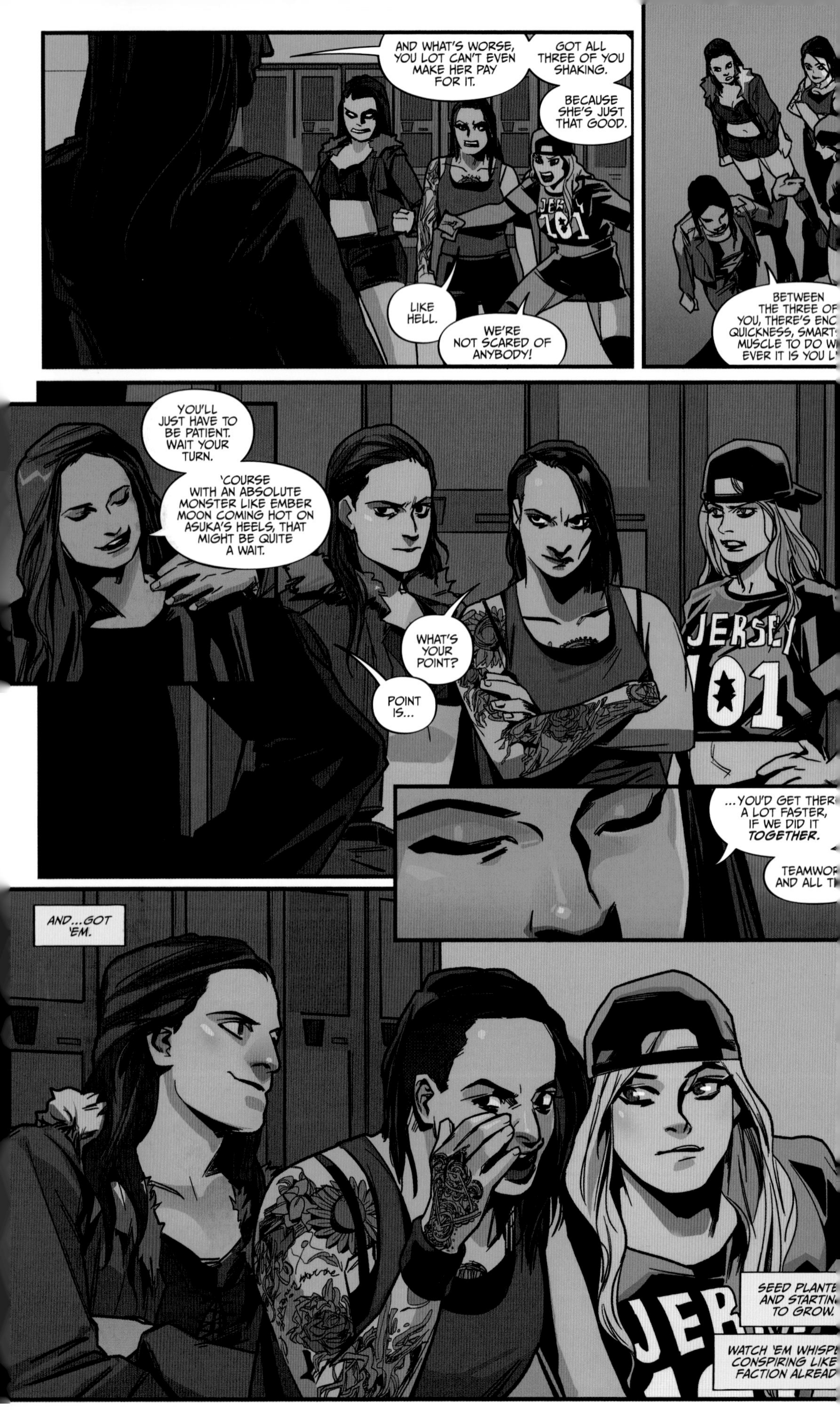
AND WHAT'S WORSE, YOU LOT CAN'T EVEN MAKE HER PAY FOR IT.
GOT ALL THREE OF YOU SHAKING.
BECAUSE SHE'S JUST THAT GOOD.
LIKE HELL.
WE'RE NOT SCARED OF ANYBODY!
BETWEEN THE THREE OF YOU, THERE'S ENO QUICKNESS, SMARTS MUSCLE TO DO WH EVER IT IS YOU L
YOU'LL JUST HAVE TO BE PATIENT. WAIT YOUR TURN.
'COURSE WITH AN ABSOLUTE MONSTER LIKE EMBER MOON COMING HOT ON ASUKA'S HEELS, THAT MIGHT BE QUITE A WAIT.
WHAT'S YOUR POINT?
POINT IS...
...YOU'D GET THER A LOT FASTER, IF WE DID IT *TOGETHER.*
TEAMWOR AND ALL T
AND...GOT 'EM.
SEED PLANTE AND STARTIN TO GROW.
WATCH 'EM WHISP CONSPIRING LIKE FACTION ALREAD

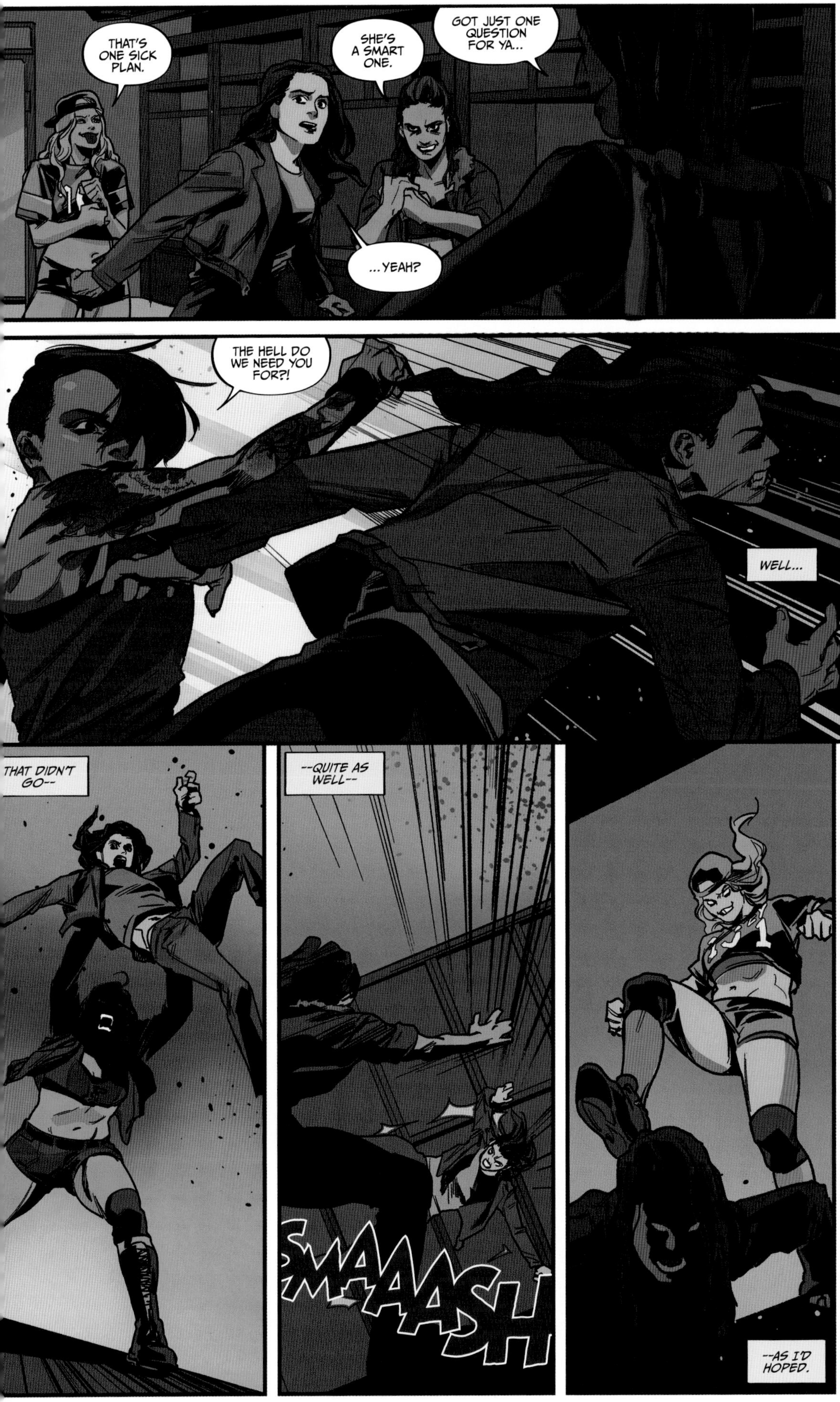
THAT'S ONE SICK PLAN.
SHE'S A SMART ONE.
GOT JUST ONE QUESTION FOR YA...
...YEAH?
THE HELL DO WE NEED YOU FOR?!
WELL...
THAT DIDN'T GO--
--QUITE AS WELL--
SMAAASH
--AS I'D HOPED.

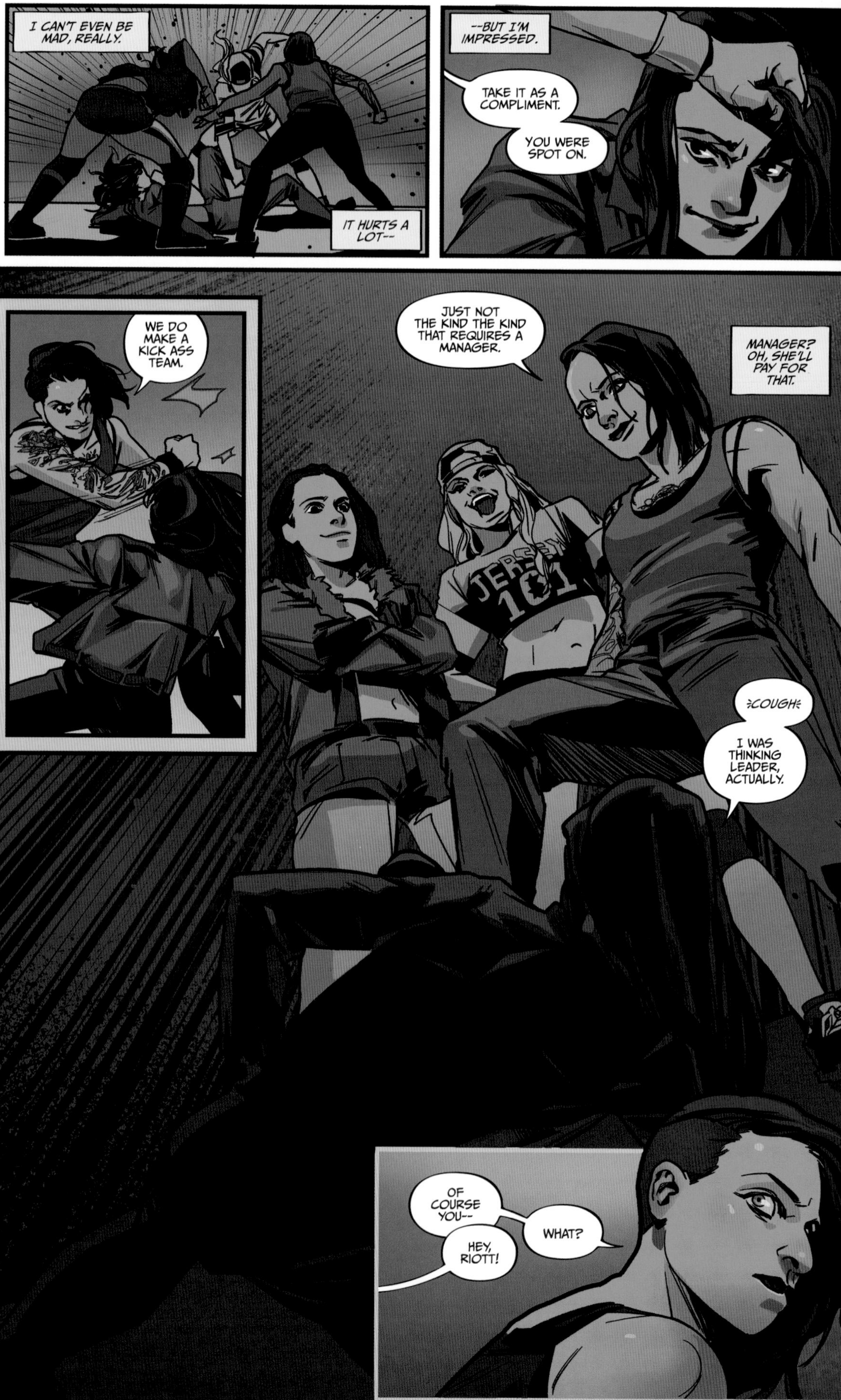
I CAN'T EVEN BE MAD, REALLY.
IT HURTS A LOT--
--BUT I'M IMPRESSED.
TAKE IT AS A COMPLIMENT.
YOU WERE SPOT ON.
WE DO MAKE A KICK ASS TEAM.
JUST NOT THE KIND THE KIND THAT REQUIRES A MANAGER.
MANAGER? OH, SHE'LL PAY FOR THAT.
COUGH
I WAS THINKING LEADER, ACTUALLY.
OF COURSE YOU--
WHAT?
HEY, RIOTT!

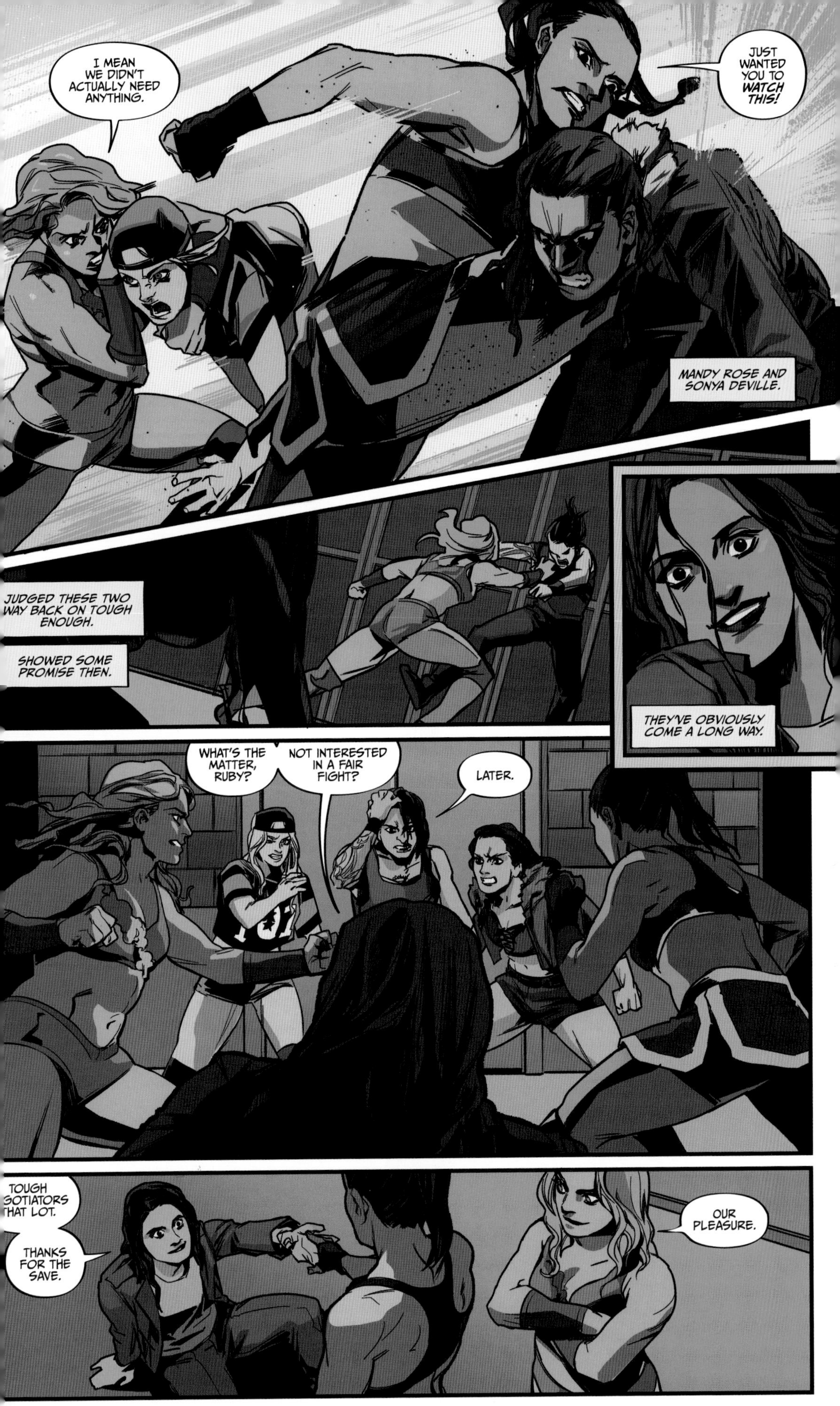
I MEAN WE DIDN'T ACTUALLY NEED ANYTHING.
JUST WANTED YOU TO *WATCH THIS!*
MANDY ROSE AND SONYA DEVILLE.
JUDGED THESE TWO WAY BACK ON TOUGH ENOUGH.
SHOWED SOME PROMISE THEN.
THEY'VE OBVIOUSLY COME A LONG WAY.
WHAT'S THE MATTER, RUBY?
NOT INTERESTED IN A FAIR FIGHT?
LATER.
TOUGH GOTIATORS THAT LOT.
THANKS FOR THE SAVE.
OUR PLEASURE.

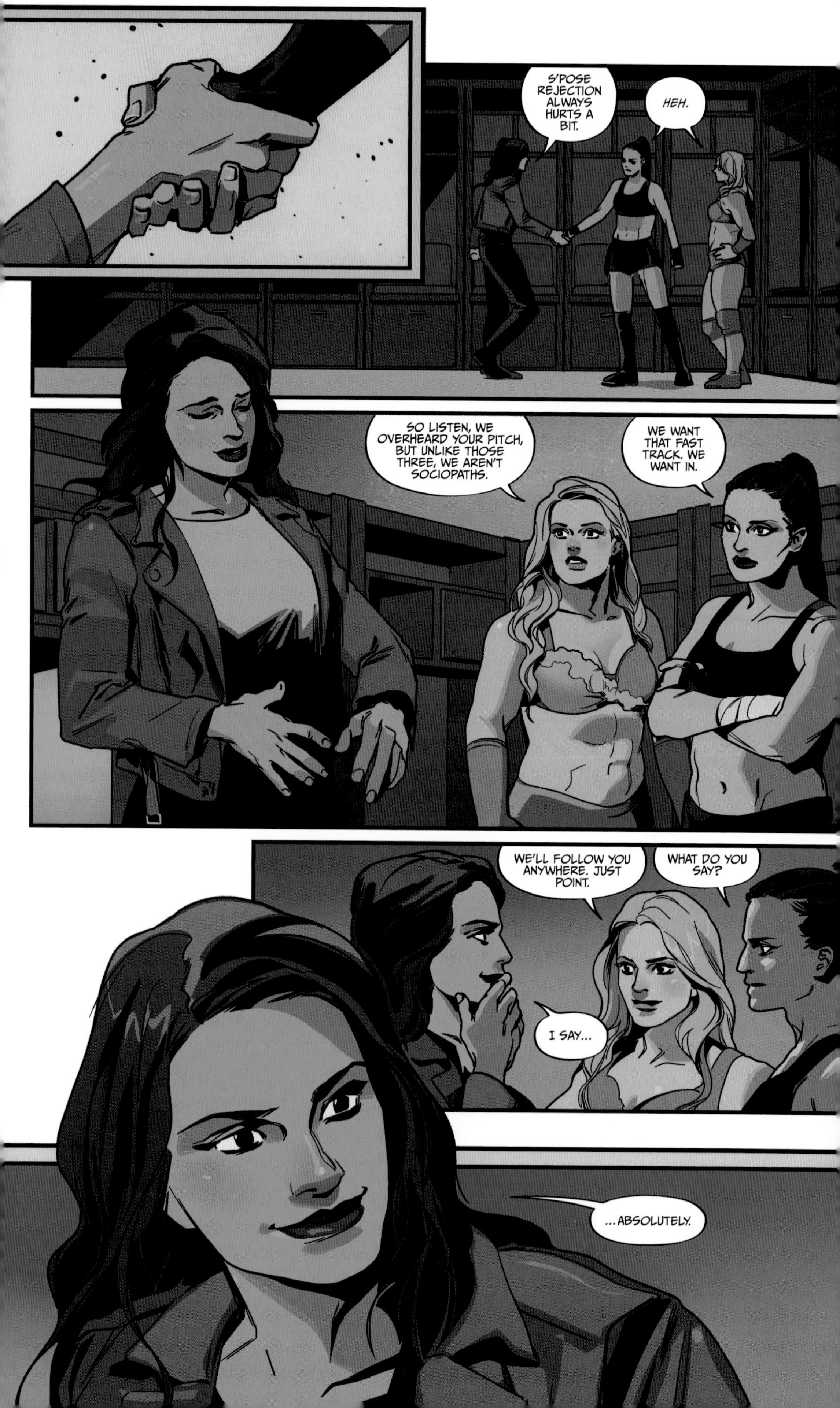
S'POSE REJECTION ALWAYS HURTS A BIT.
HEH.
SO LISTEN, WE OVERHEARD YOUR PITCH, BUT UNLIKE THOSE THREE, WE AREN'T SOCIOPATHS.
WE WANT THAT FAST TRACK. WE WANT IN.
WE'LL FOLLOW YOU ANYWHERE. JUST POINT.
WHAT DO YOU SAY?
I SAY...
...ABSOLUTELY.

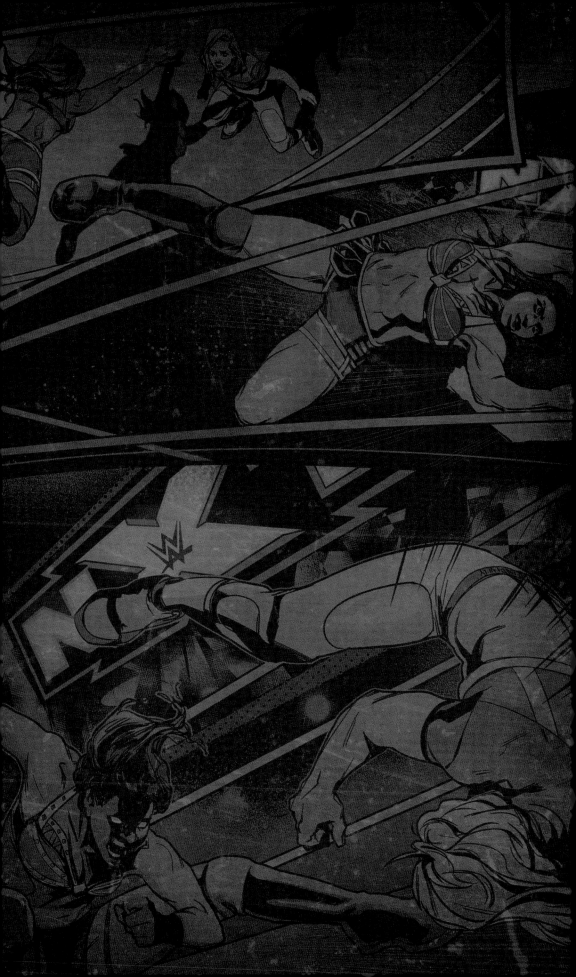

REDEMPTION

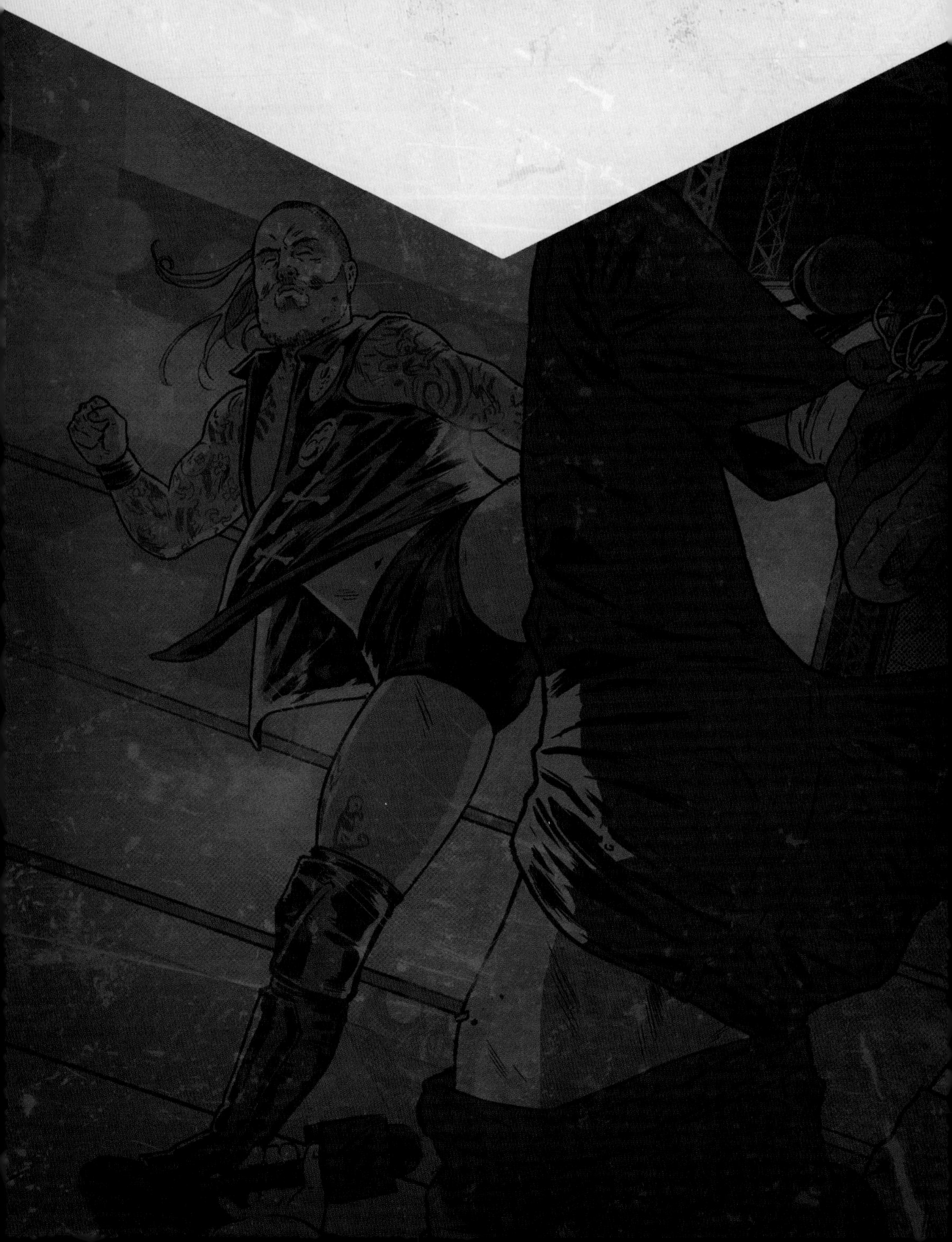

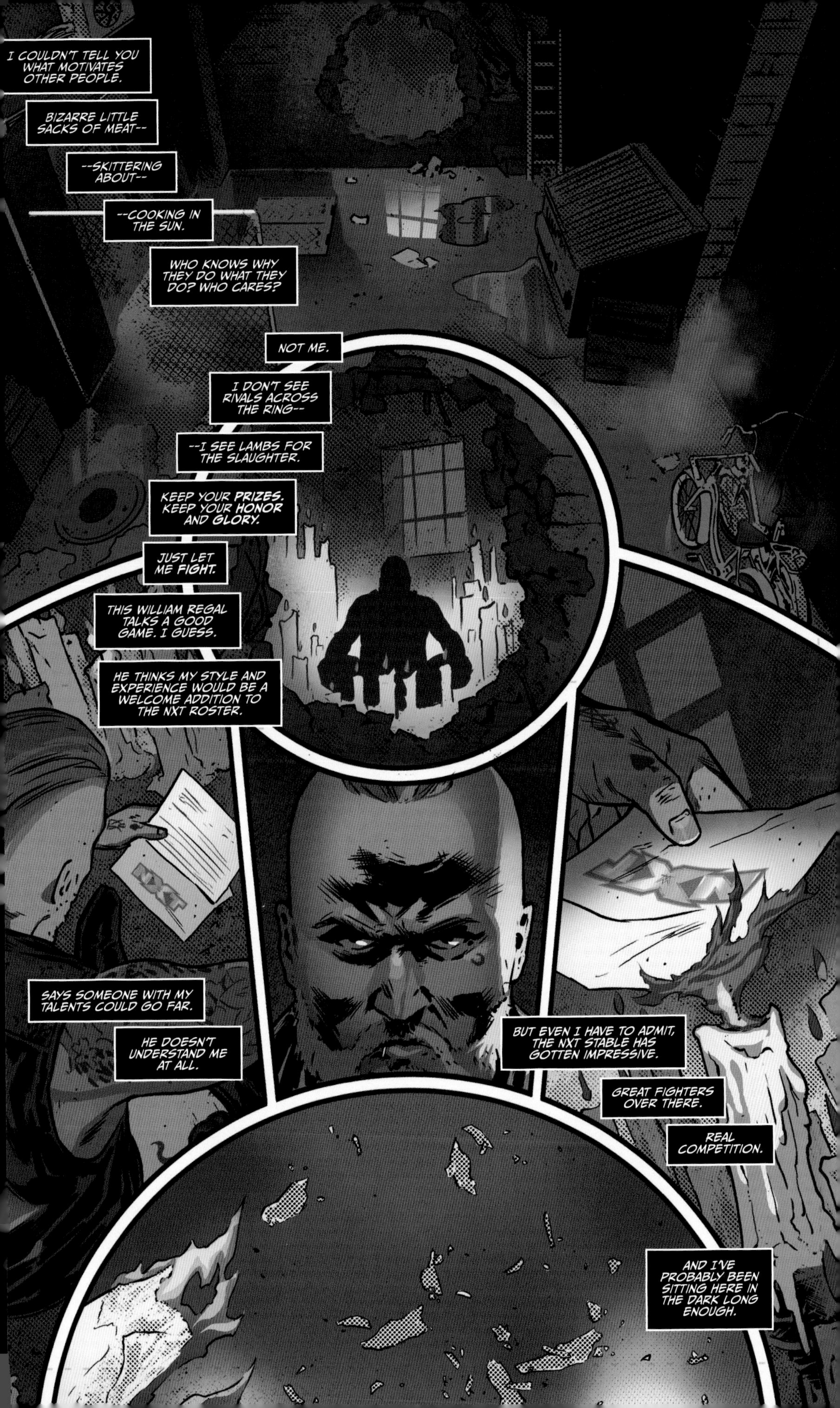
I COULDN'T TELL YOU WHAT MOTIVATES OTHER PEOPLE.
BIZARRE LITTLE SACKS OF MEAT--
--SKITTERING ABOUT--
--COOKING IN THE SUN.
WHO KNOWS WHY THEY DO WHAT THEY DO? WHO CARES?
NOT ME.
I DON'T SEE RIVALS ACROSS THE RING--
--I SEE LAMBS FOR THE SLAUGHTER.
KEEP YOUR **PRIZES.** KEEP YOUR **HONOR** AND **GLORY.**
JUST LET ME **FIGHT.**
THIS WILLIAM REGAL TALKS A GOOD GAME. I GUESS.
HE THINKS MY STYLE AND EXPERIENCE WOULD BE A WELCOME ADDITION TO THE NXT ROSTER.
SAYS SOMEONE WITH MY TALENTS COULD GO FAR.
HE DOESN'T UNDERSTAND ME AT ALL.
BUT EVEN I HAVE TO ADMIT, THE NXT STABLE HAS GOTTEN IMPRESSIVE.
GREAT FIGHTERS OVER THERE.
REAL COMPETITION.
AND I'VE PROBABLY BEEN SITTING HERE IN THE DARK LONG ENOUGH.

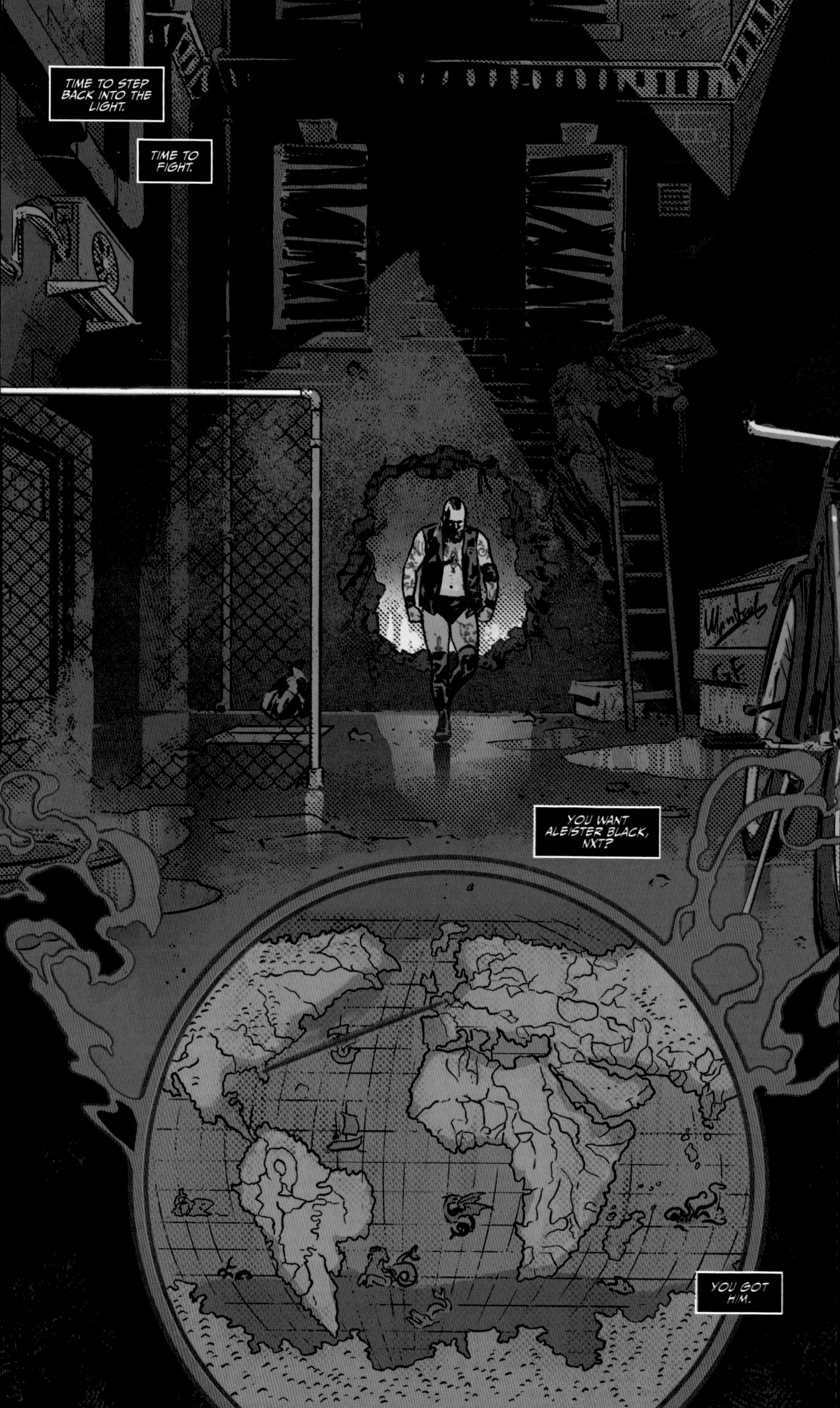
TIME TO STEP BACK INTO THE LIGHT.
TIME TO FIGHT.
YOU WANT ALEISTER BLACK, NXT?
YOU GOT HIM.

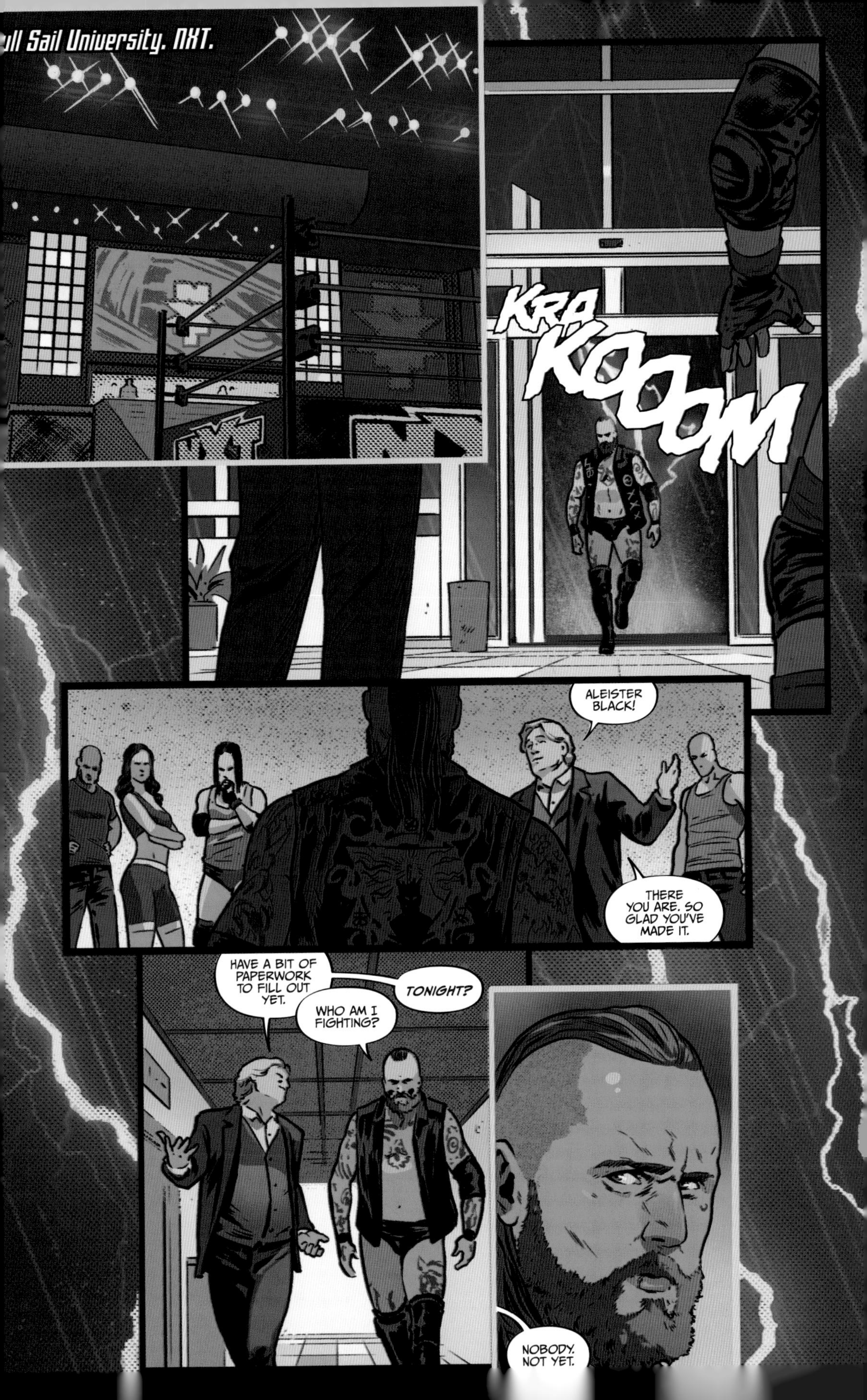

ull Sail University. NXT.
KRA KOOOOM
ALEISTER BLACK!
THERE YOU ARE. SO GLAD YOU'VE MADE IT.
TONIGHT?
WHO AM I FIGHTING?
HAVE A BIT OF PAPERWORK TO FILL OUT YET.
NOBODY. NOT YET.

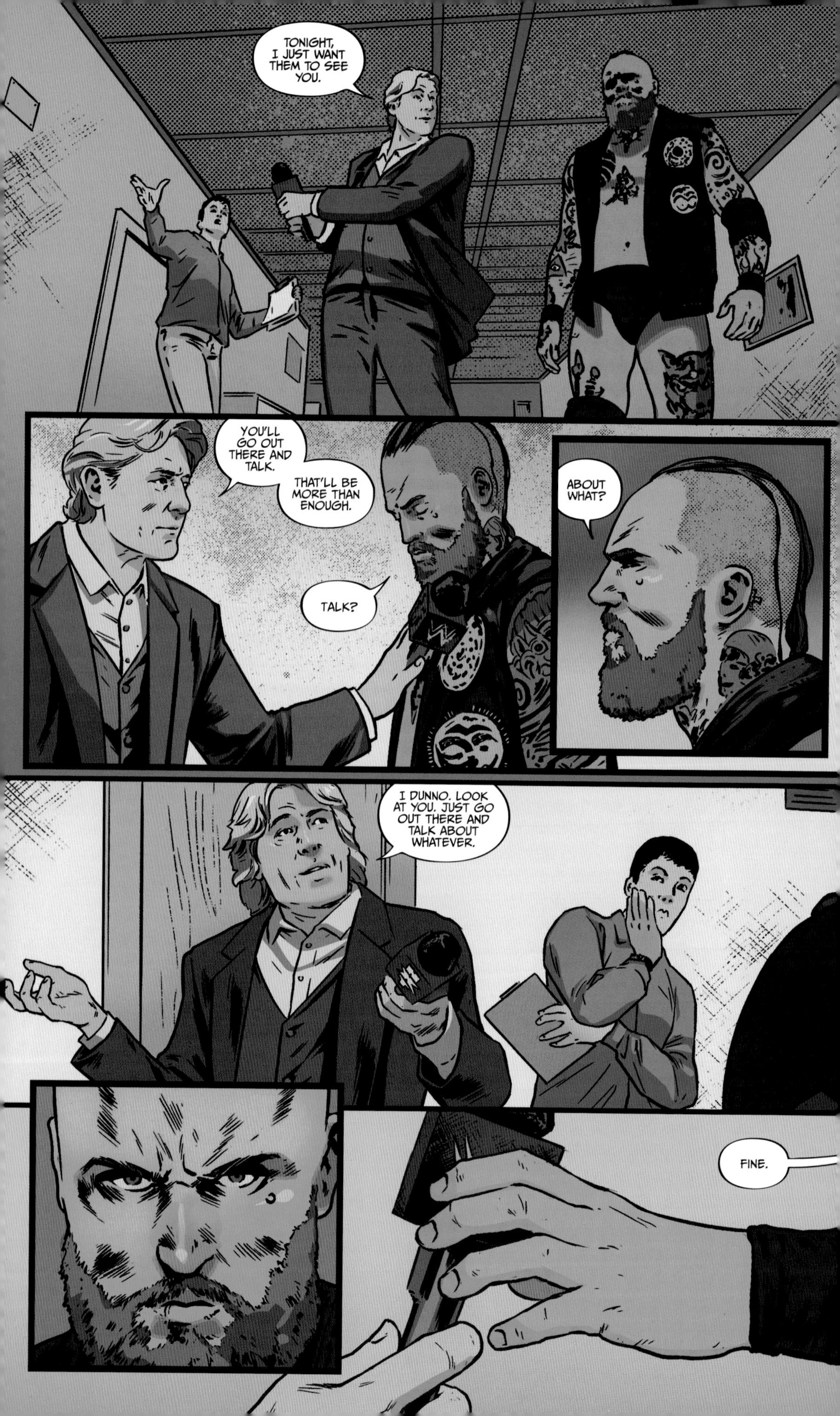
TONIGHT, I JUST WANT THEM TO SEE YOU.
YOU'LL GO OUT THERE AND TALK.
THAT'LL BE MORE THAN ENOUGH.
TALK?
ABOUT WHAT?
I DUNNO. LOOK AT YOU. JUST GO OUT THERE AND TALK ABOUT WHATEVER.
FINE.

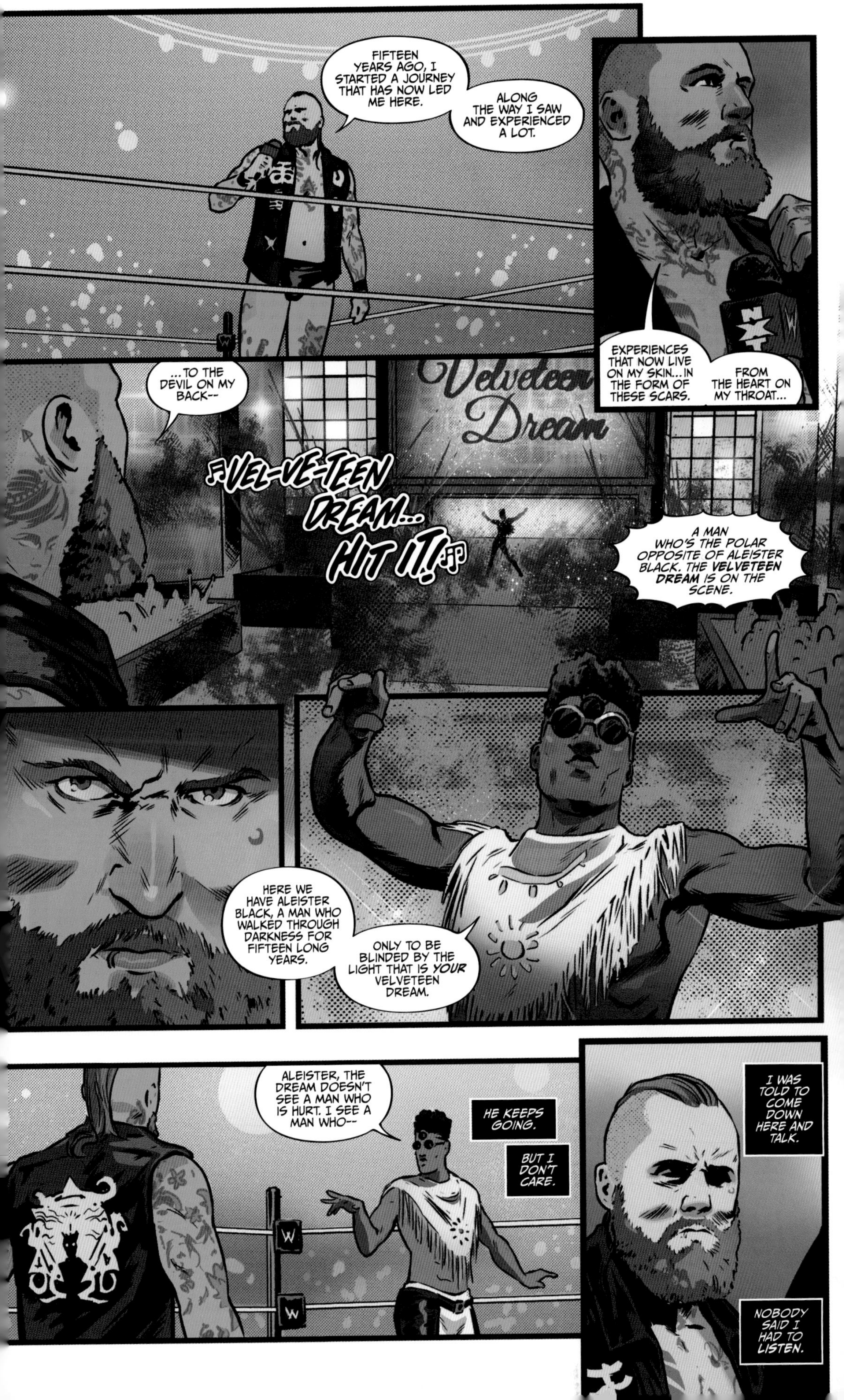

FIFTEEN YEARS AGO, I STARTED A JOURNEY THAT HAS NOW LED ME HERE.
ALONG THE WAY I SAW AND EXPERIENCED A LOT.
EXPERIENCES THAT NOW LIVE ON MY SKIN... IN THE FORM OF THESE SCARS.
FROM THE HEART ON MY THROAT...
...TO THE DEVIL ON MY BACK--
Velveteen Dream
♫VEL-VE-TEEN DREAM... HIT IT!♫
A MAN WHO'S THE POLAR OPPOSITE OF ALEISTER BLACK. THE **VELVETEEN DREAM** IS ON THE SCENE.
HERE WE HAVE ALEISTER BLACK, A MAN WHO WALKED THROUGH DARKNESS FOR FIFTEEN LONG YEARS.
ONLY TO BE BLINDED BY THE LIGHT THAT IS ***YOUR*** VELVETEEN DREAM.
ALEISTER, THE DREAM DOESN'T SEE A MAN WHO IS HURT. I SEE A MAN WHO--
HE KEEPS GOING.
BUT I DON'T CARE.
I WAS TOLD TO COME DOWN HERE AND TALK.
*NOBODY SAID I HAD TO **LISTEN.***

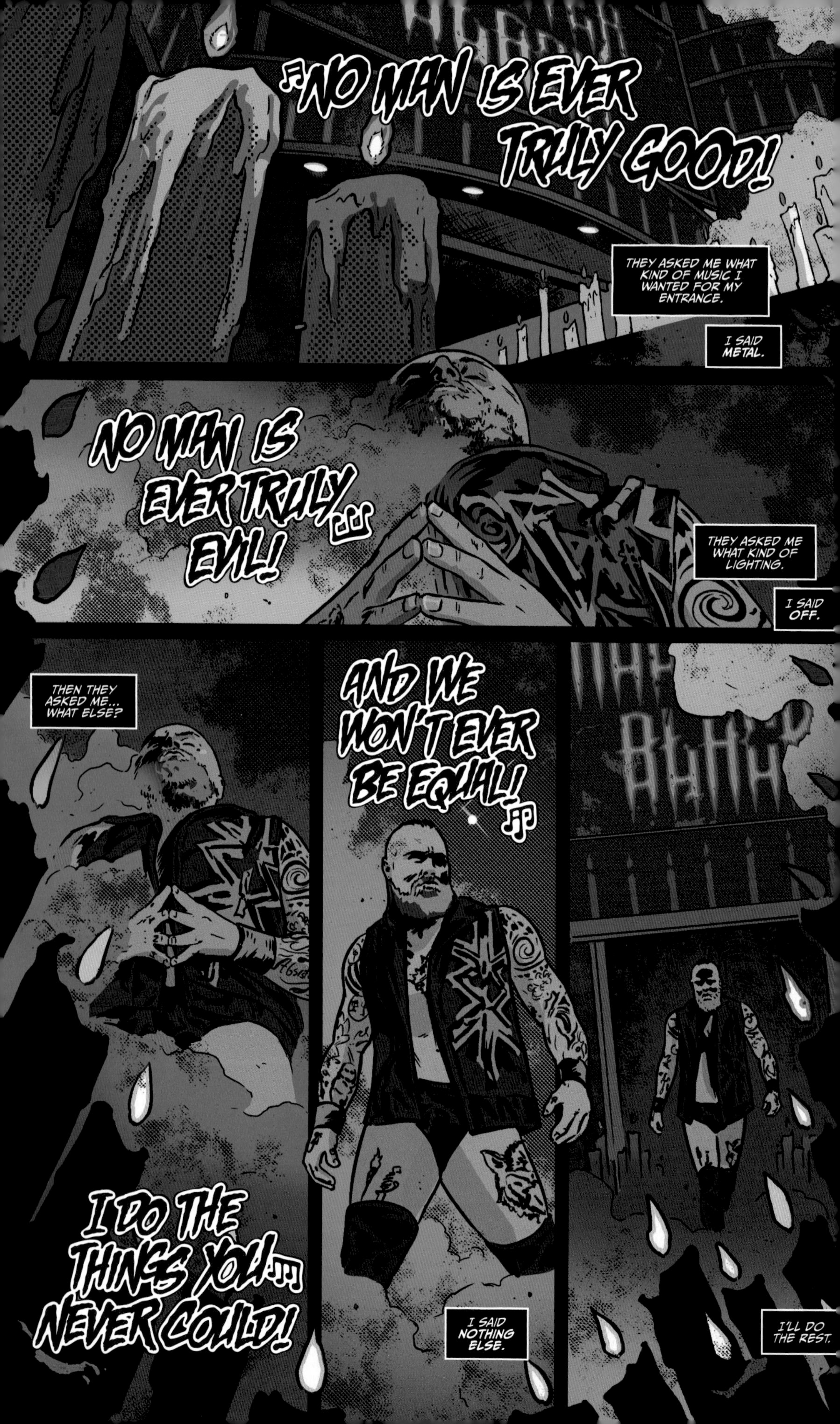
NO MAN IS EVER TRULY GOOD!
THEY ASKED ME WHAT KIND OF MUSIC I WANTED FOR MY ENTRANCE.
I SAID METAL.
NO MAN IS EVER TRULY EVIL!
THEY ASKED ME WHAT KIND OF LIGHTING.
I SAID OFF.
THEN THEY ASKED ME... WHAT ELSE?
AND WE WON'T EVER BE EQUAL!
I DO THE THINGS YOU NEVER COULD!
I SAID NOTHING ELSE.
I'LL DO THE REST.

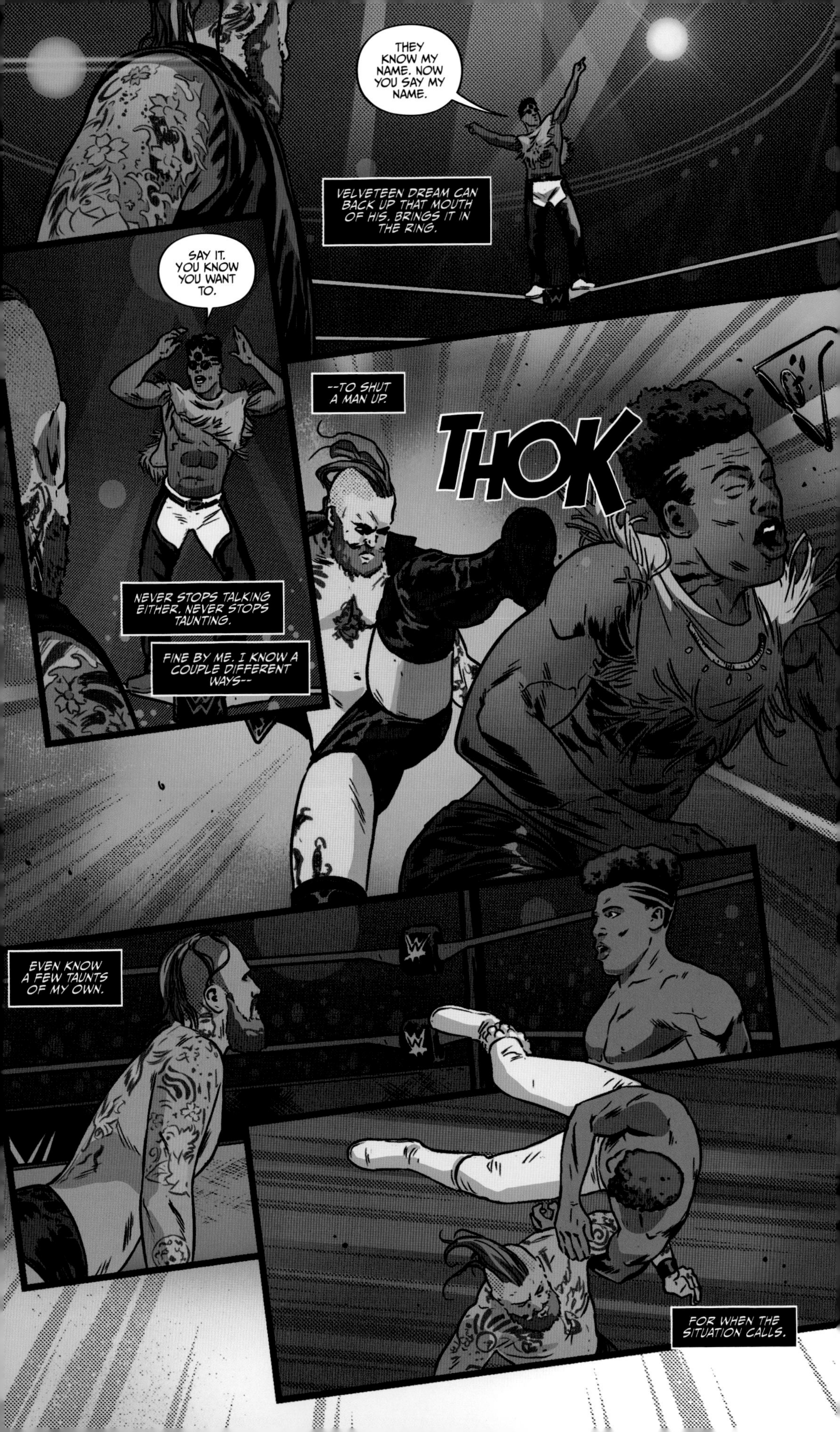
THEY KNOW MY NAME. NOW YOU SAY MY NAME.
VELVETEEN DREAM CAN BACK UP THAT MOUTH OF HIS. BRINGS IT IN THE RING.
SAY IT. YOU KNOW YOU WANT TO.
NEVER STOPS TALKING EITHER. NEVER STOPS TAUNTING.
FINE BY ME. I KNOW A COUPLE DIFFERENT WAYS--
--TO SHUT A MAN UP.
THOK
EVEN KNOW A FEW TAUNTS OF MY OWN.
FOR WHEN THE SITUATION CALLS.

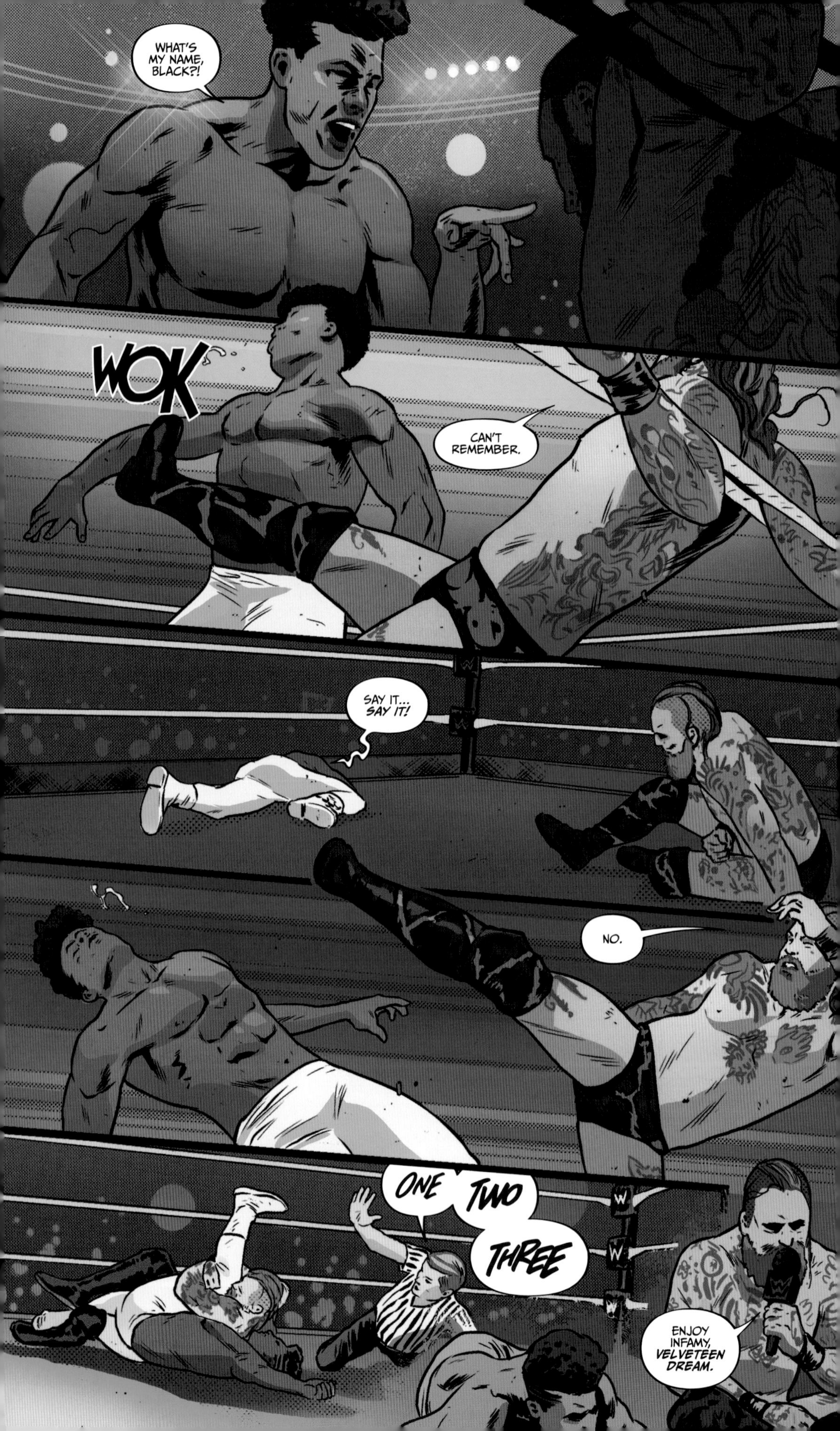
WHAT'S MY NAME, BLACK?!
WOK
CAN'T REMEMBER.
SAY IT... SAY IT!
NO.
ONE
TWO
THREE
ENJOY INFAMY, VELVETEEN DREAM.

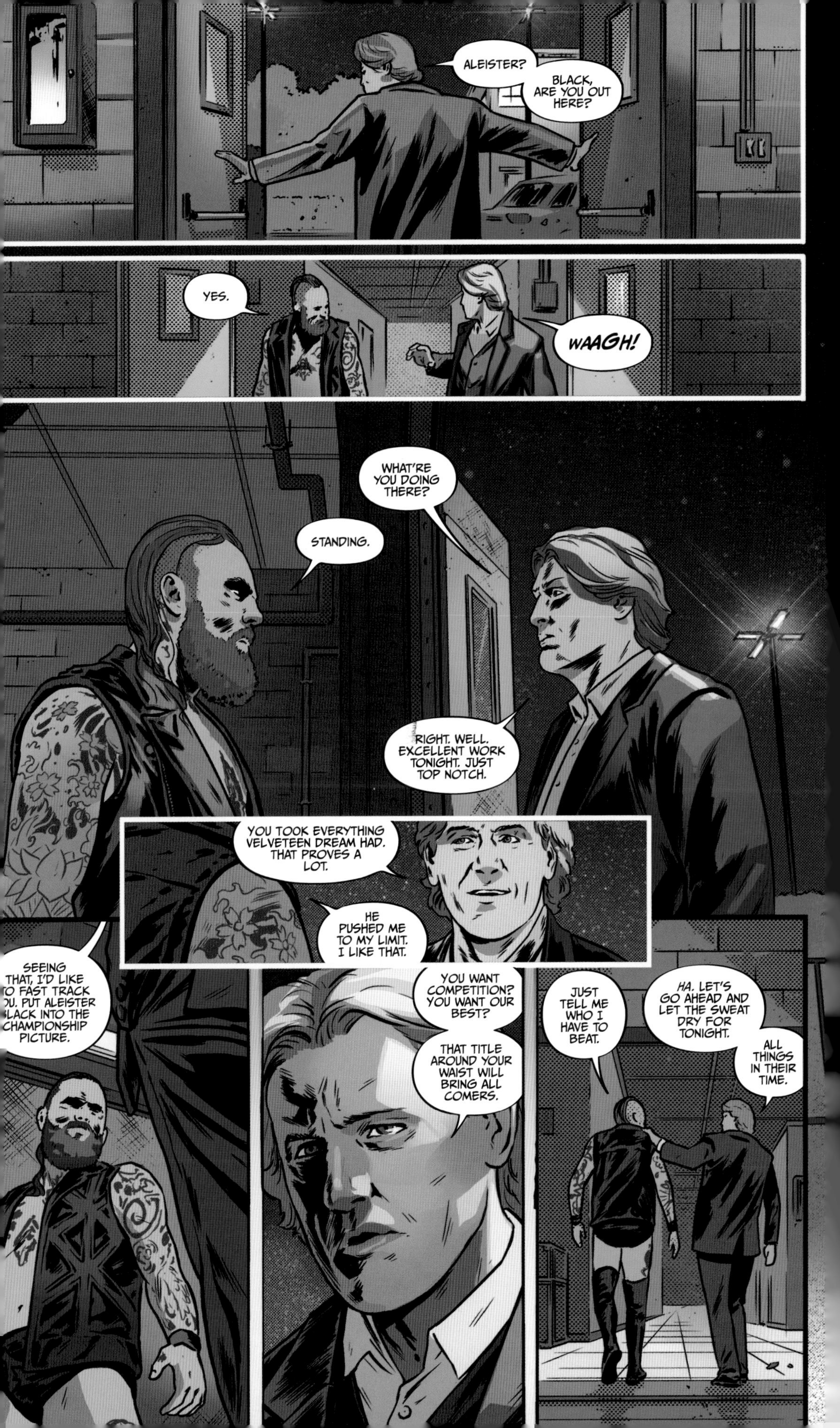
ALEISTER?
BLACK, ARE YOU OUT HERE?
YES.
WAAGH!
WHAT'RE YOU DOING THERE?
STANDING.
RIGHT. WELL. EXCELLENT WORK TONIGHT. JUST TOP NOTCH.
YOU TOOK EVERYTHING VELVETEEN DREAM HAD. THAT PROVES A LOT.
HE PUSHED ME TO MY LIMIT. I LIKE THAT.
SEEING THAT, I'D LIKE TO FAST TRACK YOU. PUT ALEISTER BLACK INTO THE CHAMPIONSHIP PICTURE.
YOU WANT COMPETITION? YOU WANT OUR BEST?
THAT TITLE AROUND YOUR WAIST WILL BRING ALL COMERS.
JUST TELL ME WHO I HAVE TO BEAT.
HA. LET'S GO AHEAD AND LET THE SWEAT DRY FOR TONIGHT.
ALL THINGS IN THEIR TIME.

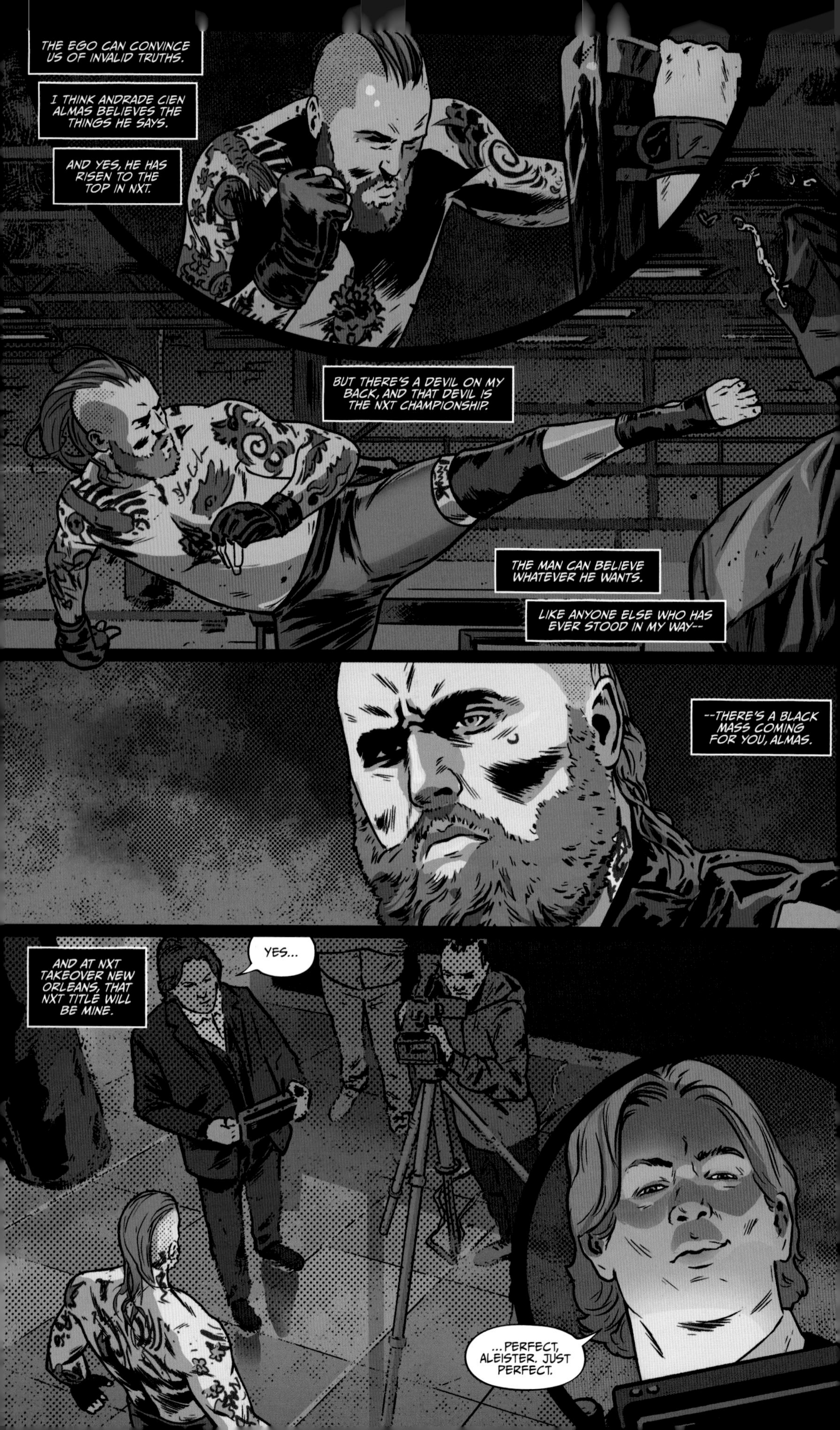
THE EGO CAN CONVINCE US OF INVALID TRUTHS.
I THINK ANDRADE CIEN ALMAS BELIEVES THE THINGS HE SAYS.
AND YES, HE HAS RISEN TO THE TOP IN NXT.
BUT THERE'S A DEVIL ON MY BACK, AND THAT DEVIL IS THE NXT CHAMPIONSHIP.
THE MAN CAN BELIEVE WHATEVER HE WANTS.
LIKE ANYONE ELSE WHO HAS EVER STOOD IN MY WAY--
--THERE'S A BLACK MASS COMING FOR YOU, ALMAS.
AND AT NXT TAKEOVER NEW ORLEANS, THAT NXT TITLE WILL BE MINE.
YES...
...PERFECT, ALEISTER. JUST PERFECT.

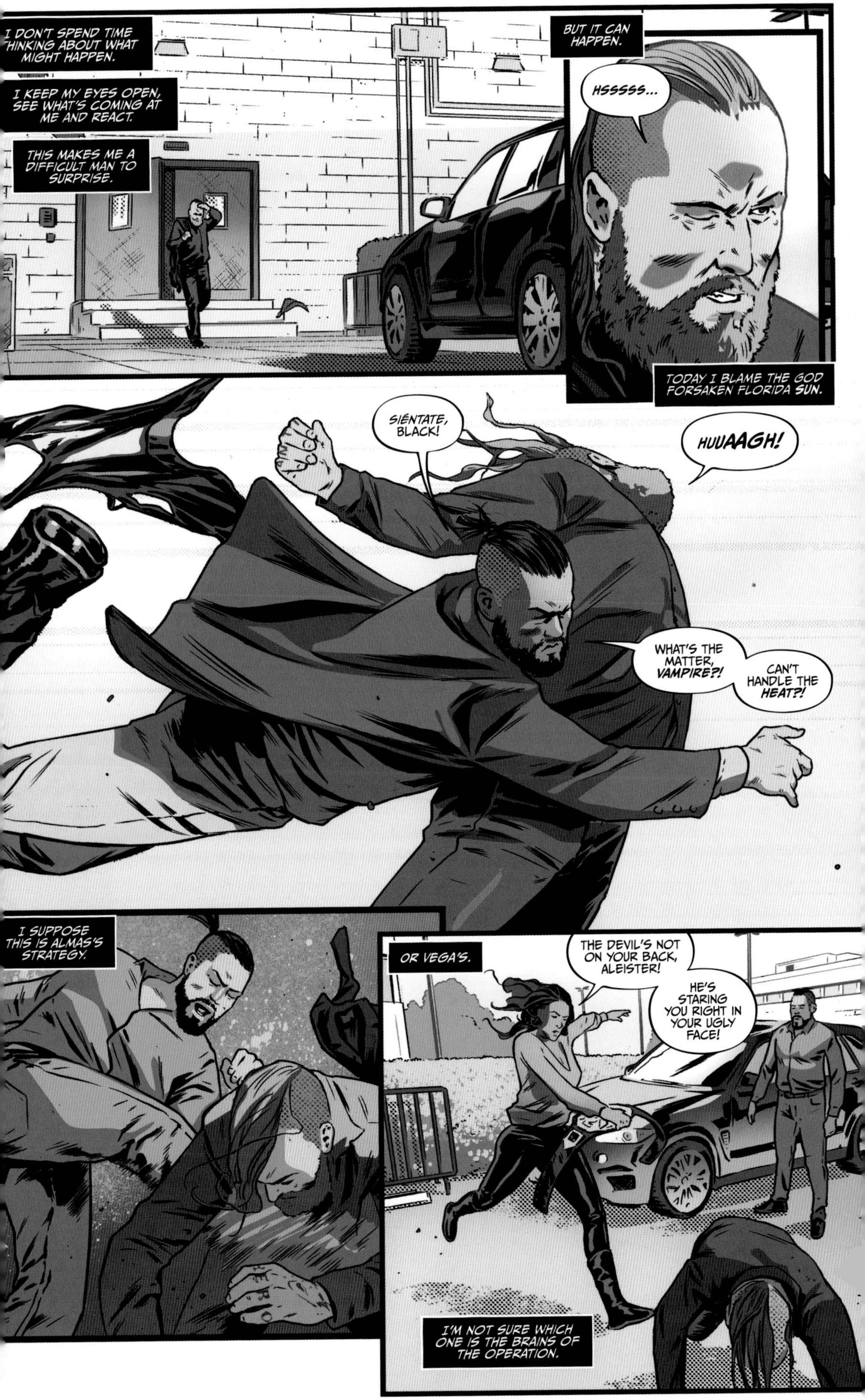
I DON'T SPEND TIME THINKING ABOUT WHAT MIGHT HAPPEN.
I KEEP MY EYES OPEN, SEE WHAT'S COMING AT ME AND REACT.
THIS MAKES ME A DIFFICULT MAN TO SURPRISE.
BUT IT CAN HAPPEN.
HSSSSS...
TODAY I BLAME THE GOD FORSAKEN FLORIDA SUN.
SIÉNTATE, BLACK!
HUUAAGH!
WHAT'S THE MATTER, VAMPIRE?!
CAN'T HANDLE THE HEAT?!
I SUPPOSE THIS IS ALMAS'S STRATEGY.
OR VEGA'S.
THE DEVIL'S NOT ON YOUR BACK, ALEISTER!
HE'S STARING YOU RIGHT IN YOUR UGLY FACE!
I'M NOT SURE WHICH ONE IS THE BRAINS OF THE OPERATION.

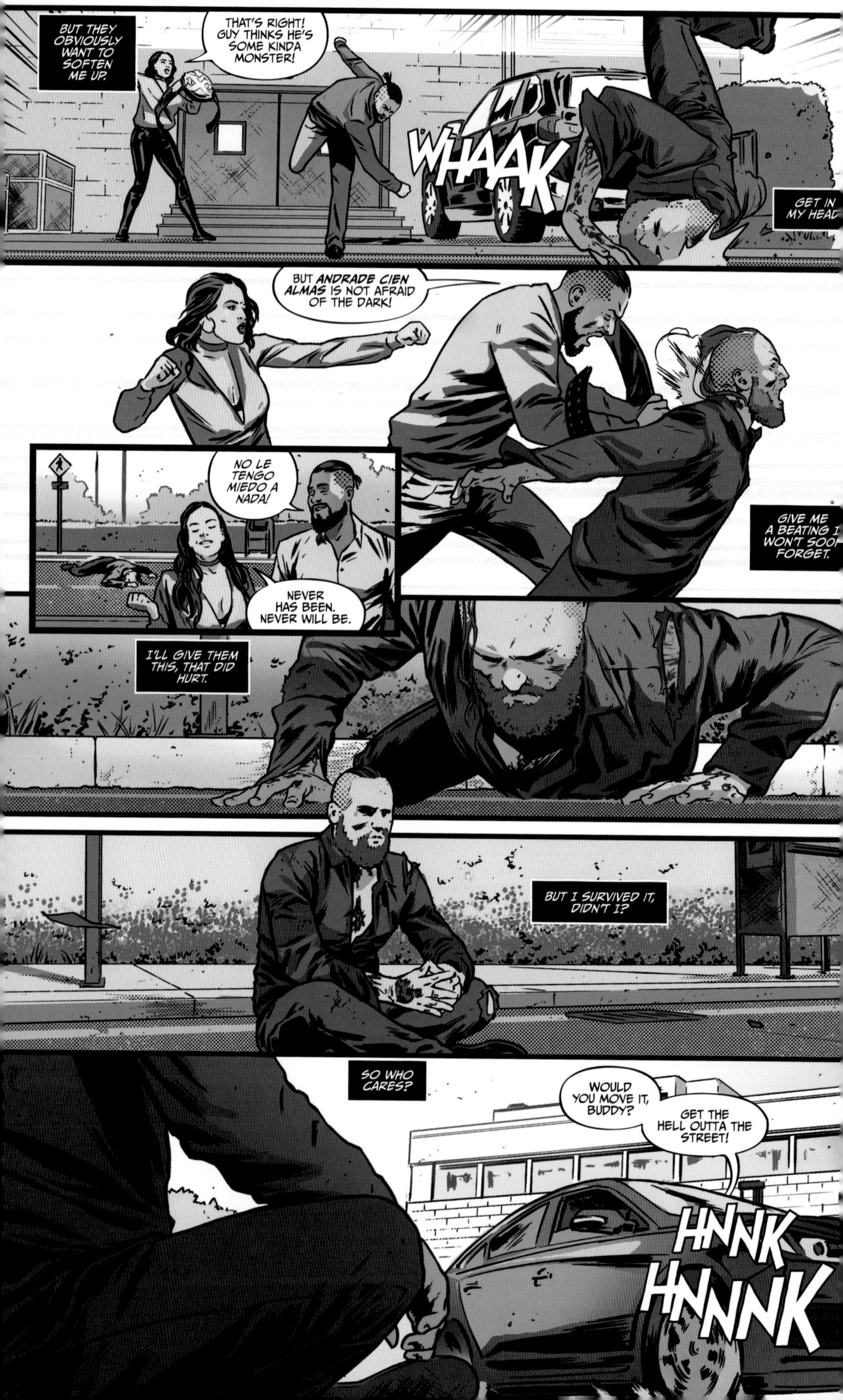

BUT THEY OBVIOUSLY WANT TO SOFTEN ME UP.
THAT'S RIGHT! GUY THINKS HE'S SOME KINDA MONSTER!
WHAAK
GET IN MY HEAD
BUT ANDRADE CIEN ALMAS IS NOT AFRAID OF THE DARK!
NO LE TENGO MIEDO A NADA!
NEVER HAS BEEN. NEVER WILL BE.
GIVE ME A BEATING I WON'T SOO FORGET.
I'LL GIVE THEM THIS, THAT DID HURT.
BUT I SURVIVED IT, DIDN'T I?
SO WHO CARES?
WOULD YOU MOVE IT, BUDDY?
GET THE HELL OUTTA THE STREET!
HNNK HNNNK

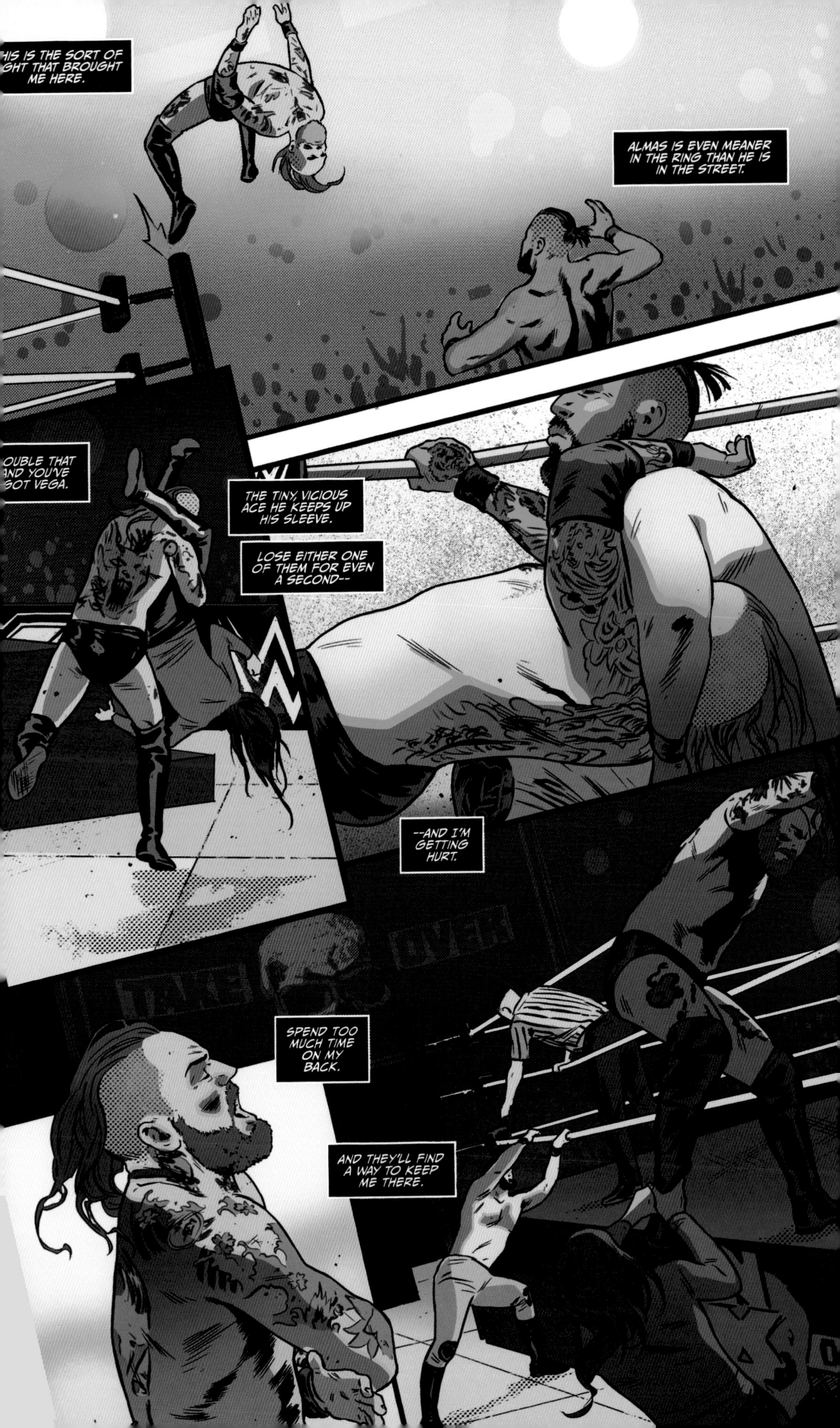
HIS IS THE SORT OF
GHT THAT BROUGHT
ME HERE.
ALMAS IS EVEN MEANER IN THE RING THAN HE IS IN THE STREET.
OUBLE THAT AND YOU'VE GOT VEGA.
THE TINY, VICIOUS ACE HE KEEPS UP HIS SLEEVE.
LOSE EITHER ONE OF THEM FOR EVEN A SECOND--
--AND I'M GETTING HURT.
SPEND TOO MUCH TIME ON MY BACK.
AND THEY'LL FIND A WAY TO KEEP ME THERE.

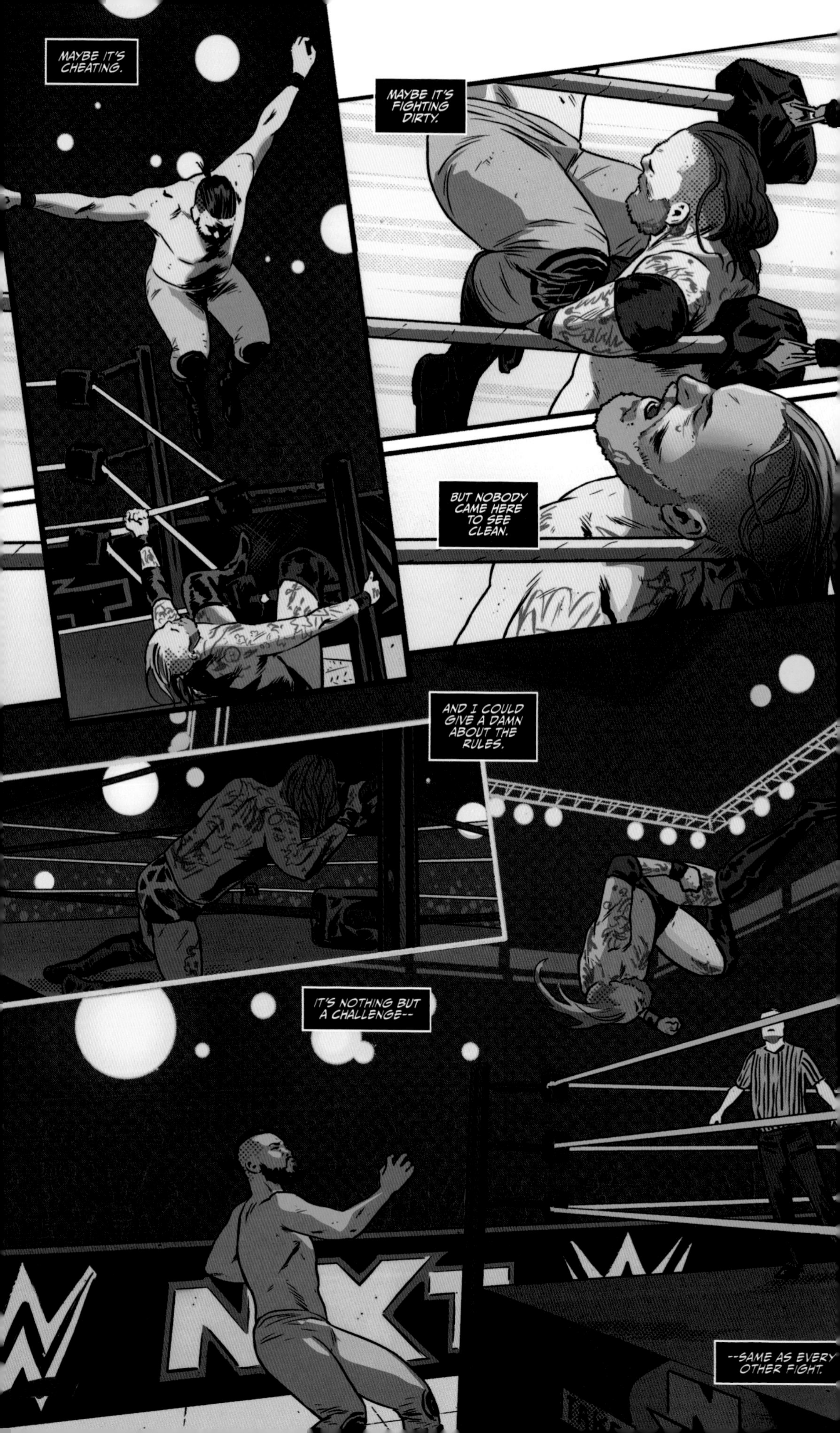
MAYBE IT'S CHEATING.
MAYBE IT'S FIGHTING DIRTY.
BUT NOBODY CAME HERE TO SEE CLEAN.
AND I COULD GIVE A DAMN ABOUT THE RULES.
IT'S NOTHING BUT A CHALLENGE--
--SAME AS EVERY OTHER FIGHT.

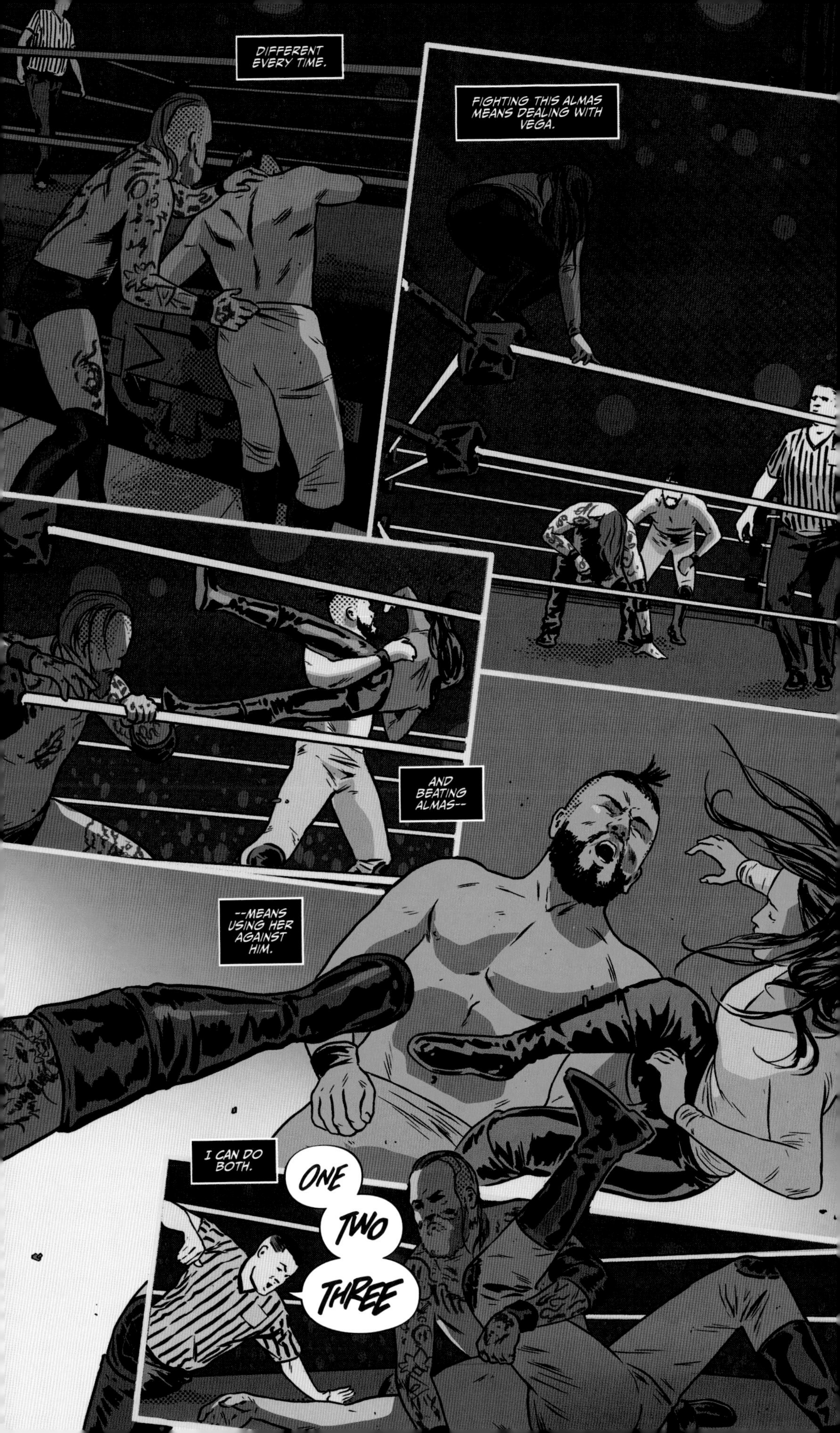
DIFFERENT EVERY TIME.
FIGHTING THIS ALMAS MEANS DEALING WITH VEGA.
AND BEATING ALMAS--
--MEANS USING HER AGAINST HIM.
I CAN DO BOTH.
ONE
TWO
THREE

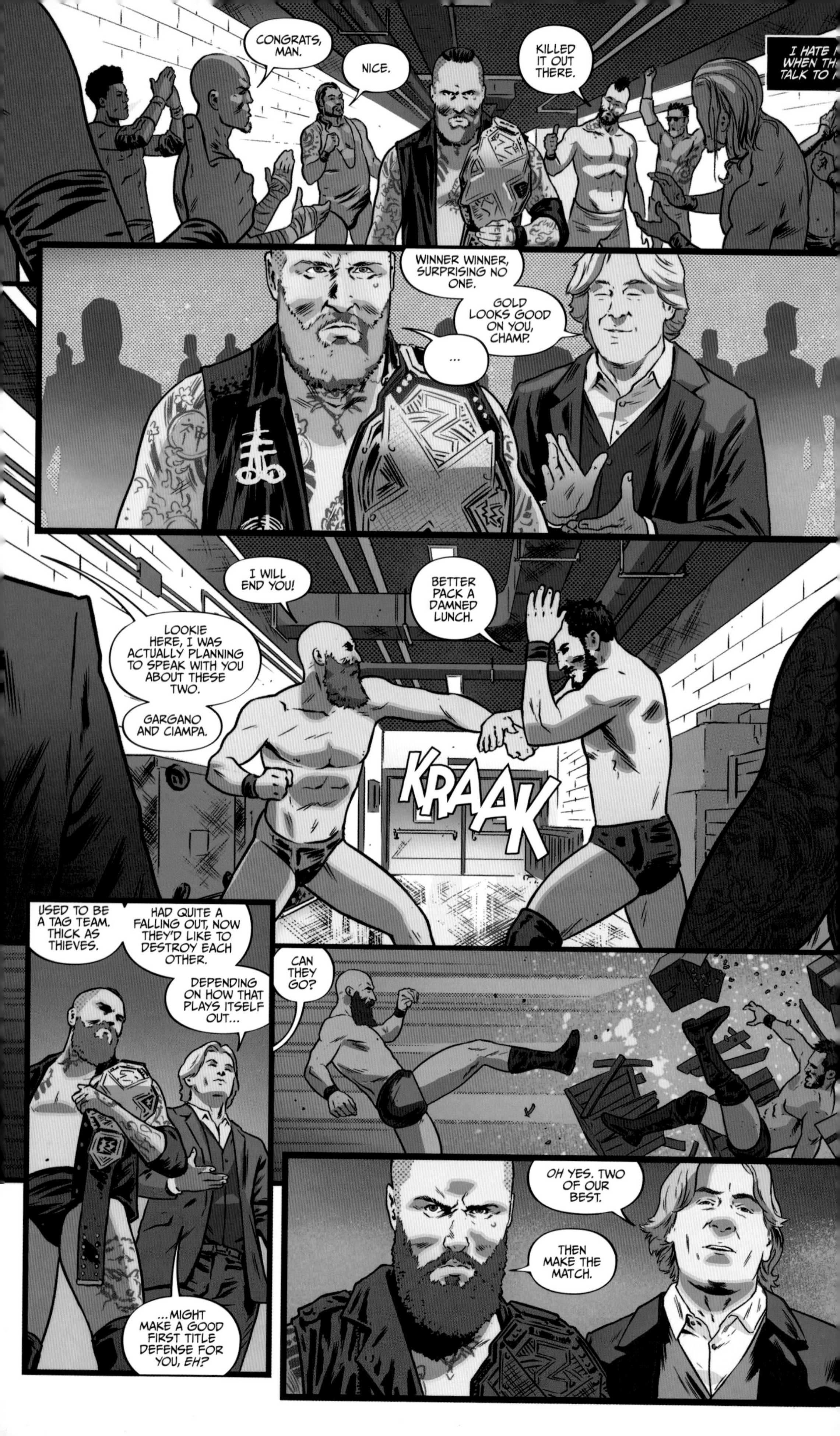
CONGRATS, MAN.
NICE.
KILLED IT OUT THERE.
WINNER WINNER, SURPRISING NO ONE.
GOLD LOOKS GOOD ON YOU, CHAMP.
...
LOOKIE HERE, I WAS ACTUALLY PLANNING TO SPEAK WITH YOU ABOUT THESE TWO.
GARGANO AND CIAMPA.
I WILL END YOU!
BETTER PACK A DAMNED LUNCH.
KRAAK
USED TO BE A TAG TEAM. THICK AS THIEVES.
HAD QUITE A FALLING OUT, NOW THEY'D LIKE TO DESTROY EACH OTHER.
DEPENDING ON HOW THAT PLAYS ITSELF OUT...
...MIGHT MAKE A GOOD FIRST TITLE DEFENSE FOR YOU, *EH?*
CAN THEY GO?
OH YES. TWO OF OUR BEST.
THEN MAKE THE MATCH.

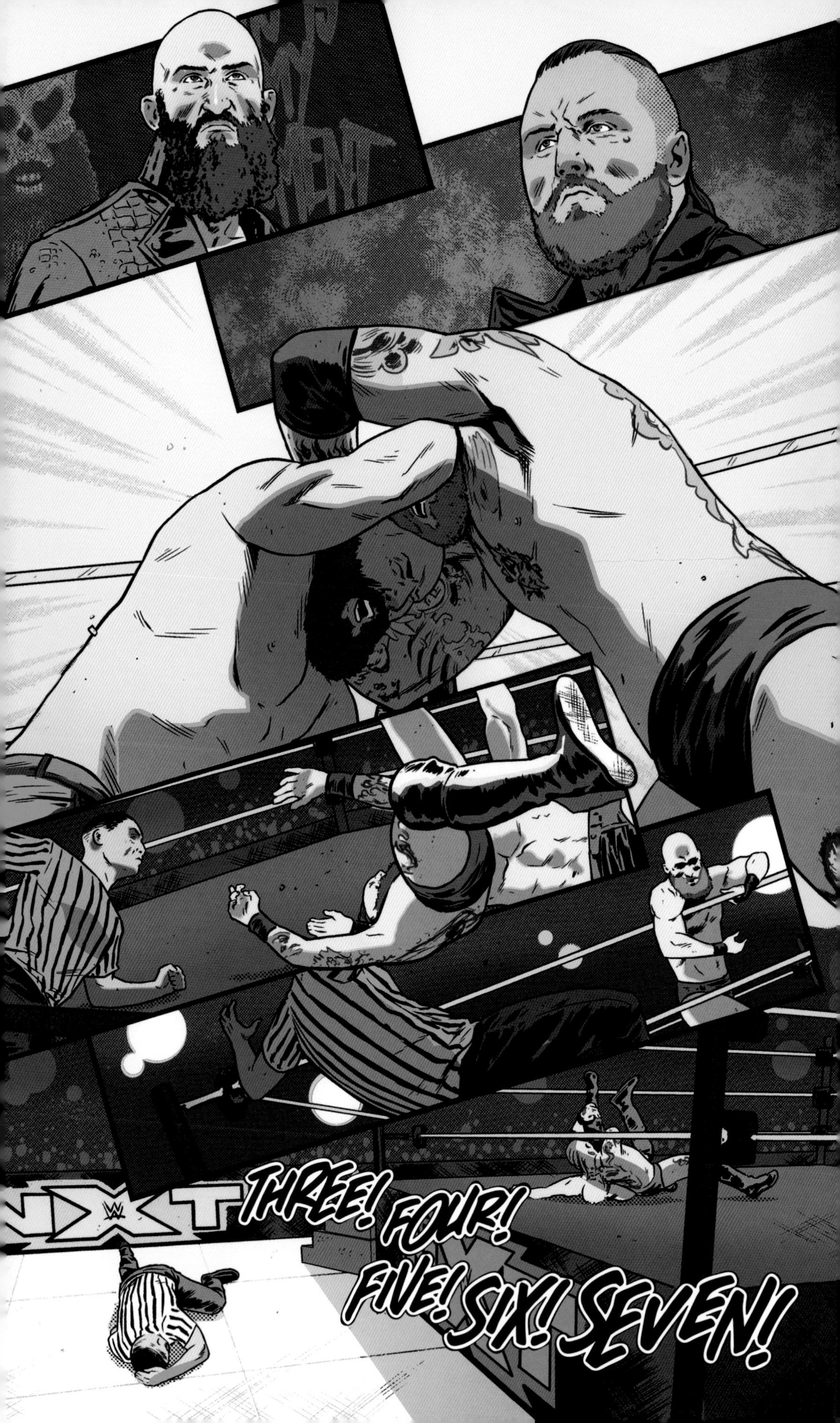
THREE! FOUR!
FIVE! SIX! SEVEN!

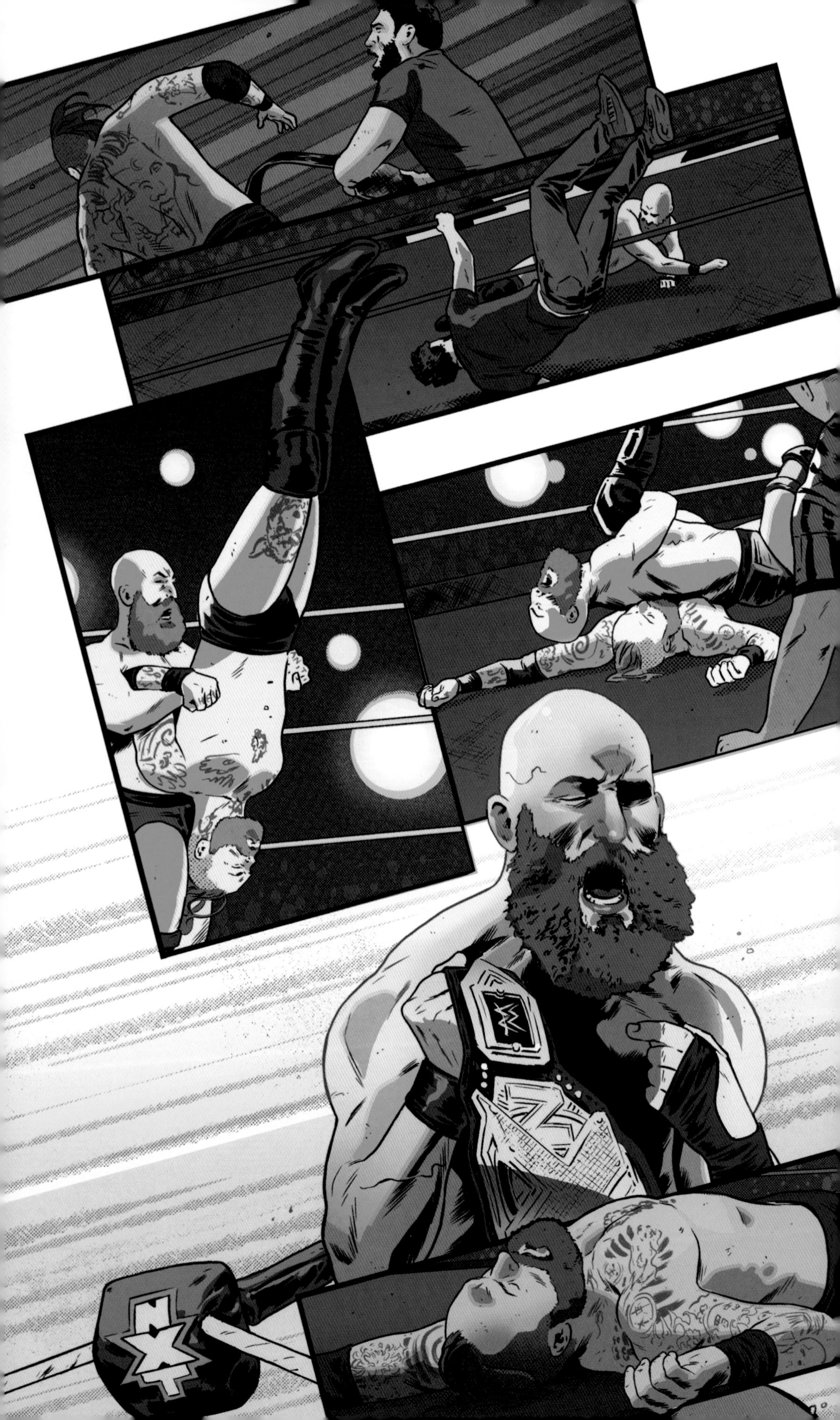

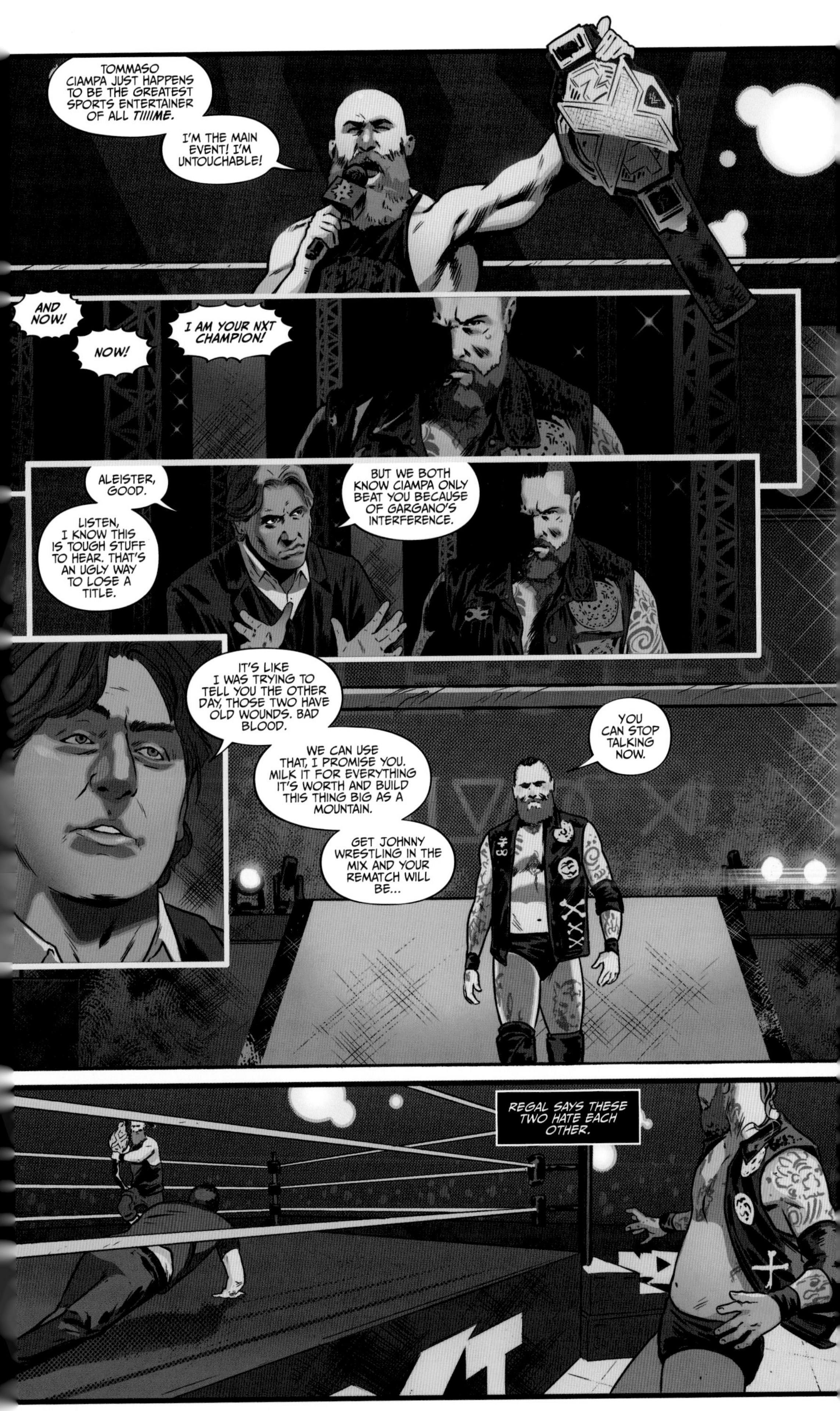
TOMMASO CIAMPA JUST HAPPENS TO BE THE GREATEST SPORTS ENTERTAINER OF ALL TIIIIME.
I'M THE MAIN EVENT! I'M UNTOUCHABLE!
AND NOW!
NOW!
I AM YOUR NXT CHAMPION!
ALEISTER, GOOD.
LISTEN, I KNOW THIS IS TOUGH STUFF TO HEAR. THAT'S AN UGLY WAY TO LOSE A TITLE.
BUT WE BOTH KNOW CIAMPA ONLY BEAT YOU BECAUSE OF GARGANO'S INTERFERENCE.
IT'S LIKE I WAS TRYING TO TELL YOU THE OTHER DAY, THOSE TWO HAVE OLD WOUNDS. BAD BLOOD.
WE CAN USE THAT, I PROMISE YOU. MILK IT FOR EVERYTHING IT'S WORTH AND BUILD THIS THING BIG AS A MOUNTAIN.
GET JOHNNY WRESTLING IN THE MIX AND YOUR REMATCH WILL BE...
YOU CAN STOP TALKING NOW.
REGAL SAYS THESE TWO HATE EACH OTHER.

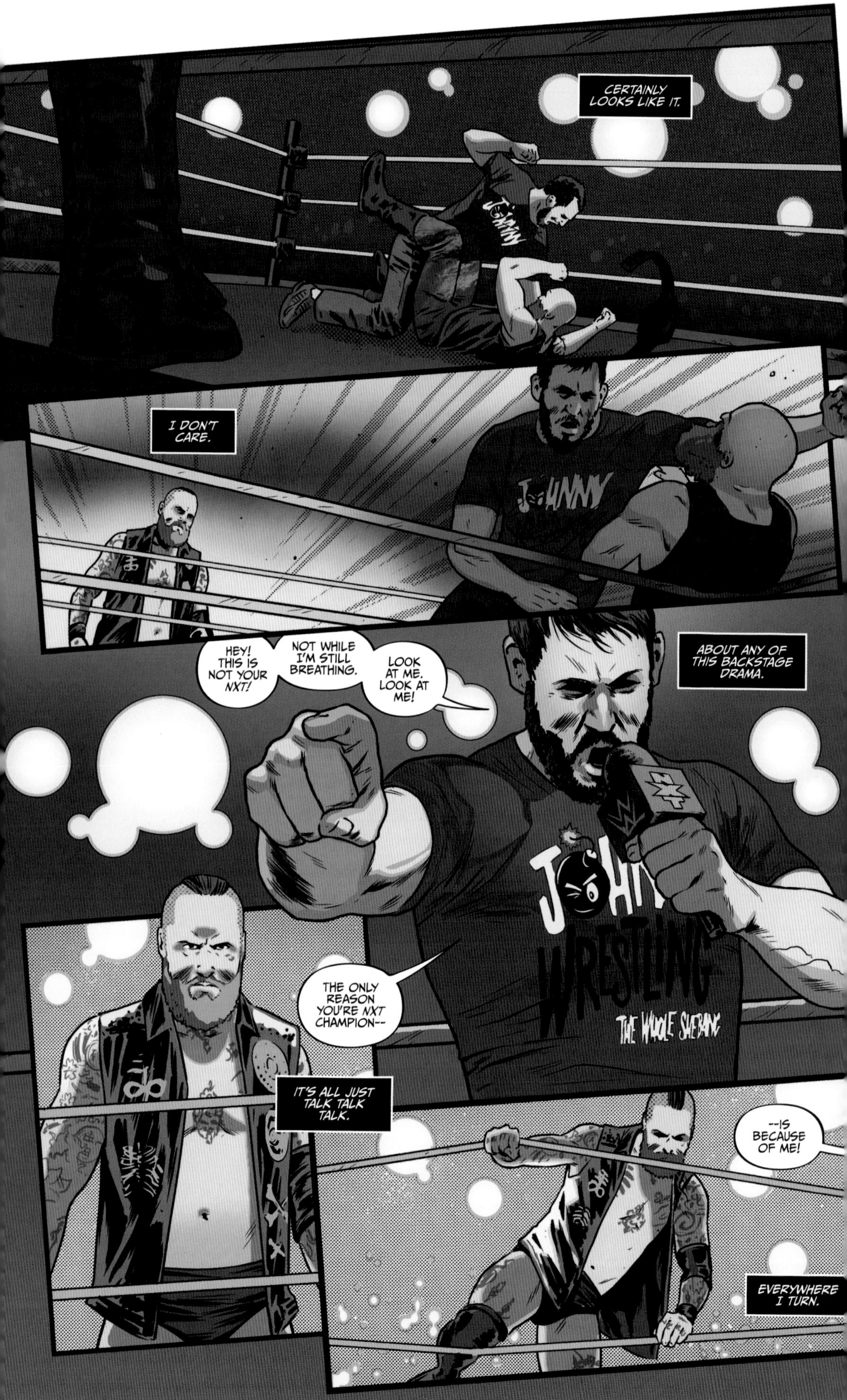

CERTAINLY LOOKS LIKE IT.
I DON'T CARE.
HEY! THIS IS NOT YOUR NXT!
NOT WHILE I'M STILL BREATHING.
LOOK AT ME. LOOK AT ME!
ABOUT ANY OF THIS BACKSTAGE DRAMA.
THE ONLY REASON YOU'RE NXT CHAMPION--
IT'S ALL JUST TALK TALK TALK.
--IS BECAUSE OF ME!
EVERYWHERE I TURN.

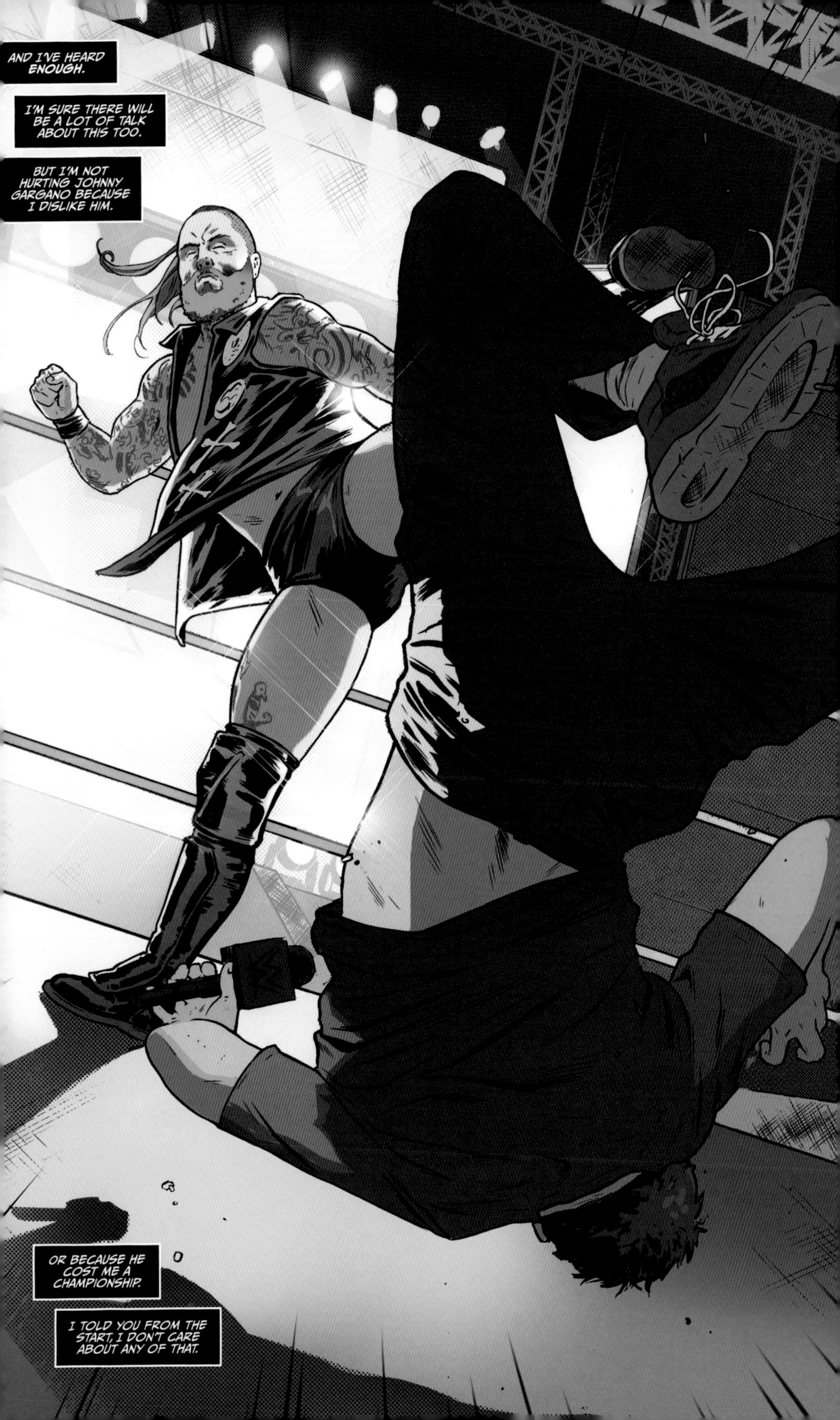
AND I'VE HEARD ENOUGH.
I'M SURE THERE WILL BE A LOT OF TALK ABOUT THIS TOO.
BUT I'M NOT HURTING JOHNNY GARGANO BECAUSE I DISLIKE HIM.
OR BECAUSE HE COST ME A CHAMPIONSHIP.
I TOLD YOU FROM THE START, I DON'T CARE ABOUT ANY OF THAT.

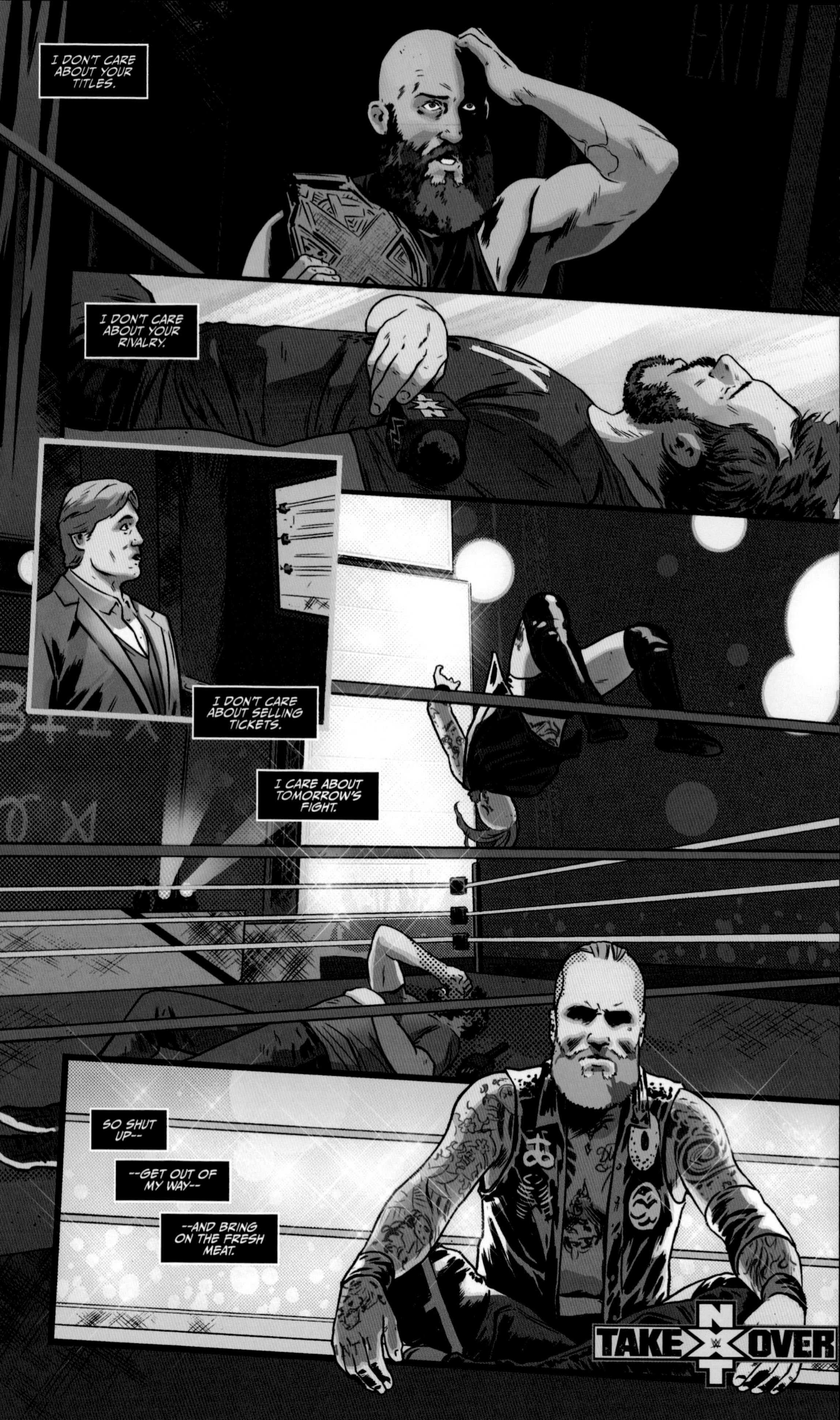

I DON'T CARE ABOUT YOUR TITLES.
I DON'T CARE ABOUT YOUR RIVALRY.
I DON'T CARE ABOUT SELLING TICKETS.
I CARE ABOUT TOMORROW'S FIGHT.
SO SHUT UP--
--GET OUT OF MY WAY--
--AND BRING ON THE FRESH MEAT.
TAKE NXT OVER

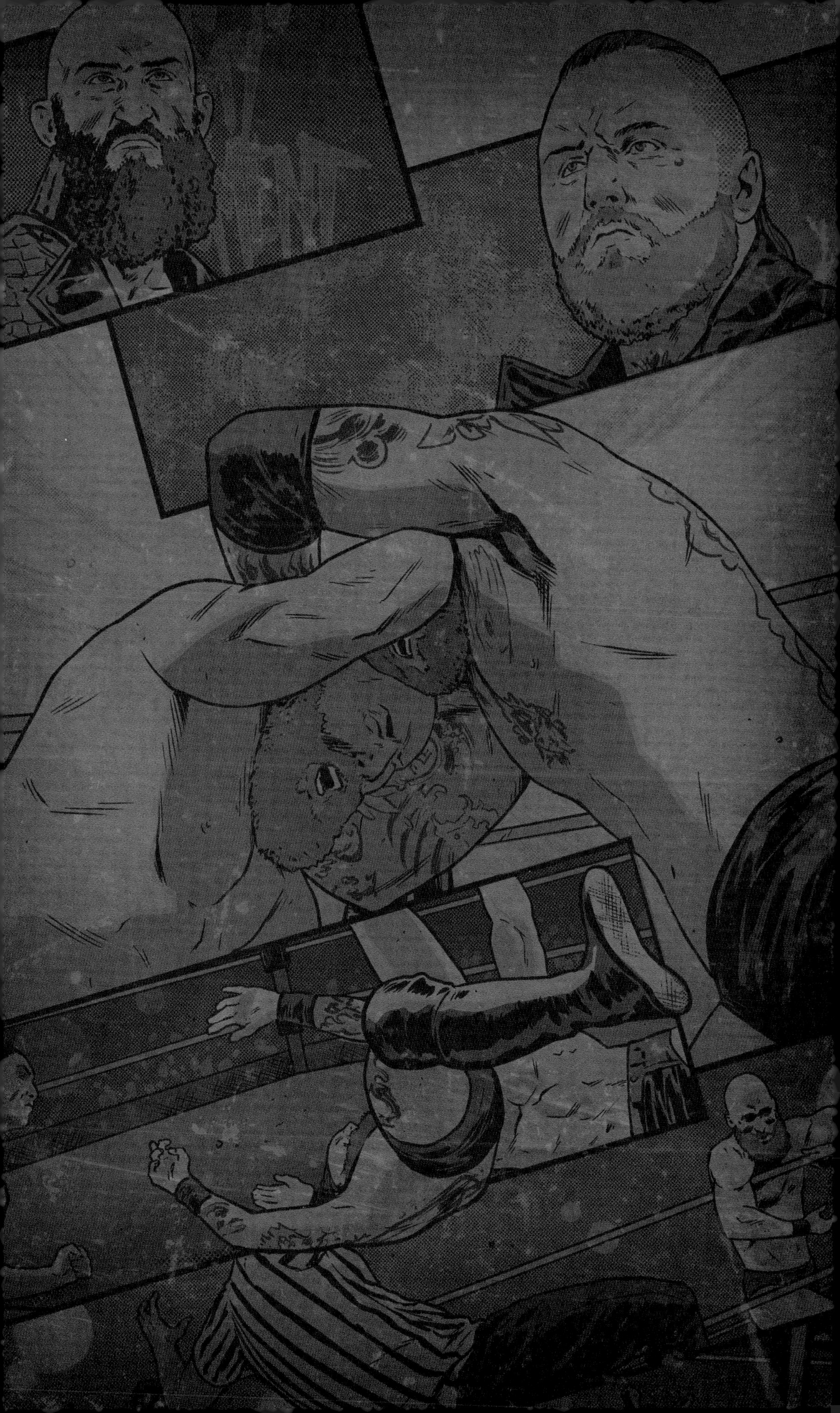

CONNECTING SUBSCRIPTION COVERS BY
MARCO D'ALFONSO

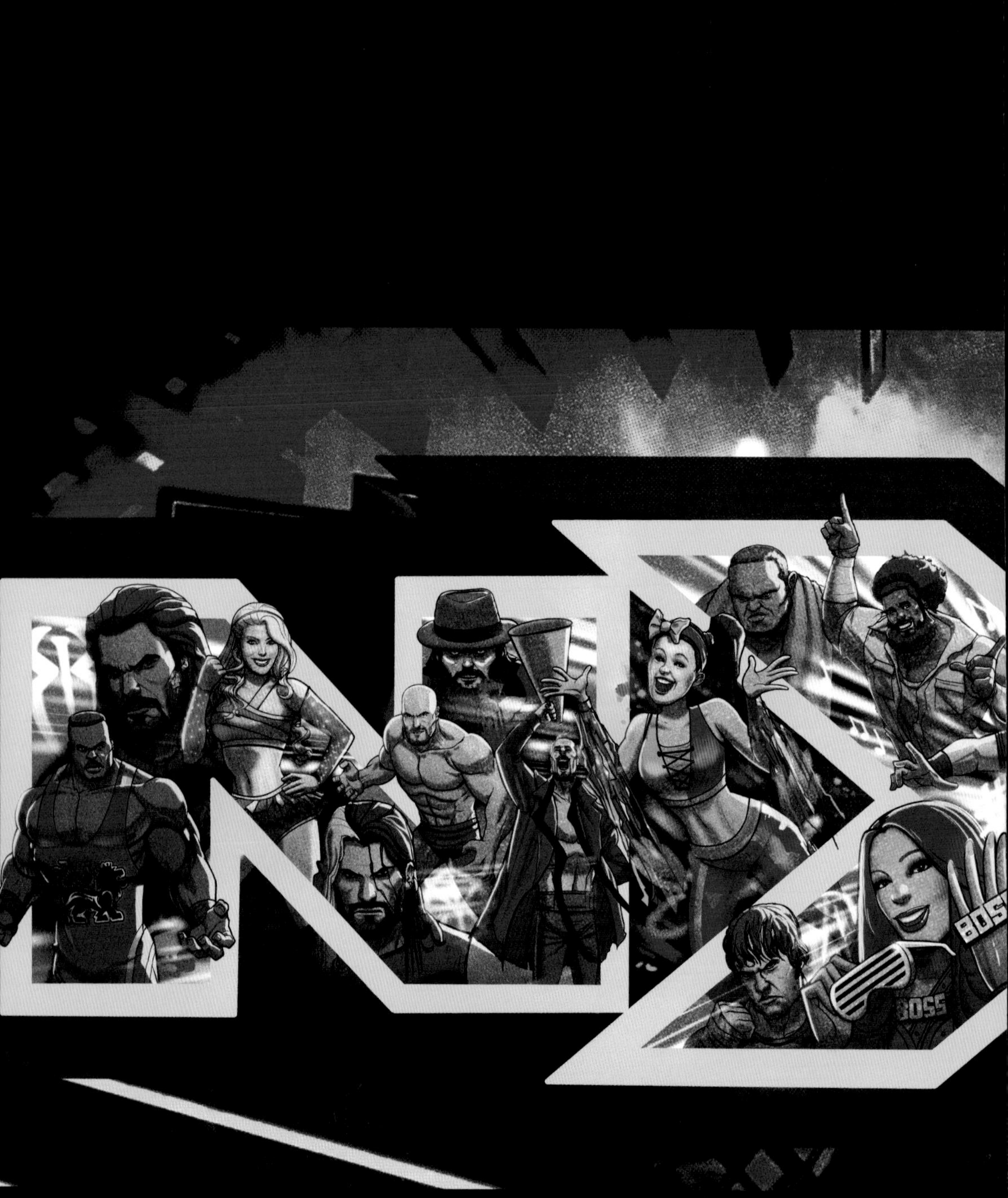
BOSS
BOSS

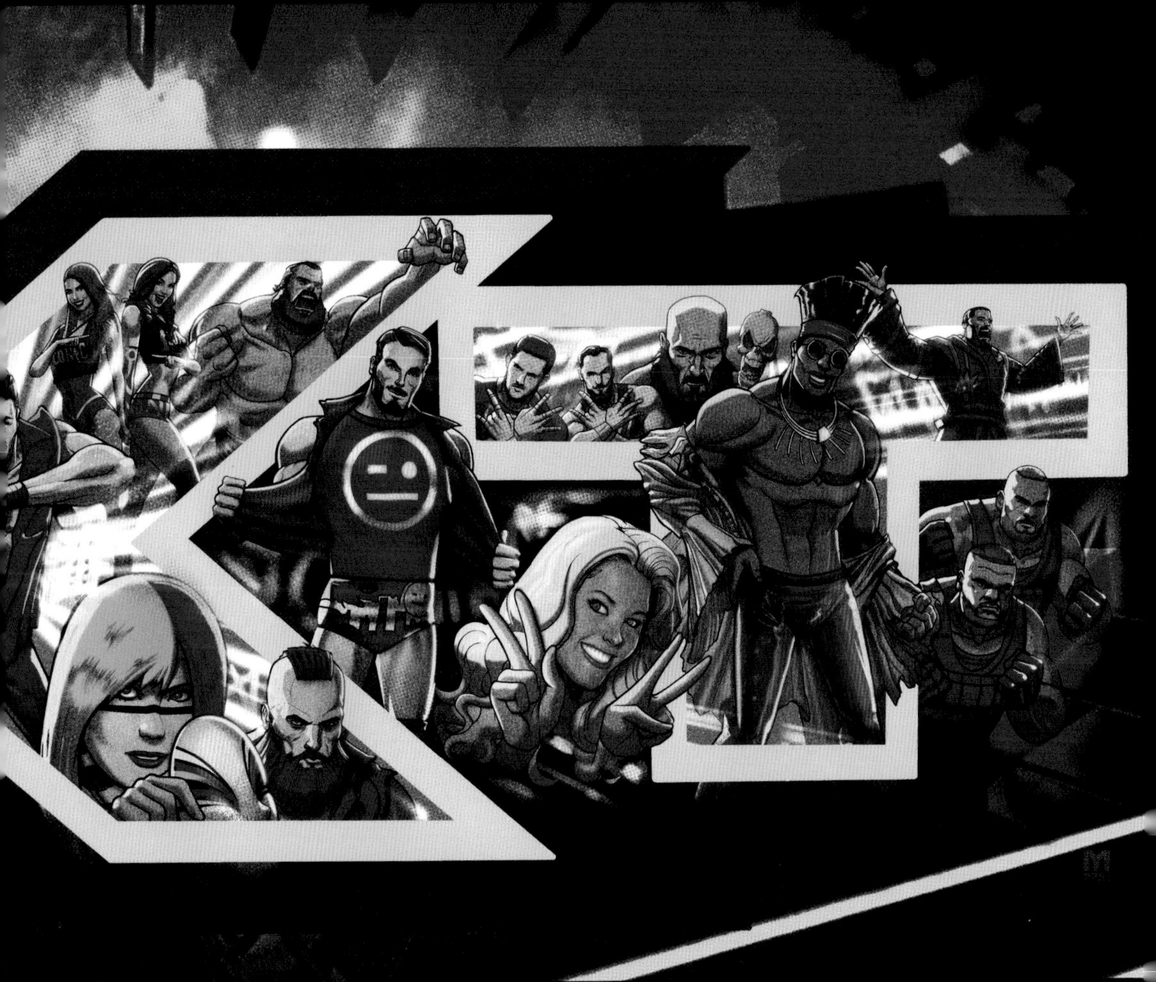

THE BLUEPRINT COVER BY
LUCAS WERNECK

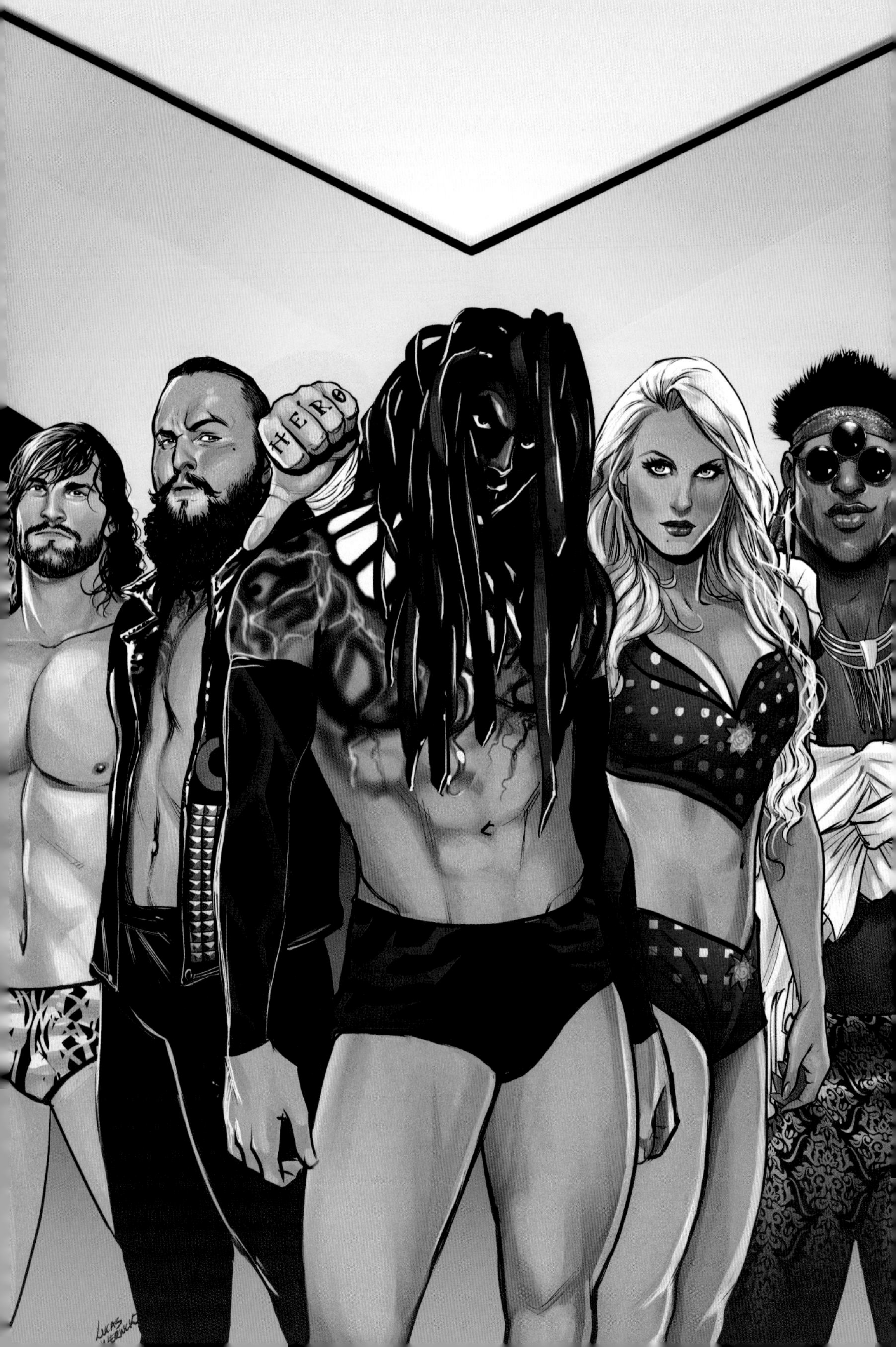

KAIRI SANE THE BLUEPRINT FNC EXCLUSIVE COVER BY
AUDREY MOK

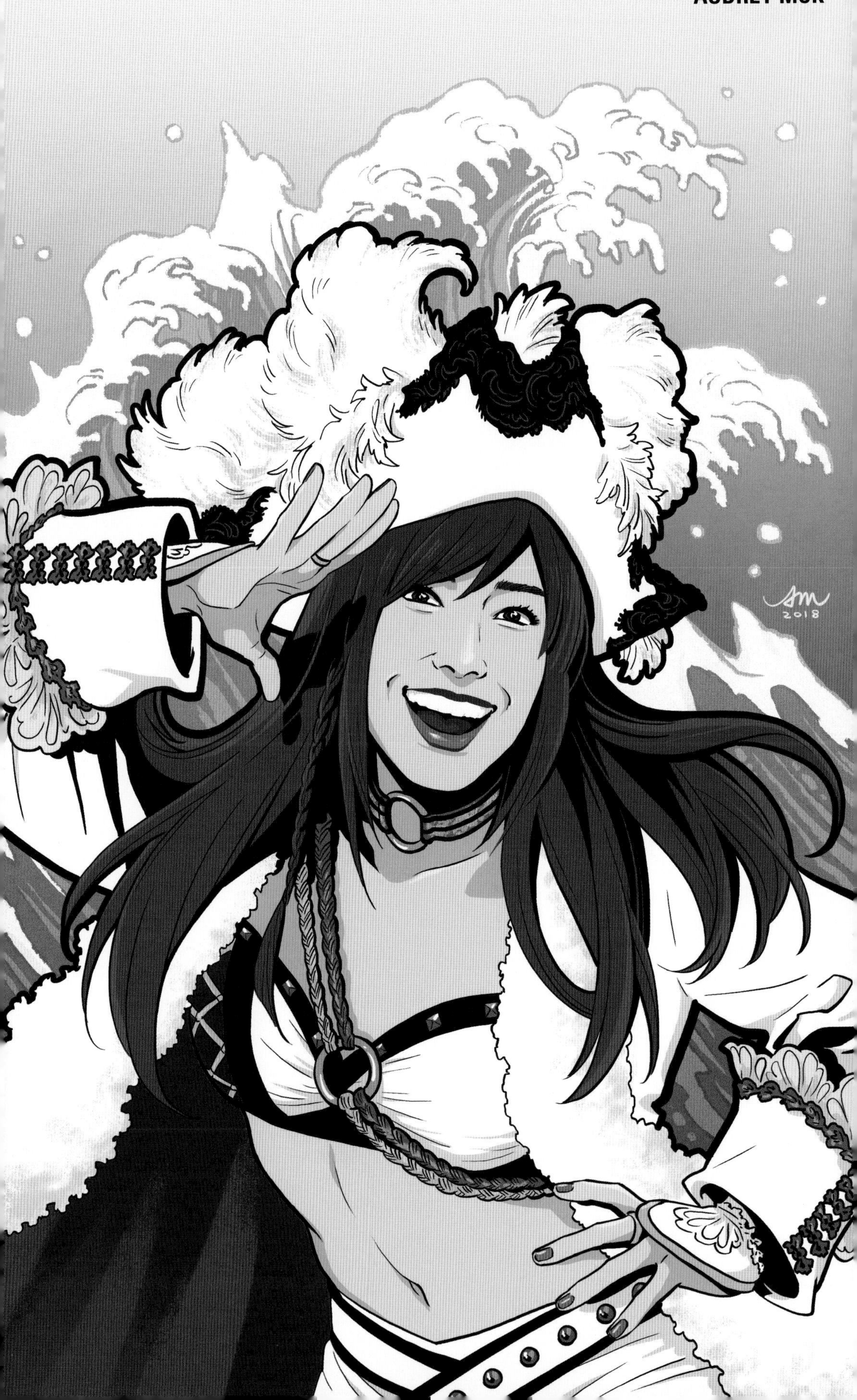

PROVING GROUND COVER BY
AARON DANA

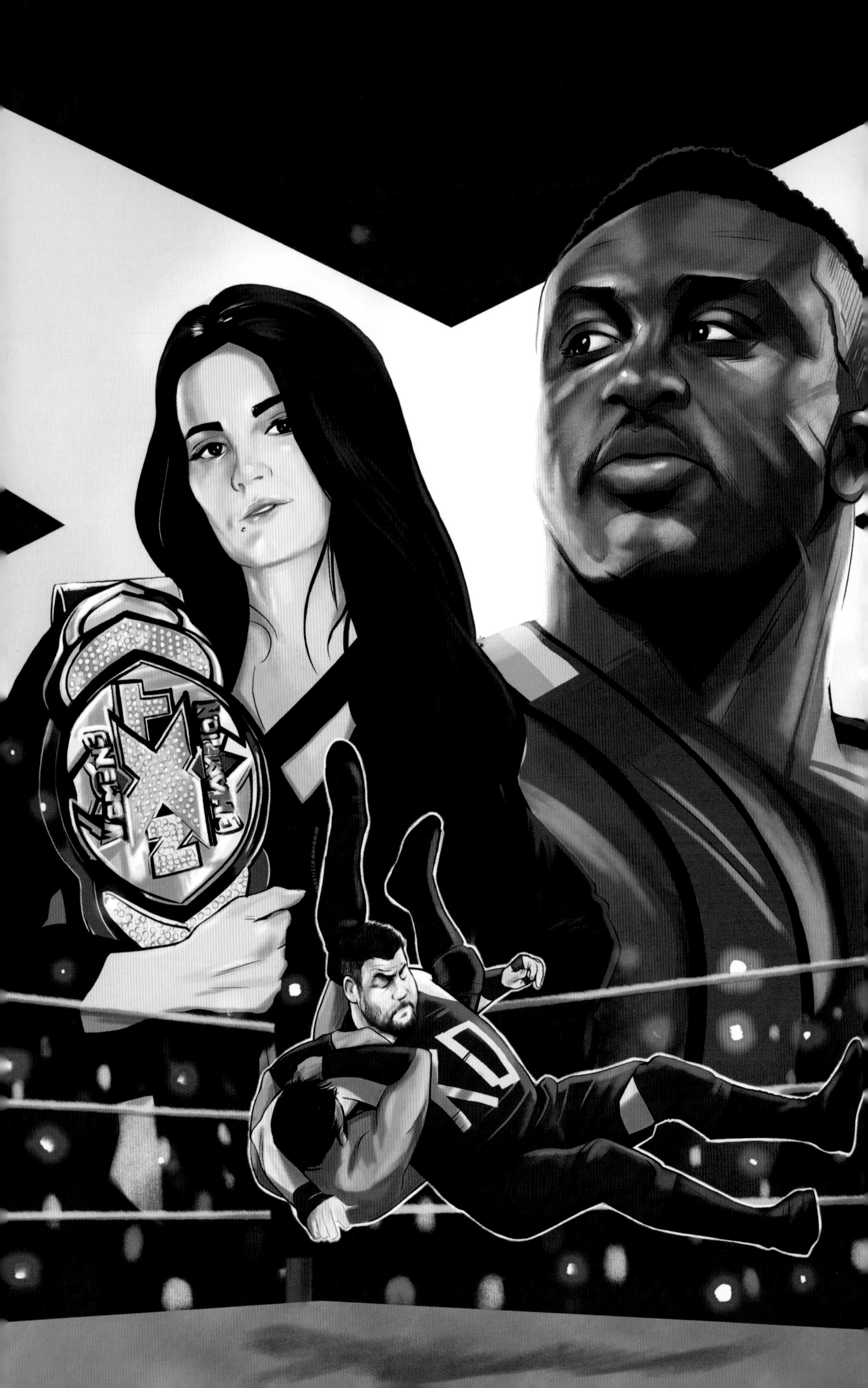

INTO THE FIRE COVER BY
DAVID NAKAYAMA

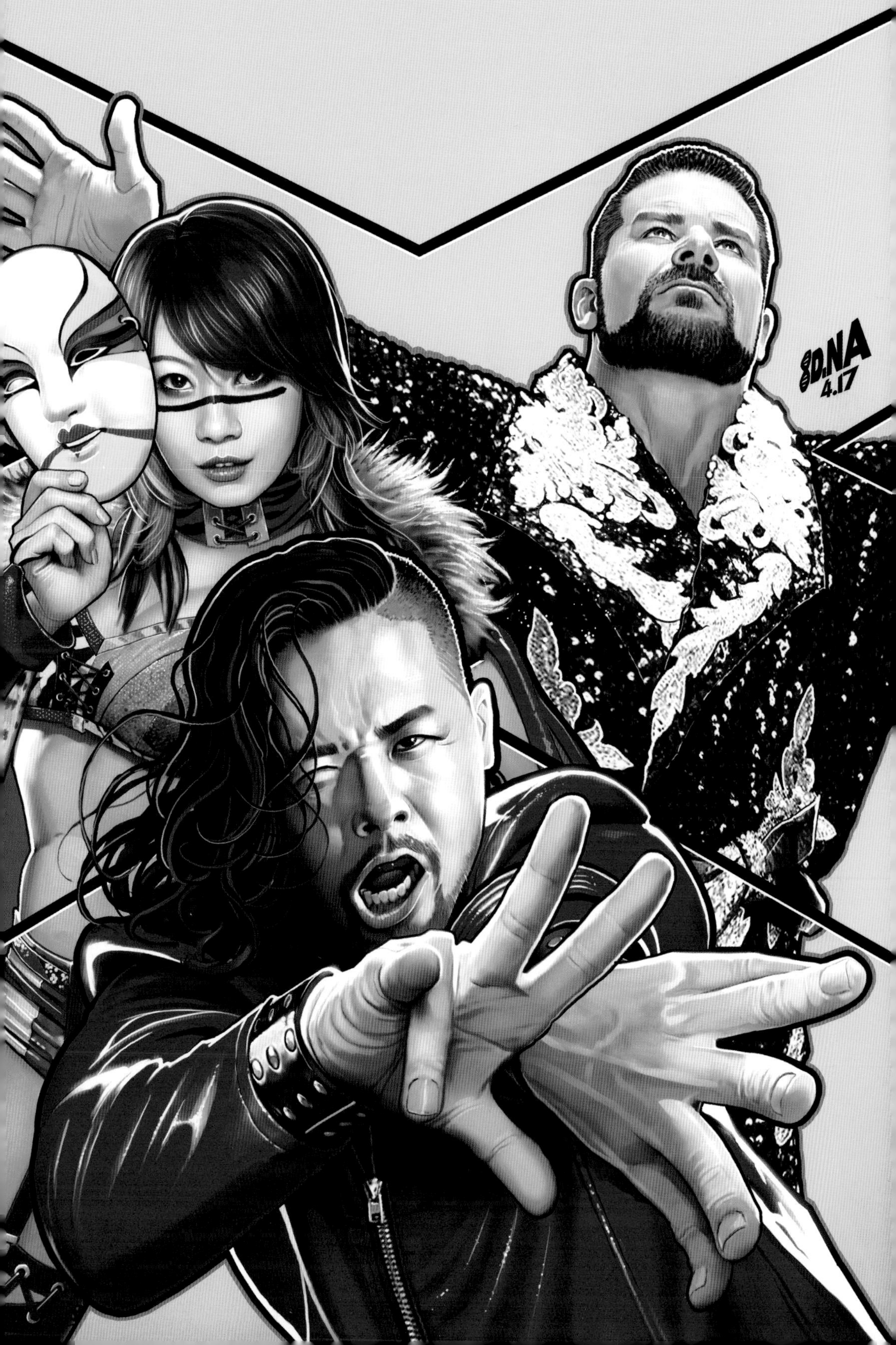
D.NA
4.17

REDEMPTION COVER BY
AUDREY MOK

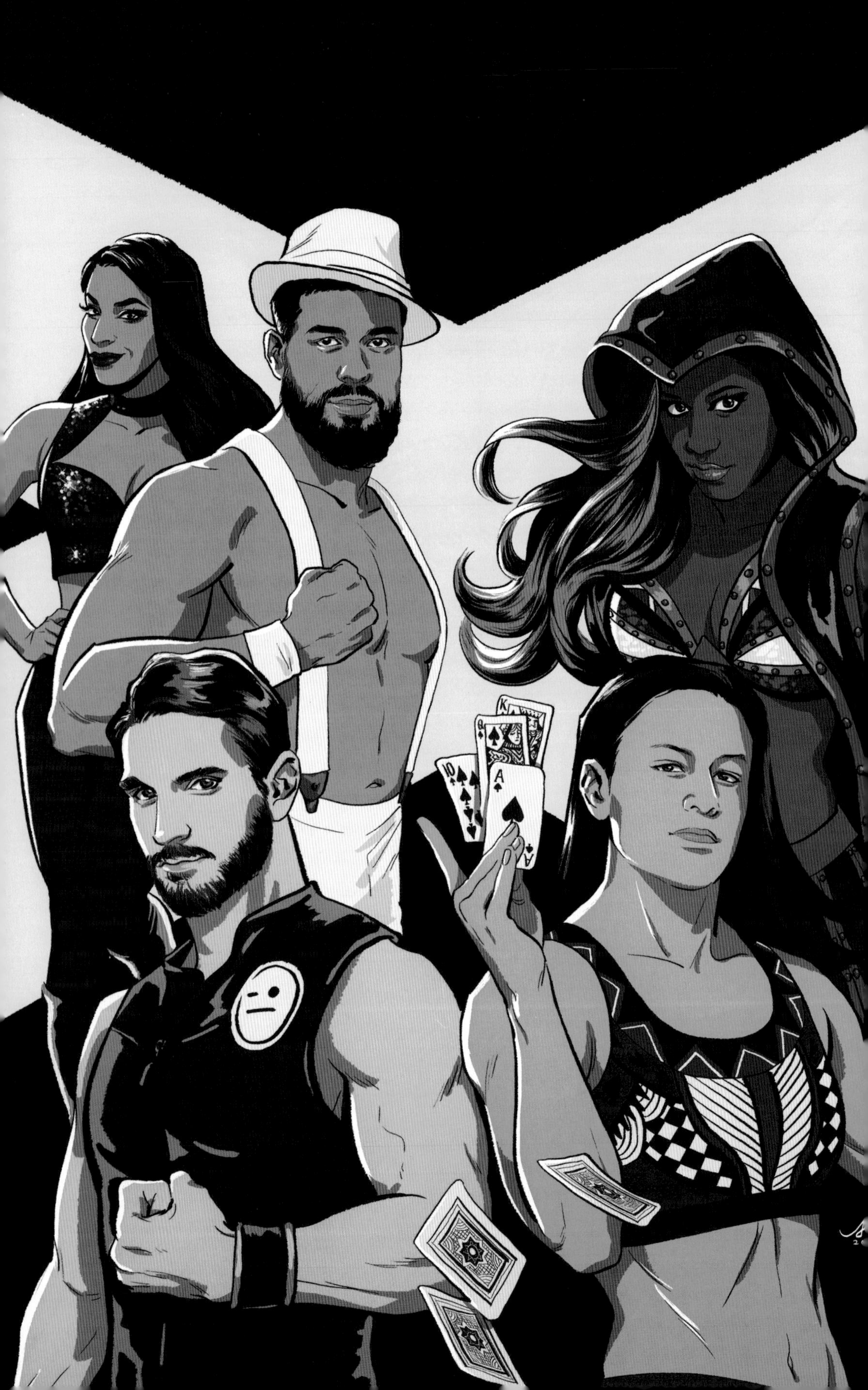

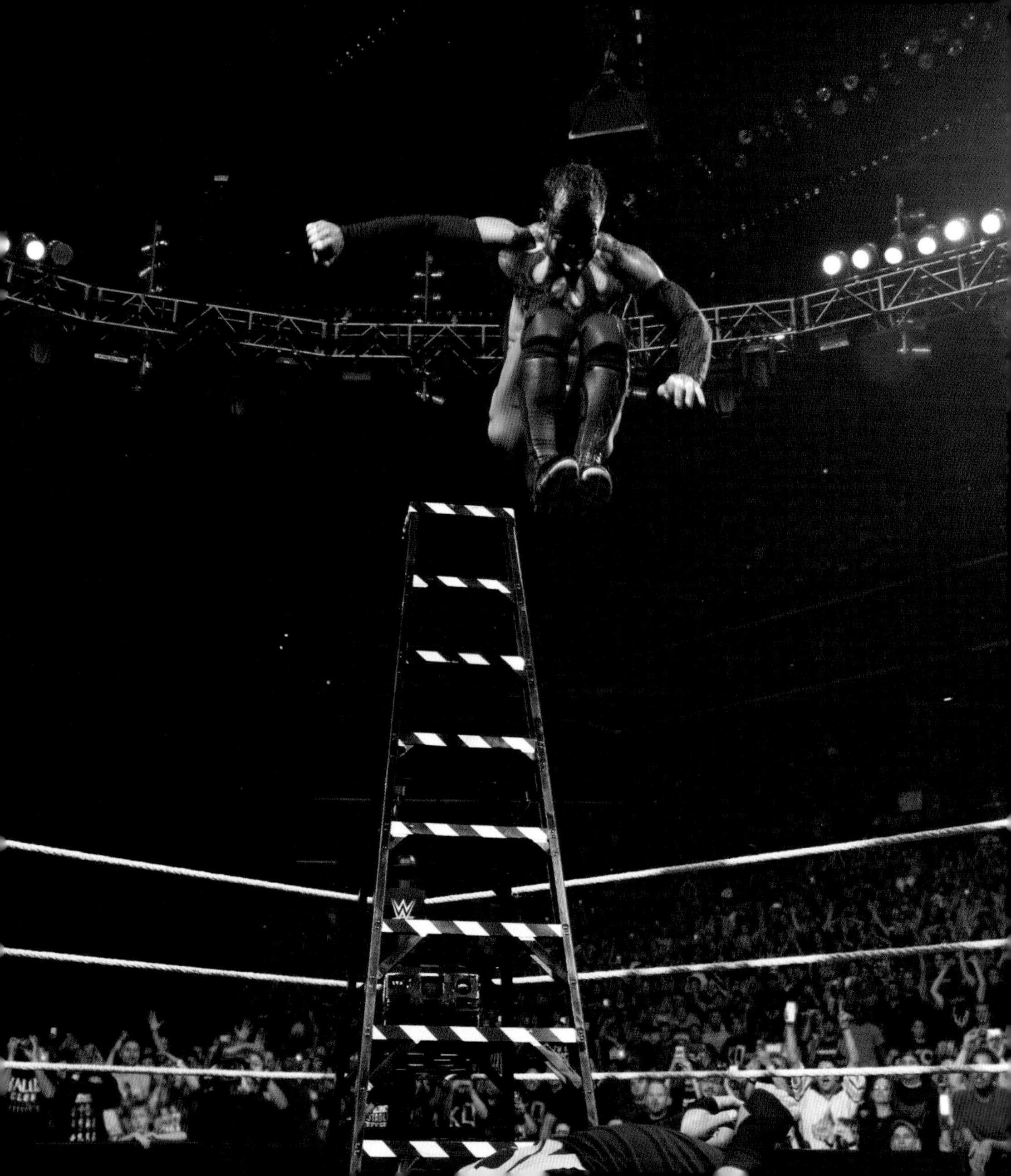

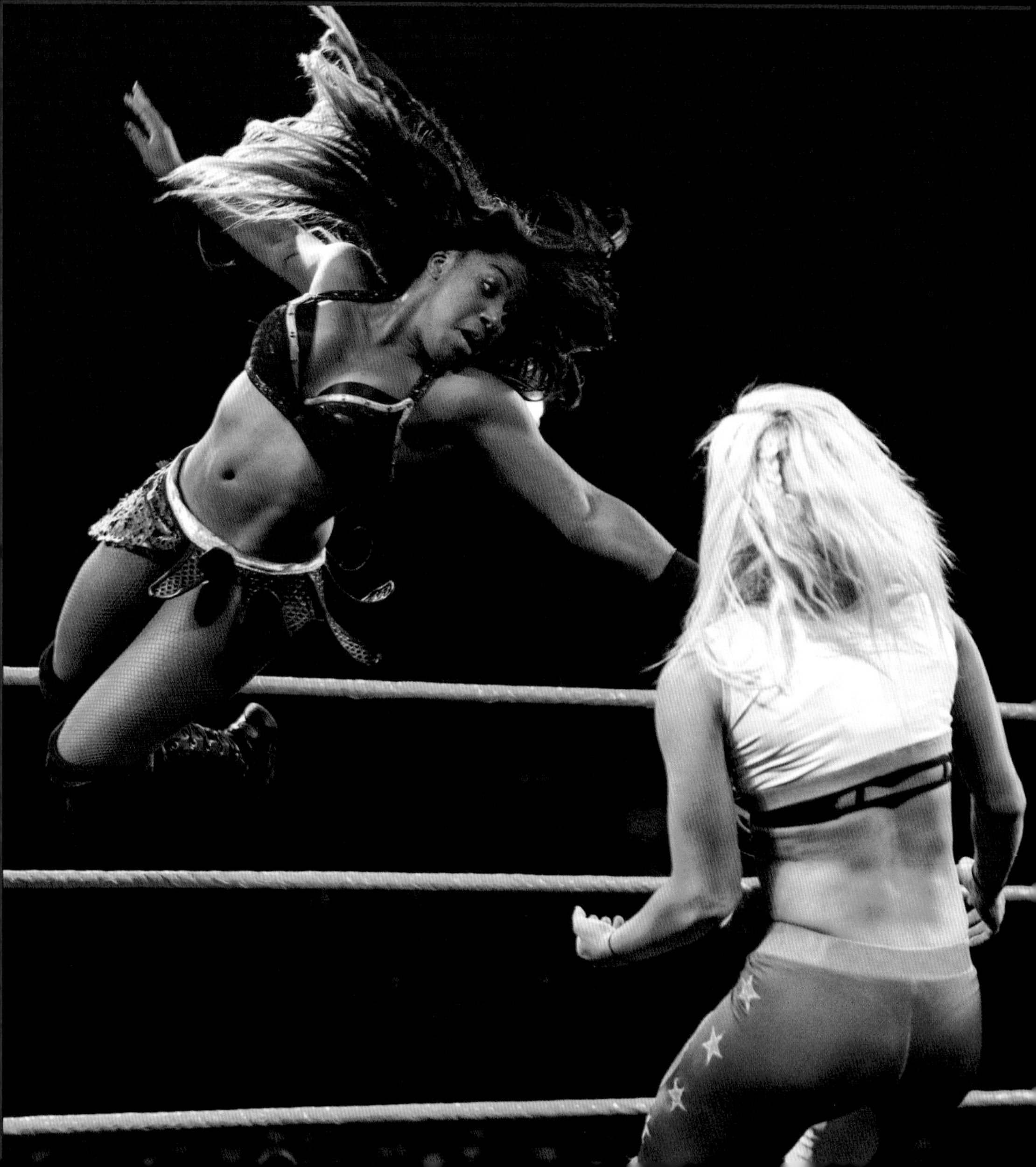

APRIL 6, 2018. NXT TAKEOVER: NEW ORLEANS

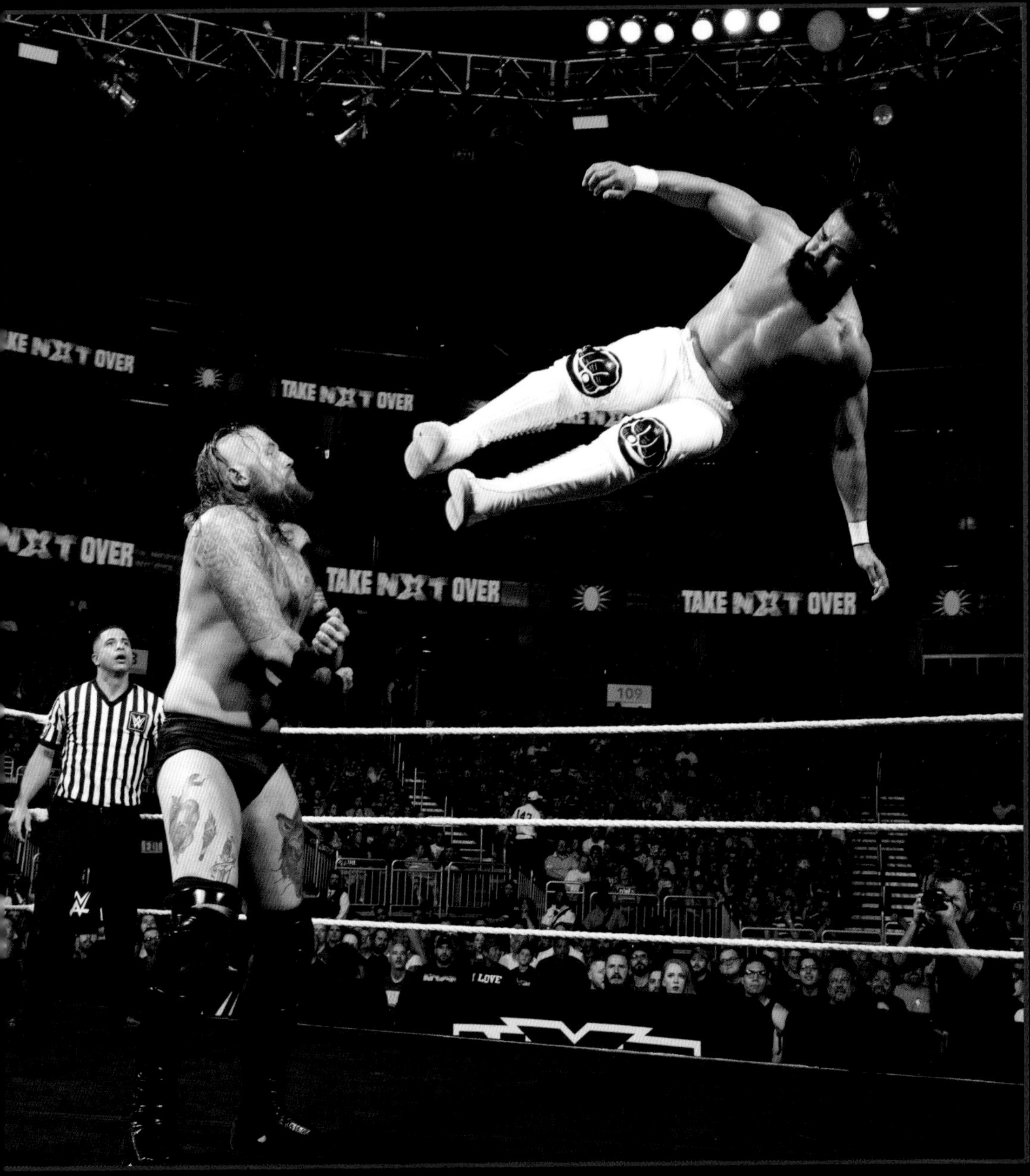
TAKE NXT OVER
TAKE NXT OVER
TAKE NXT OVER
TAKE NXT OVER
109
I LOVE

DISCOVER
VISIONARY CREATORS

THE WOODS
JAMES TYNION IV • MICHAEL DIALYNAS
VOL. 1
THE ARROW

"The Spire is fantastic! My kind of genre free-for-all." —BRIAN K. VAUGHAN (Saga)
THE SPIRE
SIMON SPURRIER
JEFF STOKELY
ANDRÉ MAY

MARK WAID • PETER KRAUSE
IRREDEEMABLE
AFTERWORD BY GRANT MORRISON

J.G. JONES
MARK WAID
STRANGE FRUIT
Foreword by
ELVIS MITCHELL

MICHAEL ALAN NELSON
DAN MORA
GABRIEL CASSATA
HEXED
THE HARLOT & THE THIEF VOLUME ONE

ABNETT & CULBARD
WILD'S END
FIRST LIGHT

BOOM! STUDIOS

AVAILABLE AT YOUR LOCAL COMICS SHOP AND BOOKSTORE
WWW.**BOOM-STUDIOS**.COM

James Tynion IV
The Woods
Volume 1
ISBN: 978-1-60886-454-6 | $9.99 US
Volume 2
ISBN: 978-1-60886-495-9 | $14.99 US
Volume 3
ISBN: 978-1-60886-773-8 | $14.99 US

The Backstagers
Volume 1
ISBN: 978-1-60886-993-0 | $14.99 US

Simon Spurrier
Six-Gun Gorilla
ISBN: 978-1-60886-390-7 | $19.99 US

The Spire
ISBN: 978-1-60886-913-8 | $29.99 US

Weavers
ISBN: 978-1-60886-963-3 | $19.99 US

Mark Waid
Irredeemable
Volume 1
ISBN: 978-1-93450-690-5 | $16.99 US
Volume 2
ISBN: 978-1-60886-000-5 | $16.99 US

Incorruptible
Volume 1
ISBN: 978-1-60886-015-9 | $16.99 US
Volume 2
ISBN: 978-1-60886-028-9 | $16.99 US

Strange Fruit
ISBN: 978-1-60886-872-8 | $24.99 US

Michael Alan Nelson
Hexed The Harlot & The Thief
Volume 1
ISBN: 978-1-60886-718-9 | $14.99 US
Volume 2
ISBN: 978-1-60886-816-2 | $14.99 US

Day Men
Volume 1
ISBN: 978-1-60886-393-8 | $9.99 US
Volume 2
ISBN: 978-1-60886-852-0 | $9.99 US

Dan Abnett
Wild's End
Volume 1: First Light
ISBN: 978-1-60886-735-6 | $19.99 US
Volume 2: The Enemy Within
ISBN: 978-1-60886-877-3 | $19.99 US

Hypernaturals
Volume 1
ISBN: 978-1-60886-298-6 | $16.99 US
Volume 2
ISBN: 978-1-60886-319-8 | $19.99 US

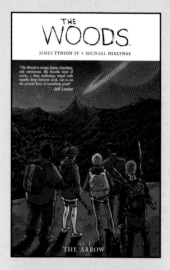

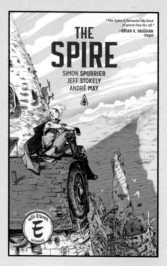

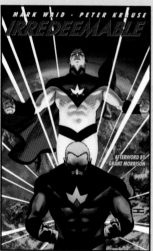

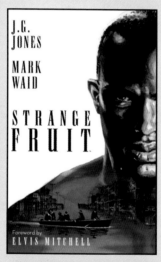

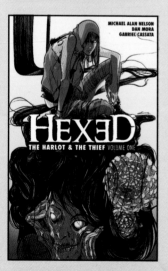

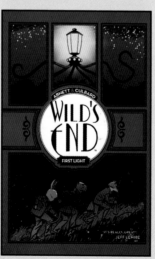

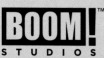